New Directions in Musical Collaborative Creativity

New Directions in Musical Collaborative Creativity

The Glasgow Improvisers Orchestra and the Theater of Home

Raymond MacDonald, Tia DeNora, Maria Sappho,
Robert Burke, and Ross Birrell

OXFORD
UNIVERSITY PRESS

Oxford University Press is a department of the University of Oxford.
It furthers the University's objective of excellence in research, scholarship,
and education by publishing worldwide. Oxford is a registered trade mark of
Oxford University Press in the UK and certain other countries.

Published in the United States of America by Oxford University Press
198 Madison Avenue, New York, NY 10016, United States of America.

© Oxford University Press 2025

All rights reserved. No part of this publication may be reproduced, stored in a retrieval system, transmitted, used for text and data mining, or used for training artificial intelligence, in any form or by any means, without the prior permission in writing of Oxford University Press, or as expressly permitted by law, by license or under terms agreed with the appropriate reprographics rights organization. Inquiries concerning reproduction outside the scope of the above should be sent to the Rights Department, Oxford University Press, at the address above.

You must not circulate this work in any other form
and you must impose this same condition on any acquirer

Library of Congress Cataloging-in-Publication Data
Names: MacDonald, Raymond A. R., author. | DeNora, Tia, author. |
Burke, Robert, 1962– author. | Sappho, Maria, author. | Birrell, Ross, author.
Title: New directions in musical collaborative creativity : the Glasgow Improvisers
Orchestra and the theater of home / Raymond MacDonald, Tia DeNora,
Robert Burke, Maria Sappho, and Ross Birrell
Description: New York : Oxford University Press, 2025. | Includes bibliographical references and index.
Identifiers: LCCN 2024045063 (print) | LCCN 2024045064 (ebook) |
ISBN 9780197752845 (paperback) | ISBN 9780197752838 (hardback) |
ISBN 9780197752869 (epub)
Subjects: LCSH: Music—Social aspects—Scotland. | COVID-19 Pandemic, 2020—Social
aspects—Scotland. | Music and the Internet. | Music—Performance—Technological innovations. |
Improvisation (Music)—Social aspects. | Glasgow Improvisers Orchestra.
Classification: LCC ML3917.S36 M22 2025 (print) | LCC ML3917.S36 (ebook) |
DDC 781.3/6—dc23/eng/20241004
LC record available at https://lccn.loc.gov/2024045063
LC ebook record available at https://lccn.loc.gov/2024045064

DOI: 10.1093/oso/9780197752838.001.0001

Paperback printed by Marquis Book Printing, Canada
Hardback printed by Bridgeport National Bindery, Inc., United States of America

Contents

List of Figures	ix
Foreword: Creating and Arranging Something Here and Now	xi
Preface: From a Quintet Who Have Never Met	xv
Author Biographies	xxiii
About the Companion Website	xxv

1. The Theater of Home and the Zoomesphere	**1**
The Creative Constraint of Lockdown or "Sheltering in Place"	2
GIO Zoom Sessions	3
Improvisation	4
Latency as Synchrony	6
The Zoomesphere and the Theater of Home	8
This is not improvised but that is	10
Previous Work	14
Structure of the Book	15
2. The Evolution of Digital Music Approaches in Practice and Care	**16**
Human-Machine Creative Cultures	16
Networked and Telematic Music	16
Human-Computer Relationships	18
Digital Identities	21
Digital Spaces	23
Digital Music Cultures: Two Examples	26
Rock 'n' Roll Music Therapy	26
Care for Music	28
New Cultures, New Futures	32
3. Opening Up Opportunities: The Shape of Things to Come	**36**
New Beginnings	36
Starting Out, Opening Up, and Boundary Objects	37
The Clap . . . and Cinematic GIO	41
Kinds of Openings	42
How Shall We Begin?	45
Opening of Confidence	46
Community Opening	48
Toward a Micro-Historical Perspective on Openings	50
Openings Unclosed	51

4. Experimentation: Habits, Habituation, Expertise, and Augmentation — 53
- The Habit[at]...uation — 53
- Lived Experiences — 55
- Habits and Habitus — 55
- Augmentation — 60
- Changing Expertise...and Habits — 62

5. Virtual Foam: Performing, Recording, and Remixing Ensemble Improvisation in the *Zumwelt* — 70
- Improvisation Within a Mise-en-Scène of Constraints — 70
- Improvisation-as-Bricolage: The "Prop-Being" of "Whatever Is at Hand" — 74
- *Umwelt* as Bubble — 76
- Forays in the *Zumwelt*: The Three Ecologies of Attunement — 78
  - Performing Through, To, and With — 79
- Gallery View, Active Speaker View, and Pin View — 80
  - Gallery View — 81
  - Meshwork and Meadow — 83
  - Speaker View ("Active Speaker View") — 84
  - Pin View — 86
- Culture of Remixing — 90
- Host and Parasite — 91
- Virtual Foam — 92

6. "I Love Lemons": Negotiating Endings — 93
- Good Endings? — 93
- Why Improvised Endings Are Important in Music and Elsewhere — 94
- "Terminal Exchanges" in and Beyond Conversations — 95
- Last Words, and When Does an Ending End? — 97
- The "Lemons" Ending — 97
- The Transcript — 98
- Talking About but Not Talking About, Finding a Way to End Serious Talk Gracefully — 109

7. New Virtuosities: This Is Our Music — 113
- New Musical Virtuosities — 114
- GIO: New Virtuosity Communities — 117
- Integrating Sound and Vision: A New Practice Emerges — 118
- Toys and Cooking: Themes for a New Modality — 120
- Conducting Improvisations — 125
- Expansion of Spaces and Development of New Realms — 128
- Theater of Home+ — 131
- Creative Developments, New Virtuosities, and New Virtualities — 137

8. An Improvising Life: Implications for Identity, Education, Therapy, and Beyond — 139
- Identity: Agency and Performativity — 139
- Improvisatory Agency — 140
- Being and Sharing: Health and Identity — 141
- Projecting Images of What It Might Mean to Be Well-in-Illness or Well Under Duress — 143
- Advancing Communicative Practices — 144
- Empowerment — 147
- Education — 149
- Implications — 151

9. New Insights into Understanding Improvisation — 155
- Post-Genre and Post-Disciplinary Implications — 155
- A Bionic Patois — 156
- Politics and New Realities: A New Imagined Future? — 159
- From Activism to Change in Music and in Life — 164
- Transforming Materialities Through Collaborative Creativities — 166
- From Experiencing the Future and Adapting to the New — 170

10. Beyond the Theater of Home: Toward Improvisational Hybridity — 171
- Duality of Identities—"I Zoom, Therefore We Are" — 171
- The Growth of the Human Archive and Its Politics — 173
- Global Connectedness — 176
- Nearly the Final Word — 179
- Final Words from the Authors — 180
  - From Raymond: Remember Fun and Relational Quantum Mechanics — 180
  - From Maria: Caring for a New Home — 183
  - From Tia: A Force for Good — 185
  - From Ross: Toward an Ecology of Improvisation — 187
  - From Rob: Experimenting with Trust — 188
- Technology, Improvisation, Collaborative Creativity, and the Mother of Invention — 190

Notes — *193*
References — *197*
Index — *209*

Figures

P.1.	List of participants.	xviii
P.2.	Authors meeting, January 2024.	xxi
2.1.	Digital and physical spaces in telematic and music practices.	23
3.1.	March 24, 2020, first online improvisation.	39
3.2.	April 14, 2020, adjusting to the Zoom setting.	40
3.3.	April 28, 2020, the first "clap."	41
3.4.	February 1, 2022, Miniature on Infinity.	44
3.5.	April 7, 2020, virtual background cat image and "The End" sign.	46
3.6.	April 7, 2020, piccolo and instrument mirroring.	47
3.7.	Player country locations from April 14, 2020.	49
3.8.	Player country locations from April 18, 2020.	50
4.1.	May 9, 2020, author Sappho with Frida Kahlo virtual background.	62
4.2.	Author DeNora GIO stick figures.	62
4.3.	May 4, 2021, kaleidoscope and visual embodied reflections.	64
5.1.	Ross Birrell & Glasgow Improvisers Orchestra, *A-111* (2020), video still.	88
5.2.	Ross Birrell & Glasgow Improvisers Orchestra, *Kokoro* (2021), video still.	88
5.3.	Ross Birrell & Glasgow Improvisers Orchestra, *Archive Fever* (2022), video still.	89
6.1.	May 9, 2020, chat piece, author MacDonald dealing cards.	99
7.1.	May 2, 2020, improvisation with hand and virtual background conduction.	119
7.2.	May 2, 2020, Robert Henderson improvising with light.	119
7.3.	May 9, 2020, toys piece.	121
7.4.	May 9, 2020, toys piece—family play.	122
7.5.	May 9, 2020, toys piece, central player holding up Welsh sign written on children's toy.	123
7.6.	May 16, 2020, cooking piece.	124
7.7.	March 2, 2021, hand conduction example.	126
7.8.	March 2, 2021, paired players—visual conduction and sonic interpretation.	126
7.9.	March 2, 2021, numbers conduction.	127
7.10.	March 1, 2022, live collective graphic score.	127

Figures

7.11. March 22, 2022, two years in lockdown "goodbye!" — 128
7.12. May 19, 2020, jumping on trampoline. — 129
7.13. May 30, 2020, experiments with body, virtual backgrounds, and sunlight. — 129
7.14. May 30, 2020, card piece, movable camera, and virtual backgrounds. — 130
7.15. June 6, 2020, Estonian forest through a movable camera and translucent fabric. — 130
7.16. September 29, 2020, Marion Treby and Faradena Affifi outdoors, and exploring the garden with Tammy the dog. — 131
7.17. May 18, 2021, Thomas Rohrer takes the orchestra on a train ride through the Italian alps. — 131
7.18. June 1, 2021, Maggie Nicols train improvisations mid-commute (Wales). — 132
7.19. August 24, 2021, Peter Nicholson brings the group to a swim on a loch (Scottish Highlands). — 132
7.20. August 31, 2021, author MacDonald travels by plane to Germany. — 132
7.21. September 14, 2021, author Sappho "breaks in" to author MacDonald's apartment. — 133
7.22. September 21, 2021, performance to the sunset at Broughty Ferry (Scotland). — 133
7.23. October 5, 2021, a cupcake riding a bike through the Scottish Highland with David Robertson. — 134
7.24. December 14, 2021, GIO's post-lockdown monthly workshops at the CCA. — 134
7.25. Cooking in the Theater of Home at the AJIRN conference, 2022. — 136
8.1. John Russell in Mopomoso TV episode 2, July 2020. — 144
9.1. June 22, 2021, The Unquiet Earth by Angela Hoyos Gomez. — 162
9.2. September 28, 2021, Apocalyptic Sunrise. — 163
9.3. June 13, 2020, Requiem for the pandemic. — 163
9.4. January 19, 2021, in memory of John Russell. — 164
9.5. *Foutraque* at GIOfest 2021, with the Noisebringers and Rachel Weiss (score and live performance selection). — 165

Foreword

Creating and Arranging Something Here and Now

Free improvisation online! The first impression from listening to the recordings might be chaotic and overwhelming. It could either turn off our attention after a few seconds or stimulate our curiosity. Upon further exploration, we might discover that there is much more happening in the music, on the screen, and between the players than we initially perceive. The following chapters reveal how improvisations hold meanings beyond the pure aesthetic or artistic aspects of the music. Engaging with the improvisational processes, as presented in this book, opens our ears and minds not only to the aesthetic qualities that this art form affords, but also to the various social and psychological consequences that arise from the act of musicking.

We have all experienced how the lockdown situation affected us. Opportunities for coming together became restricted and our ordinary social life became impoverished. The quarantine situation led the musicians into social isolation, resulting in serious economic consequences for many. Musical rehearsals were forbidden, putting serious constraints upon musical development. Many suffered from this situation of isolation and lack of communication, affecting their health and quality of life.

Online communication became a solution for many of us. The Glasgow Improvisers Orchestra started a series of online workshops on Zoom, which evolved into a global event involving over 150 participants from around the world. This initiative led to the idea of this book. Sessions were recorded, interviews were conducted, autobiographical narratives were added, and theoretical reflections transformed the process into an innovative research endeavor.

The recordings initially piqued my curiosity. Given the context of COVID-19 that prompted the project, I was surprised to observe the high level of communication among the participants. The screen revealed a multitude of signs indicating vital forms of communication. While listening and watching the large group of musicians on Zoom, I noticed a range of interactions, such as listening, adapting, influencing, responding, suggesting, imitating, filling in, waiting, silencing, hesitating, confirming, dialoguing, tuning-in, and collaborating. As evidenced in the interviews featured in some chapters, these interactions had a significant impact, both musically and socially, on the participants.

Upon further reflection, I examined the processes from various angles and disciplinary perspectives. When musicians come together for online free improvisation, we can observe the aesthetic qualities and purely musical aspects. Additionally, viewed from the perspectives of music educators, music therapists, psychologists, sociologists, or anthropologists, group improvisations offer insights into a myriad of significant ideas, practices, opportunities, and critical issues.

The book demonstrates how, from psychological, sociological, and musical viewpoints, participating in the sessions empowered the participants, both musically and socially. Socially, it created a safe weekly meeting place where individuals could share, support, and care for one another. Transformation and the narration of a new identity were integral to the process, broadening and strengthening the participants' sense of agency. The improvisations became empowering experiences.

Musically, the musicians were compelled to adapt to the new telematic situation and find solutions to technological challenges. The new online format challenged their previous method of playing, necessitating the development of new musical solutions. They learned to overcome these challenges with a form of "adaptive creativity." For instance, the issue of latency and synchronicity, inherent in playing together online, was creatively addressed by incorporating the delays and glitches into the creative output.

From a music education perspective (and my background as a former piano teacher), reading about this project inspired me to explore new teaching methods, liberating me from traditional conservatory didactics. As a music therapist familiar with free improvisation, both individually and in groups, I can attest to how agency and empowerment are enhanced through collaborative musicking. The new adaptive creativity, impacting agency, empowerment, and identity, aligns with the core tenets of music therapy. The chapters vividly illustrate how the Zoom technology offers new possibilities to engage with clients.

Improvisation, by its nature, involves creating and arranging something "here and now," utilizing available resources. The Latin root of *improviso* refers to the unforeseen. Decision-making and negotiation processes are central to improvisation, not only in selecting musical material but also in determining how to start, stop, play loudly or softly, among other decisions. The act of musicking in a group setting of free improvisation leads to transformative experiences, as evidenced in interviews and autobiographical narratives.

Viewing these transformative experiences through an ethnographic lens, they bear resemblance to "transitional rituals." The regular musical encounters function as "rites of passage," involving separation from the old position and normal time. The "Zoomesphere" serves as a transitional space where improvisers leave behind previous symbols, practices, and roles, entering a period of uncertainty, ambiguity, and exploration of new possibilities.

The transitional period, referred to as liminal, from the Latin *limen*, or threshold, involves being "betwixt and between," neither fully here nor there. Free improvisations signify change, transformation, and constant transition, akin to being in a state of musical flow or void. It is not about moving merely from one musical place to another but also from one state to another, altering relationships not only with the music material but also with others, situations, and oneself. In this sense, (free) improvisations serve as true transitional rituals, shifting states of consciousness, positions, perspectives, frames, status, and identities.

Musical improvisation transports participants into a new world where seemingly disparate sounds form unexpected connections, resembling "play." In life, play is like a prism through which we can view events from different perspectives—it can be seen as "refractive." Through play, we learn that there are multiple ways to understand situations and that things may not always be as they seem at first glance. Play allows us to consider alternative possibilities and opens our minds to different ways of thinking.

In the context of musical action, play involves framing sounds and artifacts in a way that creates cognitive boundaries, allowing for alternative perspectives and actions. A free musical improvisation can be seen as a form of play, where music acts as a framework for exploring new ideas, identities, and modes of expression. It provides a space to experiment, fantasize, and create without the constraints of traditional norms or expectations.

The online session brought musicians together in a marginal social situation, fostering sharing friendship, trust, and hope, ultimately forming a musical community. The forum facilitated a comradeship where traditional distinctions faded, fostering a sense of equality among individuals. The online platform became a space for sharing personal issues during improvisations and subsequent discussions. Anthropologist Victor Turner coined the term "communitas" to describe such unstructured or minimal communities of equals.

This new music-technological community—or communitas—has the potential to spark transformations of identities and the creation of new music genres, with far-reaching implications for musical praxis in the post-pandemic era.

The collective of writers in the book showcases a strong theoretical foundation and an ability to integrate perspectives from post-humanism, post-structuralism, current philosophy, art critique, and media theory, among others. The theoretical discourses, in conjunction with the practical examples of online musical collaborations, illustrate the innovative potential of this music-technological experiment and its impact on various disciplines.

Even Ruud
Professor Emeritus, University of Oslo and
The Norwegian Academy of Music
Oslo, March 2024

Preface

From a Quintet Who Have Never Met

> *Life is a shipwreck, but we must not forget to sing in the lifeboats.*
> —Gay (1981, p. xxvi)

On March 17, 2020, at 16:10, Stuart Brown, drummer and a founding member of the Glasgow Improvisers Orchestra (GIO), wrote the following short email to the band.

> Can we organise some sort of mass online improv "gathering" via Skype/FaceTime or something else and live stream it? Improv might be the one style of music that could still work even with internet connection time lag. In fact this might be a new GIO piece... I'm not joking. Anyone know a good way to set this up?

Thus began a series of online workshops, hosted not via Skype or FaceTime, but rather on Zoom. These workshops would spawn innovative artistic practices, provide emotional support, change lives, and have a global reach far beyond what any of us could have imagined. It was during these early sessions, exploring online improvising, set against a backdrop of local and global turmoil, that the idea for this book emerged.

This book is a celebration of collaborative creativity and, in particular, the socio-artistic creativity at the heart of the meetings resulting from the aforementioned email. In the early days of the global lockdown in 2020, we—the authors—actively participated in these online improvisation sessions, discovering new ways of working, new ways of being-apart-together, and adapting to the challenges presented by adversity. As the sessions continued, and the weeks grew into months, the meetings became a safe place for significant personal and collective engagement with the tumultuous world events unfolding. On numerous occasions when we met, we felt the weight of possibly life-changing global events touching us all. In Chapter 9 we discuss how, with significant emotional commitment, we developed new work focused on the week-by-week events taking place. Of particular importance was an improvisation in the days following George Floyd's tragic murder, and numerous improvised requiems for friends and colleagues who died during the pandemic.

The process of developing and writing this book has also been deeply and quintessentially collaborative. Until April 2024, when we finally met at Raymond's home for a meal, the five of us never shared the same physical space at the same time; during the time that this book was written, we were a quintet who had never met in person. Nonetheless, we collaborated online on every aspect of this book's development and completion, engaging in necessary writing periods of individual solitude, but also sometimes working on a section together, in real time. This way of collaborating was new for all of us. It involved a certain amount of chaos and, probably, if anyone were to examine the early chapter drafts, they could be forgiven to wonder if any kind of coherent manuscript would ever emerge from our so-called method.

That method took inspiration from the GIO sessions. We—*improvised*. We discussed the book's structure, yes. We wrote a book proposal outline and abstracts in advance for each chapter (to ensure cohesion and coverage of what had emerged as core themes). But when it came time to write, we agreed to create blank documents on Google Docs for each chapter and that we would each have license to, as it were, throw into the pot whatever we thought might belong and be worthy of development. What we initially chose to add to each chapter probably did reflect our individual disciplinary interests and training (MacDonald's in psychology, Sappho's and Burke's in performance, Birrel's in visual art, and DeNora's in sociology) and at times there was need for "translation" or further explanation of ideas or concepts—questions in bubble comments or tracked-changes elaborations with a "Is this right?" in the margins (which were themselves methods for promoting interdisciplinary dialogue). In the initial stages, each chapter was chaotic, and inchoate, but— importantly—open to newness, surprise, and mutual learning as we each entered to add, subtract, and sculpt. We even discovered the joys of working on the same section simultaneously, which happened during the writing of this very section where this exchange was inserted into the real-time prep of this, the final draft (and which we thought we would leave in to show the reader our pathway from chaos to, we hope, more clarity):

HELLOOOOOOOOOOOOOO — WE HAVE THE SAME IDEA AT THE SAME TIME:)!! HAHAHA!!!
GREAT MINDS!!! WILL LEAVE YOU TO DO IT
NO NONO YOU KEEP GOING!! — I WAS HOPING!! YOU MIGHT WRITE THIS BIT —
OKAY! I WILL CARRY ON -)
YOU MENTIONED IUN AN MEIL A:) IT MIGTH BE FUN:) I WILL GO LOOK AT REFERENCES

YES, THIS IS WHY I'm here -) I remember!!! -) I WILL TALK ABOUT THE WRITING PROCESS HOW WE ALL PILED IN UNTIL you couldn't figure out who was who in the writing

EYES! YES! EYES± YRES YES EYS EYS YES!!! THAT IS EXACLTY WHAT WE NEED IT WILL BE PERFECT FOR THE PREFACE

RIGHT. GONNA SAVE ALL THIS FUN STUFF IN A DIFFERENT FILE NOW in the "SILLY" folder, and get to it! HAH!

BIG HUG!

BIG HUG BACK. HERE GOES. OVER AND OUT

The process was iterative. We kept track of changes and used copious bubble comments, to the point that, every month or so, we had to make clean copies and archive the older messy ones. The result was a way of writing where we literally are no longer sure who added what or even wrote which sentence. We found this way of working entirely joyful. Our weekly Zoom meetings, sometimes lasting hours, were filled with laughter, over-sharing (of world events, life events, poems, artwork, music, and personal problems big and small), tangents, recipes, non sequiturs, and big ideas; we chatted about our lives, as well as the research imperatives driving the project.

Throughout, our aim was to delineate and critique new and collaborative artistic processes mediated by technology. In addition to our weekly research meetings, our ideas also stemmed from partaking in the online sessions that we investigate. Therefore, to some extent, we were participant researchers within this project, with each of us engaging creatively in the sessions, albeit with different responsibilities and experiences: some of us facilitating the sessions and others working behind the scenes, recording, observing, and editing.

Sharing thoughts, feelings, and experiences with researchers who, even in the most ethical and transparent ways possible, then use those ideas as "data" involves trust and generosity from all participants. We are therefore immensely grateful to all the musicians who freely gave their time and their permission for us to use the Zoom recordings to develop this book. We would very much like to thank all the members of the GIO who took part in the Zoom sessions. When we began the project, we had no idea that the sessions would grow to include over 150 participants from around the world, and, as of May 2024, over four years on from the first session, they continue. Figure P.1 acknowledges every musician from around the world who has taken part in these sessions; their generosity, trust, and camaraderie have been pivotal. We hope that their insightful contributions and our respect for their experiences shine through in all the chapters.

xviii Preface

Participants:

Aby Vulliamy	England	George Achieng	Kenya
Adriana Minu	Scotland	George Burt	Scotland
Ai Teranishi	Japan	George Lewis	USA
Alessandro Certini	Italy	George Murray	England
Alex South	Scotland	Gerry Rossi	Scotland
Ali Robertson	Scotland	Giles Lamb	Scotland
Alípio Carvalho Neto	Italy	Gino Robair Forlin	USA
Alister Spence	Australia	Gonzalo Carreño	Colombia
Allan Wylie	Scotland	Guillermo Torres	Spain
Alvin Curran	Italy	Guro Gravem Johansen	Norway
Amit Weiner	Israel	Hank McEwan	Scotland
Anto Pett	Estonia	Helle Lund	Denmark
Anthony Dolphin	England	Henry McPherson	England
Anne Pajunen	Sweden	Hope Young Bass	USA
Ángela Hoyos Gómez	Colombia	Isabella Ruiz Gallardo	Colombia
Armin Sturm	Scotland	Inês Rebelo	England
Atzi Muramatsu	Scotland	Iwona Wojnicka	Poland
Aviva Endean	Australia	Ian Birse	Canada
Bernd Ihno Eilts	Netherlands	James Bryce	Scotland
Betsy Wylie	Scotland	James Frew	Scotland
Blaise Siwula	Mexico	Jonathan O'Hear	Switzerland
Brice Catherin	Switzerland	José Manuel Páez	Colombia
Carl Bergstroem-Nielsen	Denmark	Juan Hernández	Colombia
Chris Parfitt	Wales	Juan Bermúdez	Colombia
Charles Ross	Iceland	Jenn Kirby	Scotland
Charlie Stone	Scotland	Jer Reid	Scotland
Charlotte Zerbey	Italy	Jessica Argo	Scotland
Christian Ferlaino	Italy	Jim McEwan	Scotland
Christine Kazarian	Russia	John Lilja	Norway
Clare Hall	Australia	John Russell	England
Cliona Cassidy	Scotland	Jose Manuel	Colombia
Colin Frank	England	Juraj Kojs	USA
Constance Cooper	USA	Kenichi Matsumoto	Japan
Cath Roberts	England	Ken Slaven	Scotland
Corey Mwamba	England	Lars Over Fosshein	Norway
Corrie Dick	Scotland	Laura Kavanaugh	Canada
David Robertson	Scotland	Lauren Sarah Hayes	USA
Daisuke Terauchi	Japan	Lin Zhang	China
Diego Herrera	Colombia	Linda O'Keeffe	Scotland
Dong Zhou	Germany	Lori Freedman	Canada
Douglas Ewart	USA	Luiz Moretto	England
Dmitry Shubin	Russia	Marek Chojecki	Switzerland
Dylan Del Giudice	USA	Maggie Nicols	Wales
Elena Inei	Scotland	María Bulla	Colombia
Emma Roche	Scotland	Maria Sappho	England
Emma Smith	Scotland	Marilyn Crispell	USA
Faradena Afifi	England	Marion Treby	England
Ferdinand Bergstrøm	Norway	Martina Líšková	Italy
Fergus Kerr	Scotland	Mia Weiss	USA
		Michael Duch	Norway

Figure P.1. List of participants.

Michael Kellett	Australia		
Mike Cooper	Spain		
Mike Harper	Scotland	Sue McKenzie	Scotland
Mike Parr-Burman	Scotland	Suzi Cunningham	Scotland
Minhwa Khoo	Japan	Natsuki Tamura	Japan
Minori Seki	Japan	Takako	Japan
Nancy Kerr	Scotland.	Tatiana Bogomolo	Austria
Naomi Watanabe	Japan	Theo Rossi	Scotland
Nicola Cisternino	Italy	Tia DeNora	England
Nicola Leonard Hein	Germany	Thomas Rohrer	Brazil
Nicolas Certini	Scotland	Tony Gorman	Australia
Noah Rossi	Scotland	Tori Kudo	Japan
Olenka Bulavina	Estonia	Una MacGlone	Scotland
Oscar Wylie	Scotland	Vinny Golia	USA
Paul Williamson	Australia	Yasmin Burke	Australia
Paul Harrison	Scotland	Yasuhiro Usui	Japan
Paul Stone	Scotland	Yasuko Kaneko	Japan
Peter Nicholson	Scotland	Yomayra Puentes Rivera	Colombia
Peter Knight	Australia	Yumi Hara	Japan
Pierre Ikenoue	Japan		
Pippin Wylie	Scotland	**Pets:**	
Qondiswa James	South Africa	Blacky (guinea pig)	Germany
Rachel Joy Weiss	USA	Chachi (cat)	Scotland
Rachel McBrinn	Scotland	Cetta (cat)	Italy
Raymond MacDonald	Scotland	Dora (dog)	Italy
Raquel Klien	USA	Kyna (cat)	Wales
Renzo Spiteri	Scotland	Lulu (dog)	England
Rick Bamford	Scotland	Honk (cat)	Scotland
Robert Burke	Australia	Lea (cat)	Italy
Robert Henderson	Scotland	Pupa (dog)	Italy
Roman Stolyar	Russia	Tigre (cat)	Italy
Ross Birrell	Scotland	Ellie Mae Bass (dog)	USA
Saadet Türköz	Switzerland	Muuma (guinea pig)	Germany
Sanae Ishikawa	Japan	Brutus (cat)	England
Santiago Botero	Colombia	Tammy (dog)	England
Sandy Evans	Australia	Stevie (dog)	Australia
Sarah Roche	Ireland	George (cat)	Australia
Satoko Fujii	Japan	Stanley (cat)	Australia
Sia Ahmad	Ngunnawal		
Steve Beresford	England	**Post-Humans:**	
Stian Westerhus	Norway	Chimere	AI
Stuart Brown	Scotland	Mushrooms	Organic

Figure P.1. Continued

Coauthorship is a fundamental aspect of the work and we aim to contribute to current debates challenging individualistic notions of creativity. Specifically, we seek to de-individualize some of the intellectual processes associated with writing. Consequently, distributed creativity is a key theme within the book. We look not only to the online sessions, but also to the process of writing this book, as examples of distributed creativity. While embracing this approach, each chapter also has, quite purposefully, its own idiosyncrasies that stem from how it was conceived and written. For example, Chapter 5 has a slightly different style, since one of us (author Birrell) had a stronger hand in writing it. In contrast, in Chapter 10 (and other places), we highlight our separate voices to help clarify particular points. Additionally, some chapters contain extracts from our interviews with GIO members, and in all the chapters, we each contribute to the drafting, redrafting, and editing.

We therefore present a book that is both collaboratively written and has space for individual voices. We are in some respects like a jazz ensemble, with each member relying on the others to help produce a cohesive sound. At times there were opportunities for solos, with one member of the group taking a little more of the spotlight, all the time being supported by the others. We hope this ebb and flow of stylistic character functions within a clear framework, highlighting our collective artistic and intellectual journey. We humbly believe this approach demonstrates how coauthorship can facilitate de-individuated perspectives, while at the same time giving room to share each author's unique understandings.

While we aim for a compelling overarching narrative, each chapter explores a separate theme that can function as a stand-alone topic for reading. To enhance the readers' experience, we have included QR codes and a web address in each that provide access to a series of short films containing extracts from our sessions that highlight key points. In addition, we have also reproduced many photographic stills throughout the book. We encourage everyone to watch the films; producing them has been a labor of love and we hope they are enjoyable and fun to watch, truly bringing the topics to life.

See the QR code and web address for access to the related website.

Please follow this QR code to the ⏵ companion website to view additional content for this book. Alternatively, you can access the content using this link: https://global.oup.com/us/companion.websites/9780197752845/.

As mentioned above, each of us brings a diverse range of backgrounds to this project including psychology, sociology, artistic research, music, and visual art, to name a few of the disciplines we closely identify with. However, this project transcends individual disciplines, focusing on cross-disciplinary and cross-boundary issues, post-genre concerns, and multimedia concepts, which are among the most important aspects of our collaborative exploration.

Preface xxi

The initial phase of this research project was titled "Flattening the curve" and was supported by a (Scottish Funding Council) Covid Rapid Response Research Grant from The Glasgow School of Art (GSA). We would like to thank Colin Kirkpatrick and the staff of the GSA Research Office and IT Department for valued advice, and also our recording assistants during the online improvisation sessions, Dr. James Frew and Rachel McBrinn. We express our gratitude to our colleagues at Oxford University Press, especially Michelle Chen, Senior Acquisition Editor, Music, and Dr. Rachel Ruisard, our project editor and Koperundevi and Dorothy Bauhoff our copy editors. Their invaluable help, encouragement, and guidance have been vital in developing this book from the initial idea to the final manuscript. Sincere thanks to Professor Oscar Odena, who provided detailed and insightful feedback on both our initial proposal and the whole book. We would also like to thank Dr. Jessica Argo, who, as well as being a constant member of online sessions, was instrumental in helping the project begin and flourish. She also made, and continues to make, a crucial contribution in organizing and hosting many of the sessions. Thanks also to Martel Ollerenshaw, who read and

Figure P.2. Authors meeting, January 2024.

commented on a final draft of the manuscript, and to Wolfgang Schmid, who read Chapter 6 and gave good comments. Author DeNora wants to acknowledge the Leverhulme Trust, who supported her research during the writing of this book. A big thank you to Gerry Rossi, who, as the general manager of GIO, calmly, and always in good humor, helps keep everything related to GIO functioning smoothly. It's been an incredible journey, not least because our working practices have been new and the friendships that developed so rewarding. Figure ii shows the authors at one of our final book meetings. Writing this book has been a joyous and exhilarating learning experience, and we hope that the following chapters not only bring some new ideas to life, but also convey the fun, the serious fun, we all had in our improvised collaborative endeavors.

Author Biographies

Raymond MacDonald is Professor of Music Psychology and Improvisation at Edinburgh University After completing his PhD in Psychology at the University of Glasgow, investigating therapeutic applications of music, he worked as Artistic Director for the music company *Limelight*, working with people with disabilities. He was editor of the journal *Psychology of Music* (2006–2012) and head of music at Edinburgh University (2013–2017). He is a co-founder of the Glasgow Improvisers Orchestra and, as a saxophonist and composer, has performed and recorded internationally for over 30 years. His co-edited texts include: *The Handbook of Music Identities*; *Music Health and Wellbeing*; *Musical Imaginations*; and *Musical Communication*. He coauthored, with Graeme Wilson, *The Art of Becoming, How Group Improvisation Works* and collaborated with an artificial intelligence on a book titled *Conversations with Chimère*.

Tia DeNora is Professor of Sociology at the University of Exeter. Her books include *Hope: The Dream We Carry* (Palgrave Macmillan, 2021); *Music in Everyday Life* (Cambridge, 2000); and *Music Asylums: Music and Wellbeing in Everyday Life* (Routledge, 2013). She was Principal Investigator on the AHRC *Care for Music* project (2019–2023). She held a Leverhulme Major Fellowship from 2021-2023 for the *Island Life and Death Project*, an ethnography of cultural change around death, dying, and bereavement. She is a Fellow of the British Academy.

Maria Sappho is a Nuyorican artist and researcher currently working in the United Kingdom. Maria's work is interested in post-human collaboration, often building new musical instruments working with AI and mushrooms. She gained her PhD from the University of Huddersfield as part of the European Research Council project Interactive Research in Music as Sound (IRiMaS) and continues this work as a postdoctoral research fellow on the Digital Playgrounds for Music project (DPfM). She is also the module coordinator for experimental improvisation at the Royal Conservatoire of Scotland, and is a Masters supervisor at the Institute for Contemporary Music Performance. Maria is a co-founder of the Chimère Communities project, bringing AI into marginalized, artistic, and activist spaces on a global scale. She is a founding member of the Noisebringers ensemble and the Brutalust duo, and long-time member of the Glasgow Improvisers Orchestra. Maria serves as the keyboard replacement for the Scottish post-rock band Mogwai. Maria is a winner of the BBC radiophonic Daphne Oram award.

Robert Burke (Associate Professor, Monash University) is an Australian improvising musician and composer. Rob has performed and composed on over 300 CDs, collaborating with George Lewis, Raymond MacDonald, Hermeto Pascoal, Dave Douglas, Tony Malaby, Ben Monder, Tom Rainey, Tony Gould, Paul Grabowsky, and Mark Helias. Books include: *Perspectives on Artistic Research in Music* and *Experimentation in Jazz: Idea Chasing* (Routledge). Rob is currently president of AJIRN (Australasian Jazz and Improvisation Research Network). His research focuses on jazz and improvisational processes investigating "What happens when we improvise?," including investigation into the phenomenology of musical interaction, experimentation, identity, agency, and gender studies.

Ross Birrell is Professor of Contemporary Art Practice & Critical Theory, and Senior Researcher (Interdisciplinary Practice) at The Glasgow School of Art. His artistic practice and research is predominantly focused upon site-specific/contextual art and moving-image/audio installation, and explores relationships between music, poetry, politics, and place. Often working in collaboration with David Harding, Birrell's exhibitions include: *documenta 14* (Athens/Kassel, 2017), *The Transit of Hermes*, CCA (2018), *Triptych*, Trinity Apse, Edinburgh Art Festival (2018), Where *Language Ends*, Talbot Rice Gallery (2015), *Winter Line*, Kunsthalle Basel (2014), *Duet*, Rothko Chapel (2013), *You Like This Garden?*, Portikus (2011), 4th Gwangju Bienalle (2002).

About the Companion Website

www.oup.com/us/NDMCC

Oxford has created a website to accompany *New Directions in Musical Collaborative Creativity: The Glasgow Improvisers Orchestra and the Theater of Home*. Material that cannot be made available in a book, namely film recordings of live improvisations, is provided here. The reader is encouraged to consult this resource in conjunction with the chapters. Examples available online are indicated in the text with Oxford's symbol ▶.

1
The Theater of Home and the Zoomesphere

Music is not a universal language; it is much more. Neither is it a commodity performed and consumed. As a unique communicative medium, distinct from language, music helps shape our identities, sustains and enhances communities, and provides a universally accessible and unique mode of expression—personal yet collective, and unequivocally ubiquitous. It is not merely a backdrop or soundtrack to our lives. Music provides a pliable aesthetic and psychological architecture that reciprocally influences, and is influenced by, how our existence is defined. These affordances of music came to the fore, as has been observed by many, during the global pandemic, which commenced in 2020.

In this opening chapter, we consider how the social isolation measures implemented during the pandemic posed challenges to musicians' livelihoods. For the musicians of the Glasgow Improvisers Orchestra (GIO), a large improvising ensemble based in Glasgow, United Kingdom, it also led to what we describe as a "creative constraint." This constraint served as inspiration and facilitated new ways of collaborating artistically. We describe these emerging practices as they manifest in a particular type of online musical activity. We outline some of the key characteristics of these sessions, focusing on the significance of latency as an essential element. Additionally, we delineate five key aspects of improvisation that are central to facilitating the online sessions. The chapter concludes with a brief overview of the book's structure and content.

The GIO was founded on October 26, 2002, during the "Free RadiCCAls" Festival at the Centre for Contemporary Arts (CCA) in Glasgow, an event curated by UK saxophonist Evan Parker and the then-director of the Centre, Graham McKenzie. The founding members consisted of approximately 25 individuals from diverse artistic backgrounds, encompassing free improvisation, jazz, classical, folk, pop, experimental music, and performance art, who were invited by author MacDonald, and although membership has evolved, the approximate size of the ensemble has remained the same since the band's inception. Collaborations with renowned improvisers and ensembles worldwide have helped develop GIO's artistic scope and have facilitated musical connections globally. GIO performs in various venues across the United Kingdom and Europe and hosts an annual festival in Glasgow, *GIOfest*, now in its 17th year. Since its inception, GIO has released 13 CDs and has gained international recognition and significant critical acclaim as one of the world's foremost large ensembles specializing in improvised music (Cook and Morton, 2008; Shoemaker, 2023). In addition to composing, recording, and performing, the orchestra is dedicated to an ongoing program of educational and outreach activities, including workshops, lectures, and master classes. This work seeks to promote diversity and inclusion and help break down barriers to artistic participation.

The Creative Constraint of Lockdown or "Sheltering in Place"

In March 2020, the United Kingdom implemented lockdown procedures mandating everyone (except for designated "key workers") to stay indoors and at home—a practice commonly referred to as "lockdown" in the United Kingdom and as "sheltering in place" in the United States; this initiative aimed to curb the spread of the coronavirus. Around the same period, countries worldwide were implementing similar measures, as the global pandemic necessitated measures of isolation for the world's population. This unprecedented situation is one of the precursors for this book. As individuals, families, and friends were confined within their homes around the globe, technology emerged as a crucial means for maintaining social networks and facilitating communication.

For musicians, concerts, rehearsals, and the daily practice of working together stopped. Many faced severe economic consequences, and their regular modes of collaboration and social-artistic engagement disappeared. GIO members began virtual meetings, performing music online using Zoom software. Unexpectedly, the sessions quickly evolved into a new way of working and collaborating artistically. Sessions were developed to include musicians worldwide, including players from Argentina, Australia, Brazil, Canada, Columbia, China, Mexico, India, Japan, Kenya, Russia, Turkey, the United States, and Europe. After three months, over 100 people became involved, and these twice-weekly sessions developed into an essential way of sustaining and enhancing a unique artistic community. It also facilitated the creation of new work in innovative ways, highlighting "adaptive creativity" in response to creative constraints, as detailed throughout this book.

"Adaptive creativity" is a term typically associated with dis/ability studies, addressing situations in which musicians can no longer use their bodies in the conventional ways related to their instruments (Lubet, 2018). This involves shifting position, avoiding certain musical techniques or materials, and exploring prosthetic or assistive technologies to ease the pain associated with performing. In this context, we extend the application of the term to the musical-social terrain. We use the term to emphasize how GIO's participants developed novel approaches to creativity while responding to, interacting with, and adapting to a set of circumstances. The creative constraint that participants encountered involved the removal of in-person interactions, which, until the pandemic, was the context for virtually all of the socio-creative work of the participants. The emerging practices during the online meetings took the form of innovative digital practices, which have produced a significant archive (over 500 hours) of recorded audiovisual materials. This book includes numerous web links to specific film examples, evidencing the different types of activities that took place during the sessions. These links underscore specific practical, technical, and theoretical points related to the overarching themes of this book, and we encourage readers to view these short clips, as this will enhance their understanding of our key points.

GIO Zoom Sessions

A musical Zoom session begins with musicians logging into a conference link. Using popular and accessible software like Zoom means that participants are not required to have any extra technical resources, such as external microphones or digital interfaces, and can access the meeting via smartphones, tablets, or laptop or desktop computers. Participation is therefore customizable, and some participants worked with a range of setups, integrating specialized equipment such as extra cameras, microphones, additional software, and green screens. In contrast, others used no extra technical equipment (see Chapter 2 for further details). As lockdowns gradually eased around the world, participants would often log into performances on their phones from diverse locations outside their homes, including workplaces, public environments, offices, friends' houses, trains, airport departure lounges, camping on a mountain with family, walks on a beach, or indeed anywhere that allowed access via a mobile network. The most important feature was accessibility, enabling anyone with Wi-Fi access and a device to "log" into the performance from anywhere in the world.

The improvisations explored various ways of interacting, with the overarching aim of collaborative exploration and the creative possibilities of large ensemble improvisation. For example, one strategy used regularly involves inviting musicians to play as much or as little as they want for 20 minutes, after which the group negotiates an ending. Sessions also included various approaches to structuring improvised interactions. For example, occasionally, text was employed, allowing musicians to type instructions using the chat feature or to write instructions on pieces of paper and display them to other participants. Small groups of musicians would frequently play in response to instructions such as "play 5 trios each lasting 5 minutes." Sometimes a theme would be suggested, such as playing for 15 minutes using food as a conceptual stimulus for the improvisation. Certain successful strategies were regularly revisited, such as the small group approach and providing musicians with specific themes for improvisation. These examples represent just a few of the numerous strategies used, including the use of text, filmic stimuli, artwork, conceptual themes, and so on, with improvisation as an enduring and key component of all these endeavors.

Improvisation

Across the following chapters, we consistently return to the theme of improvisation. Improvisation is an artistic process central to music-making and all creative endeavors and is also a universal social process fundamental to life (MacDonald and Wilson, 2020). Influential English guitarist Derek Bailey famously wrote that improvisation was the most practiced but the least acknowledged and understood feature of music-making (Bailey, 1993), and while this quote has been used on countless occasions as a starting point for papers, dissertations, book chapters, and research projects, this is no longer the case. Improvisation as a focus of study and practice is flourishing in universities, conservatoires, venues, and festivals around the world. It is recognized as a fundamental component of music-making and all artistic collaboration (MacDonald and Wilson, 2020; Onsman and Burke, 2018). Once conceptualized as the preserve of elite jazz musicians or exoticized as a "world music" practice, improvisation is now viewed as central to experimental music and a fundamental component of cross-disciplinary collaboration and an important skill for contemporary musicians seeking to forge a career within a cultural landscape that is complex, challenging, and often considered post-genre or even post-disciplinary. At last count, we noted more than 15 brother/sister improvising ensembles worldwide who use their location and the couplet "improvisers orchestras" in their title. These include: Atlanta, Berlin, Birmingham, Cheltenham, Helsinki, Krakow, London, Lucerne, Merseyside, Minsk, Norbotten, Sicily, St. Petersburg, Stockholm, and Vienna. There are also numerous "improvising" big bands and kitchen orchestras, such as in Bergen and Stavanger, and many projects that draw people from different backgrounds and abilities together in music using improvisation as their primary creative process. In summary, rather than being the least acknowledged and understood feature of music-making, the plethora of festivals, venues, ensembles, and institutional courses using improvisation as a focus highlights that improvisation is a creative process whose time has come.

Improvisation, while an elusively difficult term to define, foregrounds spontaneous creativity, interaction, and what might be called real-time music-making. It can be viewed as a social, spontaneous, creative, and universally accessible collaborative artistic process (MacDonald and Wilson, 2016). One particularly important application of improvisation is that it can help foster collaboration between musicians with different levels of experience in the same piece/ensemble. It can do this in significant ways that enhance artistic endeavors and empower participants. One reason for this empowerment is that improvisation has decision-making and negotiation processes at its core and is not predicated upon advanced instrumental technique, although technical mastery is unquestionably crucial to many improvisers' professional practice. The decision-based foundations of improvisational processes have been discussed by numerous researchers, and this can take the form of selecting, in real time, what notes, rhythms, melodies, and scales to focus on (Berkowitz, 2010); from a more psychological perspective, decisions such as when to start, when to stop, how loud to play, and what material to play can be viewed as fundamental building blocks of improvisation (MacDonald and Wilson, 2020). These social and psychological decisions also underpin much of the improvisational work presented in this book, particularly when the online sessions involve "free improvisation" contexts and where there are no notated elements to the music and very often no instructions beyond "play what you want, whenever you want."

The importance of adaptive creativity, improvisation, and experimentation was central to the online sessions, particularly since there are limited examples of how this type of work is undertaken outside of specialized areas of study. There were no examples of this work taking place in mainstream culture and no recognized canon of work to perform. Also, there were no general guidelines about how previous performers had negotiated this type of music-making and, therefore, no correct way to perform online and, equally importantly, no incorrect way to perform. The online sessions, therefore, facilitated the development of adaptive creativity using experimentation and improvisation, as when the sessions began, there were no artistic or social templates to follow. Experimentation is linked to the development of innovative practices because it allows experiences that create new possibilities by way of trial and error and in-the-moment observation and action (Onsman and Burke, 2018).

Latency as Synchrony

While many musicians, artists, filmmakers, and creative practitioners were experimenting with online virtual working during the early stages of lockdown, the GIO sessions included a number of key features that made these sessions distinctive. Unlike many other projects, the GIO sessions involved synchronous activity. By synchronous, we mean that musicians were interacting and collaborating online at the same time. In contrast, much online work included asynchronous activities in the sense that musicians would record and film themselves separately. The separate parts were assembled into a multi-person, multitrack recording at a later stage. The edited and integrated separate recordings would then be presented as a whole ensemble "performance." Orchestras and choirs would thus appear to perform together, creating the illusion of a synchronous performance, but in reality, each individual recorded their own part separately. Contrastingly, GIO sessions involved people performing at the same time and developing, through an adaptive experience with varying forms of latency, a new form of synchrony, as we propose below.

Much has been written about the particular way in which "latency" influences online music-making. For example, when a saxophone player plays in a particular location, it takes time for the signal to travel across the internet and be heard by the other musicians taking part in the session. Those musicians may be in a different city, a different country, or a different continent. The further the distance, the longer it takes the signal to travel. Therefore, being "in time," in the conventional sense of the word, is not possible. However, all musical engagement involves latency of some sort since it takes time for sound to travel from one location to another, whether digitally or not. Think of a choir singing in a large cathedral or a band playing a stadium rock concert. It will take some time for the sound to travel from the choir pews or the stage to the back of the cathedral or stadium. This is one of the many reasons why concert halls require careful attention to the acoustic properties of the venue. Using an improvisatory approach allows the specific context of online music-making latencies to be embraced as an emergent feature of the unfolding music and not a hindrance to the ongoing interactions.

Imagine for a moment that latency was "merely" understood as a form of impediment to "real" or "good" or "satisfying" musical praxis (i.e., it blocks what GIO members used to be able to do). In that sense, the members of GIO might be understood, or understand themselves, as "injured" musicians, that is, as musicians suffering a "loss" of ability—a "dis-ability," in other words. While it is true—and borne out again and again in interviews we undertook and discuss throughout the book—that the members of GIO who ventured into the new, online, socially distanced version of improvised music did feel a sense of "loss," it is important to clarify that the experience of a sense of "loss" was associated with social contact, and not the ability to continue to be creative improvisers.

On the contrary, and this is what we mean by the term "creative constraint," the loss gave birth to a new resource, namely new aesthetic practices that embraced, rather than sought to paper over, the latency "problem." Key here, then, to the story we will tell is how a potentially "dis"-abling situation became ultimately "en-abling," being reconfigured as an empowering situation of adaptation, adjustment, and real aesthetic adventure. The following chapters detail how these aesthetic adventures produced creative breakthroughs, positive effects on health and well-being, new knowledge about the nature of collaborative creativity, and the importance of improvising within these developments. We also place these developments within a broader context regarding the nature of collaborative creativity.

While discussing these new collaborations, latency is a key theme in three senses: first, as a technological aspect to be navigated during the sessions; second, as a new resource or condition to be explored for improvisation; and third, as a metaphor along a number of dimensions. These dimensions are relational latency (communicative acts were delayed, but individuals' visual presence is both heightened and democratized), and temporal latency, which is a delaying or asynchronizing condition that can be reduced through adaptation. So, for example, when improvisation occurs, the relational aspect of collaboration and possibly of human interactions are foregrounded and more immediate. We can see people's faces more intimately than when, as in the past, they might be ten meters removed, and we can often see into their domestic surroundings in ways that never before were possible (this relationship between visual and sonic material is discussed in detail in Chapter 5). This relational latency is particularly important and accentuated when improvising online—and only possible as a resource for *improvisation* when improvisation happens online.

In addition, the project also had a very short research latency due to the COVID context—from initial idea to first dissemination was a matter of nine months. Further, GIO's focus is on improvisation, which includes the sharing of some important understandings of music-making and interaction that are shared with the key features of social life. This includes initiating new ideas and making a series of decisions in real time—decisions that are made consciously and unconsciously or concurrently. Latency plays a limited role in this approach, as GIO does not improvise in constructed parameters of playing parts/roles in a composed (determined) synchronized time feel.

Developing this theme of the metaphorical importance of latency, the technical latencies also produced a heightened interactive immediacy within the improvisatory context. Given that the musicians cannot rely on what might be called "conventional time-based synchrony," they must utilize other strategies in order to achieve satisfying creative interactions. This need for other strategies takes the emphasis away from the energies normally associated with achieving synchrony—for example, being precisely together within a musical score or tight rhythmic, melodic, harmonic synchronization linked to a *groove* in the broadest sense (Duman et al., 2023). It shifts the balance to other aesthetic priorities—resources are deployed in assessing and responding to the developing visual and sonic array. This multimodal attention involves a heightened sensitivity; it involves responding to the immediate digital environment—beyond sound per se. Thus, technical latencies present in online improvising can activate a more holistic form of interactive synchrony, one that is fully immersed in the present moment in time (Stern, 2004). Because participants must forgo attempting to synchronize sonically in "real time," they place heightened salience on interacting with a wider array of features in the present moment. The resultant enhanced synchrony arises from the participants' integration of sonic and visual material on a moment-to-moment basis. The analysis of this integration necessitates contributions from multiple disciplines, a topic to be further elaborated upon in subsequent discussion.

The Zoomesphere and the Theater of Home

These unique features of the online creative environment were termed the *Zoomesphere*, which produced particular affordances enabling us to stay "connected," while at the same time making significant artistic breakthroughs.

Notably, a key feature of the sessions involved the domestic context in which the vast majority of musicians were engaging with the Zoom sessions. Globally, people were confined to their homes, and musicians attempted to remain creative while their movement was restricted. This produced some unique features as the technical affordances of Zoom interacted with the domestic location of the sessions. It led to the unique location that we have termed the "Theater of Home." This term is used to recognize how many features of the domestic environment were deployed within the creative setting. For example, as we will highlight, kitchenware was utilized in the Zoom sessions, with musicians playing pots and pans and using food, cups, glasses, and cutlery, not as a frivolous gimmick, but as a serious aesthetic choice, occasionally with humorous undertones but never losing the gravitas of the communicative and aesthetic imperatives of the performance. Family members also appeared within the unfolding improvisations. Moreover, there was a blurring of the boundaries between what might be considered a formal performance space and more private domestic space as the private domestic space often merged with the performative online environment. Thus, the term "Theater of Home" encapsulates the fusion of what conventionally might be considered a formal performance space with the inherently more informal domestic environment.

The sessions also produced a range of new compositions and research interviews that highlighted the benefits of the ongoing collaborative practice. The compositions foregrounded the types of strategies that can be used to structure creative endeavors online and in particular the merging of the visual with the musical. For example, author MacDonald began working on a series of audiovisual compositions with Miami-based composer and musician Rachel Joy Weiss. The collaboration was titled *Duet for Two People Who Have Never Met*,[1] and includes a piece commissioned and performed at the Huddersfield Contemporary Music Festival (Weiss and MacDonald, 2020. Importantly, this and indeed all the new work developed in the sessions emphasize the distributed nature of creativity. A distributed view of creativity sees artwork emerging from social interactions rather than from individuals (Schroeder, 2013). With this approach in mind, the online environment facilitated moving beyond the idea of the singular composer. In these collaborative endeavors the ideas, innovation, and new practices emerge not from any one individual, but rather from the social context and collaboration of all participants.

As evident from the aforementioned descriptions, the sessions involved a considerable amount of cross-disciplinary collaboration: this is particularly important when considering the improvisational context within which the musicians are working. A pivotal transformation in improvisational practices took place in the first few weeks of the lockdown sessions. Some musicians began to use the visual features of the online environment as a key component in their interactions. Consequently, improvisation facilitated a move away from purely musical interactions to music and visual/film interactions mediated by the technical affordances of the online environment. This marked a crucial "moment" in the development of the collaborative practices of the ensemble and one that we will discuss in detail in the forthcoming chapters. The unique visual display presented within the Zoom session, where each member of the group occupies the same-sized rectangle, also created a new interactive context for the group. This meant that musicians were not arranged in the more conventional "horseshoe shape" setup of in-person performance, but rather the individual screens were presented in what became the well-known Zoom format. We called this feature "flattening the curve" for both literal and metaphorical reasons (MacDonald and Birrell, 2021).

This is not improvised but that is

This book describes a particular type of improvisation, namely improvised music within the context of GIO, occurring in a distinct situation and historical time frame—improvised music in GIO online during the 2020 pandemic and its aftermath. However, from the outset, it is essential to clarify that our exploration of online improvisation in GIO is driven by a broader objective. We seek to explore the meaning of what improvisation and improvised music can be, examining the potential social, political, and aesthetic implications inherent in engaging with music in this manner.

In terms of exploring the wider implications of improvised music-making, in 2019, author MacDonald "presented" a piece with the title: *This is not improvised but that is*. The piece, delivered as a conference lecture with musical accompaniment, was dedicated to deconstructing the dichotomy of "improvisation" versus "pre-composition" (MacDonald, 2019, 2020[2]). This acknowledgment resonates with the prevalent belief in a dichotomy, wherein certain activities are perceived as scripted and are closely tied to the parameters of a text and/or to a highly specified codex of rules. In contrast, other things we do are viewed as being "freely" improvised. Author MacDonald's piece sought to question the differences and similarities between, on the one hand, reading a pre-composed text aloud ("this is not improvised"), and, on the other hand, speaking about whatever might enter our mind, perhaps even in ways that might not "connect" with whatever someone else said before.

If we think about this dichotomy and how it is manifest in everyday practices, we quickly find that it dissolves. In its place is something not quite "free" and not quite "structured," around which are myriad practices that help to make it look "as if" it were spontaneous, or "as if" it were pre-planned, and this feature of improvised, not quite free and not quite structured, is absolutely central to the sessions that we study across the whole book.

There are five themes that we have found to be useful for setting out before we embark on our main task. These themes connect to the deconstruction of the "improvised"/"pre-planned" dichotomy, and they draw our consideration of musical improvisation close to more overtly sociological and social psychological and political issues linked to expression, creativity, and communication. These themes are: (1) indexicality and rule following, (2) order and retrospective sense-making, (3) individual creative abilities, (4) the politics of experience, and finally, (5) identification and boundary work

The first theme, indexicality, captures the incompleteness of all rules. Think, for example, of a recipe for an omelet: "First break four eggs into a bowl." To the uninitiated, it may not be clear by this instruction that one is to break the shell on the edge of the bowl and tip the liquid inside it into the bowl, discarding the shell. Most recipes do not bother to explain this because they rely upon the reader's "common sense" or tacit understanding of what the instruction means. But even when the instruction is clear ("throw away the shells and do not leave pieces of shell in the bowl") there can be ambiguity. For example, some cookbooks will tell you that you should crack the egg with a knife, gently open it up in your fingers, release the liquid into the bowl, and then discard the shell. This ineluctable ambiguity of all rules means that, ultimately, the meaning of a rule is always enacted, that is, brought forth in and through collaborative action and peer-to-peer learning ("I'll show you what I mean," we might say). This theme has been considered in many domains, for example, conversation (Sawyer, 2016 [1997]), and sporting results (DeNora, 1992). It has also been considered in music, specifically around the issue of how to interpret a micro-feature of a musical score (Hennion, 1997).

The second theme of order and retrospective sense-making follows on from indexicality and rule following and has implications for how we are to understand order—as an interpretation and a social achievement. When we say that a rule "was followed," we are imputing a particular causal logic to events. A great deal of that logic, if not in fact all of it, derives from how we produce accounts about "what happened" and "what it meant." We make a particular sense of events that is inevitably selective—our account ("you have followed the recipe for omelet very well, and this is a great omelet") places a particular (possible) spin or complexion on what has happened. It is linked to real, physical events (how an egg is cracked or a liquid stirred), but it couples those events with slanted ways of appreciating, defining, and arranging them in relation to many other things, including values. This arranging is itself improvised, most obviously when it is done through the real-time medium of talk, but also when done through the medium of retrospective critique, and that improvisation involves placing a particular frame around "what happened" earlier.

So even when actions are deemed to be closely following rules or texts, there is a kind of wiggle room, space for agency, and space for improvisation. And that space and the actions that claim to be un-improvised are anything but. The appraisal of those actions is also improvised. And yet, in both cases, we may be acting "as if" we are "merely" carrying out rule-based actions where the rules are "obvious"—"easy to follow," "what anyone would know"—and "as if" in appraising that action we are "merely" recognizing the degree to which an action "conforms" to preordained rules. By that logic, skill, craft, technique, and even creativity can be defined in terms of the degree to which they match predetermined criteria of judgment.

The comparison with cooking also extends to many music talent shows on television where conventional aesthetic hegemonies (e.g., how "in tune" or how "normal" a singer appears) are often used to ridicule and humiliate contestants. Notions of rules to be followed and constraints also highlight the possible connections with concepts of freedom. Writings on improvisation often discuss issues of freedom and how improvised activities provide opportunities to explore creative freedom. However, in all improvised activities, including music, the notion of freedom is relational. In other words, from what are musicians free? Are they free, for example, from more rule-bound forms of making music? And what are musicians free to do . . . anything, or . . . ? Freedom to improvise normally includes certain norms or expectations. Perhaps those norms and expectations are broader in improvised music in comparison to what might be called non-improvised music, but they still exist. The online sessions are somewhat different because there were no previous online sessions undertaken by GIO, or by any ensemble, which might have acted as a benchmark or gold standard. Thus, the sessions provided a completely new context for exploring creative interactions, a context which, to some extent, was free from expectations and rule-bound notions of making music.

By that logic, moving to the third theme, it is individuals who exhibit creativity that is "merely" recognized by others who do not contribute to the value of that creativity by their acts of judgment and response. So, for example, if I make an omelet and you, acting as a judge on a TV cookery contest, taste it and comment upon its excellent texture (but do you prefer fluffy or creamy omelets, and which one is "better"?) then the "excellent" omelet is due to my skill at making an omelet and your discernment at being a critic. This way of thinking about creative ability masks the ways that your declaration that this is hereby an excellent ("eggsellent") omelet is a particular kind of performative utterance, one that foregrounds some—of potentially many and potentially contradictory—criteria, and backgrounds other criteria. It brings into being the reality of the goodness of the omelet and the chef, while hiding the fact that the goodness was co-produced, performed in and through the improvised act of proclaiming goodness as "in" that omelet (and creative ability "in" the chef).

From there, it is perhaps easy to see how the fourth and fifth themes (the politics of experience, and finally, identification and boundary work) follow—and interrelate. The fourth theme calls attention to the politics of experience, how, in being creative, we draw upon and sometimes wish to assert features and concerns from our personal lives ("the personal is political"). How I make my music (or my omelet) will have much to do with my habitus, my quasi-conscious, habitual patterns of action, reflexes, and tastes. The fifth theme calls attention to how, in judging what I produce, you may be doing symbolic violence to my work, asserting your definition of the situation of creative production "as if" it were the only correct one and, by implication, "as if" my skills as a musician (or a cook) are deficient. You are also upholding your own status as a critic by making the claim that there "is" a "right way" to make music (or an omelet). And from there, in failing to recognize the inherent indexical, retrospectively produced, collaboratively performed, political nature of creating something, we are also solidifying the boundaries around types of identity, as if they are preordained (I become "a bad musician/cook," you become a "good critic") and in ways that—when repeated and repeated—allow reputations and identity entitlements to become entrenched.

If, however, we can manage to hold open the idea that whenever we make something, define something, do something, or say something, we are engaging in a kind of improvisatory activity that is, at that moment, bringing possible realities into being, then we are also holding open the possibilities of difference and of change. And in this sense, improvisation is, as MacDonald and Wilson (2020) say, "the art of becoming."

Previous Work

The analysis presented in the following chapters draws significantly on a series of 29 research interviews undertaken by authors MacDonald and Burke several months after the Zoom meetings began in 2020. All interviewees were regular participants at the online sessions, and ethical approval for this project was granted by Edinburgh University. Interviews were recorded on Zoom and fully transcribed and analyzed in accordance with recognized criteria outlined by Denzin and Lincoln (2005). Importantly, all coauthors were involved in the analysis of the data and the development of the key themes and implications. For a detailed outline of this part of the overall project, see MacDonald et al. (2021).

There are three publications that outline our initial research in this area, detailing the processes and outcomes of these sessions and our early research interviews (Burke et al., 2024; MacDonald and Birrell, 2020; MacDonald et al., 2021). This work emphasizes the emergence of Zoom software as a resource in qualitative research (Toma and Bidet, 2024). The GIO online sessions also feature as a major case study in author Sappho's PhD dissertation (Sappho, 2022). These publications highlight a number of key features of the online environment. For example, participants at the sessions were, in effect, both performers and audience. Taking part in a Zoom session involves looking at a screen and watching and listening, in a similar way to which an audience member might watch an online performance, while also making a choice about when to play. Therefore, musicians are performing and also listening and watching as an audience member. This work also highlighted that not only were there creative breakthroughs, but that the ongoing meetings provided a variety of social and psychological benefits as well. The sessions proved to be not only creatively rewarding but also psychologically important for the participants. These benefits (which included reduced feelings of social isolation and positive effects on mental health) and their implications will be examined throughout the course of this book. Additionally, the social and psychological advantages arising from the capability to maintain connections through both technological and artistic avenues will be explored.

As the world emerged from this period of extreme social isolation, the assumption was that we would return to pre-pandemic modes of interaction. However, the online sessions taught us new ways of working together, new ways of collaborating, and new ways of sustaining and enhancing our community, and it is these new ways that this book focuses on.

Structure of the Book

This book is structured into 10 chapters and three sections. Section 1, Chapters 1 and 2, presents an introduction, including our initial research and practical work in this area, focusing on the GIO online sessions. We also position this work within wider contexts of online music-making and telematic artistic collaboration, including examples of other types of online musical collaborations taking place during COVID restrictions. In other contexts, technology was being used around the world as a means of staying connected, and we draw out some parallels between GIO's work and other musicians and individuals seeking to sustain their community through collaborative artistic endeavors. Section 2, Chapters 3–7, focuses on the analysis of these online sessions. These chapters draw out specific ideas and contextualization within broader debates regarding collaborative creativity. Chapter 3 focuses on how openings are negotiated, while Chapter 4 investigates specific important moments within the sessions. Chapter 5 explores the relationship between the visual and sonic material with an emphasis on how these two elements were integrated to produce new creative practices, while Chapter 6 discusses how endings are negotiated. Chapter 7 explores the range of new practices that developed during the sessions with an emphasis upon what we term "new virtuosities," that is, new and/or previously undervalued musical or artistic practices fundamental to successful creative work. In Section 3, Chapters 8–10 discuss the wider implications of the results. Chapter 8 explores the implications of the results in terms of creative identities and educational and therapeutic practice, while Chapter 9 draws together the findings from the analyses chapters in Section 2 to discuss new understandings of experimentation in improvisation through the experiences and discoveries of the participants performing in a virtual environment. Finally, Chapter 10 focuses on the possibilities of numerous hybrid environments becoming normalized in a post-pandemic global landscape, and we discuss how creative practices in the future could be influenced by online experiences.

Throughout the book, we highlight the interconnectedness of social, artistic, and psychological factors, emphasizing how technology and improvisation can facilitate artistic collaboration. Indeed, the collaborative process not only enables the sustainment and enhancement of communities but also fosters artistic breakthroughs that can be life-affirming and inspiring. We combine our own research with the research of others to show the fundamental importance of artistic collaboration and how technology can facilitate collaborative endeavors during exceptionally difficult times. The following chapter emphasizes how artistic engagement can facilitate creative, psychological, and social developments mediated by technology.

2
The Evolution of Digital Music Approaches in Practice and Care

This chapter presents an overview of digital music-making in relation to telematic and networked musical creativity. Two case studies are then analyzed to highlight specific examples of how online music-making has been used in broad contexts to meet the challenges of the global pandemic. The first example covers a virtual collaboration between a Glasgow-based music company and an Austin-based music therapy center (Quigley and MacDonald, 2024), and the second outlines a hospital-based community therapy study called Care for Music.[1]

Human-Machine Creative Cultures

There are two core relationships with technology at the heart of the practices that were developed by distanced digital creative communities working during the pandemic. One deals with the enmeshed collaboration of working with computers within a creative network (human-machine interaction). The other relies on the use of the internet as a mode for expanding ensemble/community possibilities. The practices that developed during the pandemic therefore sit at the crossroads of computer music and telematic or networked music and respond to new materialist perspectives regarding the impact and role of technology in developing new creative cultures.

Networked and Telematic Music

Discussions around online creative collaborations are topical and ongoing, but they have been taking place ever since the internet began: "Telematics will affect the major instruments of culture: language, in its relations to the individual, and even in its social function; and knowledge, as an extension of collective memory" (Nora and Minc, 1980, p. 128). Free improvisers have reportedly been using digital conferencing software (*CU-seeme*) for networked music meetings since the early 2000s (Lewis, 2020). Many forums and groups for telematic improvisation populate the community, including Pauline Oliveros's *Telematic Circle*,[2] the Telematic Improvisation Resources on *The Improvisers Network*,[3] and the *Avatar Orchestra Metaverse*,[4] a group that meets entirely digitally (forming their own characters/instruments/identities) entirely within the video game *Second Life*. Notable ensembles include "The Hub," founded in 1986, which was one of the first networked music ensembles (and is still running today):

> The telematic musical experience embodied by The Hub is inextricably bound up with two crucial elements: real-time improvisation and networked agencies of interaction. And now, because of the recent pandemic, we are all telematic, rendering the vision of the hub both prescient and urgent. (George Lewis quoted in Brümmer et al., 2021, pp. 157–158)

A key feature of approaches to telematic music-making, or online music-making, is that these previous (pre-pandemic) approaches were essentially for "specialist" practitioners, and the accounts published were catering to individuals who already had expert knowledge or an interest in what might be considered a "niche" practice. The pandemic produced a seismic shift in how people globally utilized online communications since, for a significant period of time, people were confined to their houses; thus what had been the preserve of a small group of interested parties suddenly became the only means of group communication. For people working in the creative industries, this presented, quite unexpectedly, an opportunity born out of necessity.

Networked music practice enhances an awareness of a human-machine relationship, often involving an indeterminate property that affects the ways ideas are managed within a group. The design of the system in which creative practice meets with technology greatly affects the form of work created. During the explosion of pandemic-related networked music practices, a number of meeting models emerged between players. Most notably, these include the use of online meeting platforms and digital conferencing software, including Zoom, Google Hangouts, Microsoft Teams, and Twitch; stand-alone network music platforms such as Jamkazam and Sonobus; and intermediary programs for software enhancement, including Max MSP, OBS, Snap Cam, and Camtwist. Furthermore, it is also common for players to combine the use of software; for example, the use of Sonobus and Zoom affords a focus on enhanced sound and latency (Sonobus), while still retaining in-time visuals (Zoom).

As discussed in Chapter 1, all GIO online sessions took place within Zoom, which coincided also with many of the internal updates of the software adapting to global needs. Zoom was the best available option as it is accessible, no expert knowledge is needed in order to use it, and it is possible to access via a range of devices (phones, tablets, computers). Perhaps most importantly, the functionality of Zoom meant that people could quickly and easily master the basics and commence online communication with ease. GIO decided to use Zoom software for these reasons—it seemed to be the easiest way to facilitate group communication, and we decided to stick with it for these reasons of accessibility even while many musicians were experimenting with other platforms which offered lower latencies and higher production values. We felt that ease of use would allow more people to sustain engagement with their sessions. Once again we felt the drawbacks of Zoom's longer latency and a general "thinning out" of the musical material could be viewed as emergent features of the ongoing improvisations and not necessarily as a drawback to the musical interactions—we welcomed these glitches and latency as important features of the creative performance (Nachmanovitch and Krueger, 2022). There are also wider concerns of a multinational business's corporate software becoming integral to community practice, Including consideration of the ways in which these kinds of technologies are entering society and surveillance culture more broadly. These subjects are discussed further in Chapter 9.

Human-Computer Relationships

The human-machine relationship has a rich history in improvised music practices where improvisers have been actively engaged in exploring the possibilities of inviting computers into improvisational spaces (Mills, 2019). Working with a machine as if it is another stimulus echoes the strong relationship in improvised music which acknowledges the post-humanist perspective of the importance of non-human/more-than-human actors within the creative setup (Frank, 2021; Reardon-Smith et al., 2020; Rottle and Reardon-Smith, 2023; Sappho, 2020). To this end, players have designed several important computer-improvising systems that contextualize the contemporary use of computers in the GIO digital sessions.

Depending on how a computer-improvising system is designed, there are various affordances given to the human and the machine; the differences in the setup therefore impact the relationship between the actors—what kind of control they each have within the music. How a system is designed highlights many components of improvisation theory that might be implemented within a computer program. Several examples are described below which outline the use of these machines to investigate musical parameters and techniques, hierarchies in ensembles, and understandings of sonic identities.

Building a machine-improvising system requires consideration of structural logics of practice which might be developed toward a notion of "machine musicianship" (Mills, 2019; Rowe, 1993). For example, in the Cypher program, a complex analysis of compositional and listening techniques is implemented so that the output of the machine is readily apparent to a human listener (Rowe, 1992); that is, sense-making between human and machine creative outputs is achieved through the reflection of innate human listening and cognitive processes. In another way, Lewis's pioneering Voyager system was designed to challenge the relationship between "human leader/computer follower" (Lewis, 2000, p. 35) toward non-hierarchical notions of ensembleship central to free improvisational practices. Voyager is often installed on a Disklavier, meaning that the machine has direct access to a live acoustic instrument and therefore has largely equal sonic agency within the improvisational space. Finally, another important element of human-computer improvisational work is that which focuses on the augmentation of live human contributions, for example, IRCAM'S OMax software, which recycles performer-based phrases to generate a notion of expanded self-ensemble, allowing players literally to play with a previously recorded version of themselves as ensemble partners. This approach was extended by the Donohue+ system, which develops the musical content of the live player by specifically designing a bespoke extension of that player's practice logic, thus producing a mirror of that player's sonic signature. With Donohue+, author Sappho's improvisational logic as a pianist was utilized to train the machine to play like Sappho, allowing Sappho to play alongside a fictional, yet recognizable version of herself live as an ensemble partner (Gillies and Sappho, 2021).

In contemporary practice where telematic music enhances the possibilities for the human-machine relationship, players are variously adapting their setups to create bespoke and diverse computer-enhanced improvising setups. For example, GIO players have reported using a wide range of technical setups in joining a Zoom call, ranging from simply joining on a phone while in transit, or to intricate amplification, multi-camera, green-screen productions which afford a complex and interdisciplinary approach to audiovisual improvisation (MacDonald et al., 2021). While all players might not be joining a GIO session specifically with electronic instruments or complex setups, they are all nevertheless noting the enhanced relationship of working with Zoom as a machine element within the improvised setup. The players consider Zoom in this setting variously as a new collaborator, a new instrument, and a new member of the ensemble, and many of the compositional works that the group has developed reflect a consideration of the kinds of parameters that can be highlighted/seized by the central role of a machine. As with the evolution of telematic music histories, the rise of the use of Zoom and digital conferencing software for group improvisation settings affords the group new opportunities to explore new and accessible ways to develop work in technology-assisted creative practice. GIO's members understood these points and described the new possibilities, relationships, and selves afforded by the new technologies. For example:

> I then started to have this relationship with Zoom itself, you know, in terms of its pauses and stuff... all sorts of things that have agency, and I'm of the mind that everything has an agency in its own way. Just because something is non-human doesn't mean that the presence to do something is not there.... So for example, there's the agency of Zoom itself to select based on criteria. It could be that there's not necessarily an intelligence behind what it selects, but there is a method to how it selects, and it's partly based on volume and partly based on frequency. Sonic frequency. So, I think it's massive. I think agency is really important and especially since we've got this other instrument, which is Zoom. Each of us has Zoom as an instrument and it has its own ideas. (Corey Mwamba, quoted in (MacDonald et al., 2021)

> Zoom is somehow almost like the final participant or the kind of the moderator of the improvisation.... Zoom is like an additional player or conductor or something that's choosing what we all hear. (Stuart Brown, quoted in MacDonald et al., 2021)

In both audio and visual editing (selecting short film extracts from longer sessions, moving between gallery, speaker, or "pin" view functions, post-production, and credits) the software effectively became a "non-human collaborator," in Bruno Latour's terms, an equal actant in producing the final recording (MacDonald and Birrell, 2021).

In Chapter 7, this theme is revisited, delving into these new developments that contribute to an understanding of the new virtuosities made possible by this setting. These developments include the development of improvisational tactics such as conduction and graphic scores, exploration of concepts involving more-than-human actors like toys and objects, the presentation of augmented and personalized versions of identity and self through video augmentation and costume, and the creation of bespoke performance spaces and hybrid events.

Digital Identities

One of the marked changes in the availability and accessibility of these new digital meeting forms has produced a contemporary demographic shift in networked music practice. That is, with the rise of these new easy-to-access non-specialist technologies, which might be run with simple hardware, a new generation of international, gender-diverse, and non-age-specific electronic and network music players is emerging. This reflects a practice-based shift that has organically altered the often noted Western- and male-dominated presence in electronic musics and telematic music historical practice (Rodgers, 2010). While these changes emerged without a conscious intent toward the diversification of technology-assisted creative practice, the results nevertheless reflect wider sociocultural research investigating the power of digitality in expanding and empowering the development and assertion of more diverse identities (Russell, 2020). This subject is further explored in Chapter 5 and Chapter 9, delving into the implications of digitally enhanced work in a number of sectors. In essence, online music collaboration quickly, and globally, shifted from a niche specialist activity to a mainstream activity. Many people with no previous experience are engaged with new technologies and new creative processes in order to continue working and to remain connected to their communities.

The emergent practice developed within digital creative platforms imitates a wider shifting role for technologies in social culture. These developments reflect a growing body of research that is investigating the expansion of human possibilities present within the advent of digital and internet communities (Coleman, 2011; Haraway, 1991; Russell, 2020). Essentially, this signifies an expansion of the known and logical world through the implementation of self- and community-generated realities that retain agency to independently agree upon their own social norms and ethical constructs. This is an element of contemporary society that Beth Coleman considers the "X reality," a point in which technology aids the ability to construct social spaces that exist outside traditional physical limitations—expanding opportunities for those with protected or marginalized characteristics or disabilities to live in ways that would not be possible in the "real world" (Coleman and Shirky, 2011). Coleman and Shirky propose that the influx of digital realities in everyday life produces a bifurcation of possible realities—multiple realities that are experienced and which affect daily life in parallel—layers of human social interaction may coexist within the wide variety of digital media experiences that influence a person's daily life (internet, social media, video games, or forms of virtual and augmented reality) and which also afford the drawing across digital and physical realities—for example, experimentation with gender identity "online" before a "real-world" presentation (Russell, 2020).

These views of identity move beyond anthropocentric representations of self, that is, where individual humans might be seen as non-central to a web of much greater human and more-than-human intra-actors (Barad, 2007). The pandemic produced a new lens through which to explore these new materialist perspectives of identities intermixed with the rise of digital technologies' prominence in global communication and the creative activities at the center of this book. In other words, we were all forced to use technology to stay connected with our extended social networks (socioeconomic status notwithstanding). This enhanced use of technology created a shift in our understanding of the embodied nature of communication, including our relationship with our physical bodies, as communication became virtual. Thus post-human or new materialist notions of "self" became normalized and "on show," possibly much more quickly than they would have in the absence of the pandemic, and digital and physical realms of identity and creative development flourish, influencing both online and offline practice. And in this new creative space we (a mixture of specialist and non-specialist technologists) explored and became familiar with our digital avatar and co-developed methodologies for these digital avatars to interact with other digital avatars; responding again to Coleman and Shirky, a flourishing x-artistic practice could be said to have emerged (Sappho, 2022, 2023). As Legacy Russell proposes, we evolved into "digital natives" and users of a new "bionic patois," as the very notion of continuing to develop a socially motivated creative practice sought adaptation in the only available (digital) spaces possible during this period.

> The passage of glitched bodies between the internet underground and the AFK (away from keyboard) arena activates the production of new visual culture. A sort of bionic patois, fluent to the digital native. Suspended between on and offline. Eternally traversing this loop. (Russell, 2020, p. 45)

Hence, the confluence of a "need"—a means to continue to meet and make music and sustain community in an uncertain time, and the possibilities of contemporary technology, afforded GIO's exploration within the multiple realities available in digital social worlds. We propose that three key influences and shifts have affected GIO's community over this time which contributes toward the central claims of the contemporary practice at the heart of this book: first, the understanding of the effect of the specific blend of digital and physical space in which players and prospective audiences are meeting

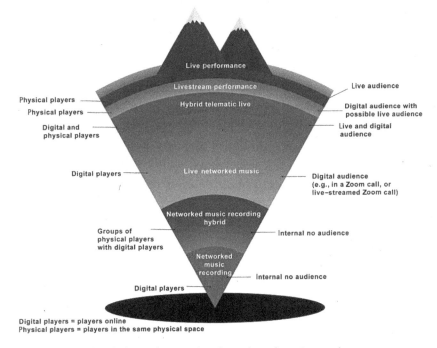

Figure 2.1. Digital and physical spaces in telematic and music practices.

(highlighted in Figure 2.1); second, the mediation and development of new social constructs and practices which are necessitated via the now expansive possible physical and digital meeting points (discussed in Chapter 3); and third, the resulting impacts on individual and community identity expression which emerges with the possibility for bespoke control over surroundings—including instrument design, embodiment, exploration and development of new techniques, and contextual influences (discussed in Chapter 7).

Digital Spaces

With the global proliferation of digital interaction driven by pandemic needs, different social groups carry different interactive needs for the spaces and places in which they wish to build their society's shelter. The wealth of software and approaches aforementioned suggests an array of options for global communities to create art, share ideas, and connect during challenging times. The diversity of these digitally enhanced social spaces has a great impact on the nature of meetings taking place and is therefore important to outline here, with particular regard to those that have emerged as central new identities for GIO in recent years. Figure 2.1 outlines the extent of the digital and physical mixture in these working practices, with specific regard for the options of "audience" and "performer" interaction. These range from entirely digital meeting spaces, where players meet in a closed space for the recording and practice of works with no audience present, to hybrid spaces which combine digital and physical players with digital and physical audiences. On the accompanying website, Figure 2.1 is presented with exemplar videos (▶ Films 2.1–2.6); on this page the reader might engage with each "layer" of digital performance practice and its corresponding example combination of digital and physical creative space use.

QR Code: Please follow this QR code to the ▶ companion website to view additional content for Chapter 2. Alternatively, you can access the website using the link provided in the front matter.

The difference between the above-noted digital and physical spaces is important, as the makeup of the presence of audience and player embodied-ness affords different social outcomes and, in turn, requires diverse new considerations surrounding the care needed to mediate between digital and physical bodies. In spaces that operate with digital-only human presences, players and audiences have similar needs: that of the creation of a space that affords hearing and seeing the necessary digitally present bodies. Nevertheless, contingent upon the setup and intention of the work at hand, different social interactions can be encouraged. For example, in a live-streamed Zoom session where players are present together within the software, while the audience is viewing on a separate stream (on platforms like YouTube, Twitch, Facebook, etc.), players manifest as physical bodies. There is also the further possibility of internalized text chat within the software among the players. In contrast, the audience presence is more abstract, with individuals coming and going, and are only present through the "viewer" count and any possible "live commenting" function available on the chosen live-streaming platform. Conversely, in live performances conducted entirely digitally, where both players and audiences are present within the chosen digital performance space, a different dynamic unfolds. Audiences are actively invited within a shared space, potentially appearing on screen between or even during performances (audience interactive works). In some cases, audiences have direct access to the internal working processes of the artist's approach to mediating the digital space, including a view of internal chat. This matters because it is a function of digital involvement that expands the choices of proximity in the presentation of artistic works and, in turn, generates new avenues for the framing of "concert." In all cases in digital-only work, participants have more agency over their presence in the work, which does not require physical travel or adherence to traditional concert etiquette aesthetics.

In contrast, hybrid digital meetings must instead redefine the performance space in order to accommodate a wide variety of performer and audience digital-physical needs. In these settings, there is a greater need for specialist knowledge and gear to achieve. This includes savvy technical support in amplifying physical space sounds with those that are transmitted digitally, often including careful attention toward feedback and level balancing. In GIO's 2021 and 2022 festivals, it was important for the digital players to be visible in space. This necessitated the setup of both multiple cameras in space (for digital players to see physical players) and for the projection of digital screens (for physical players and audiences to see digital players). Moreover, the performances were live-streamed on the GIO website using separate cameras in the space, adding further layers of complexity to the notion of "liveness." Digital audiences had access to views of both the stage and digital performance, which would be less apparent to live audiences in the space with the musicians, and vice versa. These outputs, along with others, are further elaborated upon in Chapter 7.

This short overview of the many forms of technology enveloped in the contemporary digital practices explored by GIO assists in understanding what is trying to be achieved by the group and the kinds of "meeting" places chosen to achieve these goals. This includes both the wishes of the ensemble to seek new forms of practice and to continue to make music together. It also includes an expanded interest in the kinds of audiences and communities which these practices are being produced for. Considering the contemporary era of digital music-making therefore allows for an understanding of the emergence of new kinds of ensembles and forms of membership, new instruments, techniques and tools, new possibilities for audiences and outputs, and adaptive and unique methodologies employed by groups that facilitate these collective goals. In the case of GIO and the many experiments with digital and hybrid performance spaces, it is possible to witness an ensemble that is continuing to seek opportunities to involve its now expanded global artistic pool within the wider range of the group's outputs. This includes the involvement with a much wider set of artistic practitioners and global audiences, as well as the now important roles of collaborative videographers and live-stream directors who have become innate to the new working practices. The following explores two further examples of groups working with similar digitally enhanced music setups using online conferencing software where the community, audience, and tools respond to alternative goals than those of GIO, proposing the further wider implications of the implementation and development of these new creative cultures.

Digital Music Cultures: Two Examples

Rock 'n' Roll Music Therapy

During the pandemic, various forms of online music therapy and community music developed as a way of maintaining ongoing interventions for vulnerable groups while respecting physical distancing guidelines and rules (Carvajal, 2020). Like the GIO Zoom sessions, these projects utilize communication-based technologies. There is a long history of using these types of telemedicine technologies to provide access to care and interventions where geography, time, and/or sociocultural barriers might make in-person work difficult (Wootton, 1996). While various types of technologies have been used, an important point is that there is an expanding body of evidence highlighting that music can play a key role in maintaining and enhancing health in both clinical and non-clinical contexts; therefore utilizing technology to facilitate musical engagement can have both education and healthcare benefits, and technology can play an important role in the maintenance of musical activity (MacDonald et al., 2012).

Quigley and MacDonald (in press, 2024) studied an online music project for individuals with disabilities that employed both music therapists and community musicians. Participants and facilitators were based in either Austin, Texas (USA), or Glasgow, Scotland. Utilizing Zoom software, over a two-month period, facilitators ran 16 music workshops where participants wrote, recorded, and participated in an online event that broadcast these new compositions via a series of films. Interviews with participants and facilitators highlighted several key themes suggesting that the project facilitated the development of important personal narratives for the participants. There was clear evidence that participants experienced feelings of achievement, mastery, creativity, and self-expression, in part due to the unique socio-creative online environment and the unique manner in which the online community work developed.

Rather than the online environment hindering communication, results suggest that the home environment (Theater of Home) in which the participants were working enhanced creativity. Possibly participants experience an enhanced sense of agency and control in their more familiar home situation.

> They were allowed to stay in their familiar and comfortable environment, again, the musicality, and the contributions and the flow from Michael and Trey was [sic] so much more natural. But they were always in their own comfort zone, so I think that allowed much more energy to go into the creative process. (music therapist, quoted in Quigley and MacDonald, 2024)

The project highlights a number of key features regarding how online music sessions can be tailored to meet the specific needs of participants and successfully delivered. Facilitators and participants do not need to travel long distances; therefore new opportunities for collaborative music-making are created by using online technology like Zoom (Lorweth and Knox, 2019).

The participants also reported that the online environment facilitated the creation of both lyrics and musical accompaniment and in particular reported that an important aspect of the workshop was being able to express personal stories when songwriting. This included seemingly mundane everyday themes (a kite stuck in a tree) which facilitated the expression of important emotions. This type of psychological process, where music can communicate feelings that might not otherwise be expressed, is an important feature of the overall musical communication process.

It was also clear that improvisation was an important part of the sessions, and there were many examples of lyrics being generated via improvisation by the participants.

> "In the Park" came from Michael just improvising his own lyrics. We were playing, and he just was making up all these kinds of scenarios, something that was happening in a park. And we didn't know that he was improvising at the time, I thought that he was singing a song that he had already learned before. (music therapist, quoted in Quigley and MacDonald, 2024)

Additionally, improvising appeared to help the musical style of the composition emerge during the sessions:

> If you're writing in a group situation improvisation is a good way of creating the vibe of the song. . . . I mean obviously every song is written in a different way, but the things that we did helped us to find the style that would suit the people in the band. (community musician, quoted in Quigley and MacDonald, 2024)

The extracts above highlight the important role of improvisation in the online session and illustrate how improvisation processes promoted the exploration of both musical and narrative ideas. This raises questions that, ultimately, are about values—questions about the nature of musical sound, the degree of multimedia content, the importance of synchronous moments, the value of random features, and the degree of "control" over a sound or work. Moreover, these questions carry implications for what comes to count as "capability." They prompt considerations about how, when, and whether to "compensate" or "enhance" forms of capability or capacity, and the means by which such compensations or enhancements should be implemented. The parallels drawn resonate with ongoing discussions in the dis/ability literature. For example, should hearing "impairment" be addressed through technologies such as cochlear implants and hearing loops, or should "everyone" learn sign language? These questions delve into the social distribution of adaptation—determining who needs to adapt and change, and in relation to what and whom. We now consider these themes through descriptions of ongoing projects where the issue of latency and holistic present-moment attention are explored.

Care for Music

The Care for Music Project ran from May 2019 to May 2023. It focused on how, in care homes and hospices, and often *in extremis*, people still care for music. The project's aim was to flip the usual focus on music "for" care. Instead of asking how music might work as an "intervention" or to manage behavioral or physical symptoms, it asked how caring for music—engaging, participating, and savoring music—might enrich lives in ways that might thereby also enrich the quality of life in otherwise constrained circumstances.

Methodologically, the project used micro-ethnographic observation, video analysis, discourse analysis, and gestural analysis to examine how, in musical situations, relations, atmospheres, and identities took shape, were transformed, and allowed for meaningful interaction. The site of the study was Hill House, a "neurodisability" care home in a major metropolitan area in the United Kingdom.

Music therapist Gary Ansdell and sociologist Tia DeNora began working on this project at the care home "Hill House" in 2017. Subsequently, live music sessions have been consistently held for a couple of hours one afternoon each week. The music includes anyone who's there at the time, including residents, family members, and staff, who may join briefly or simply dance through to the kitchen. Most weeks the ambience in the sitting room typically turns gradually from sleepy to lively. There is also unexpected musical participation as people sing, dance, play instruments, or just tap a foot. On occasions, residents silently mouth the words to a song: residents singing to their next-chair neighbors. Staff members observed residents exhibiting behaviors they had never seen before. In moments of rare intimacy, the wife of one resident may hold hands and sing with her husband who, once eloquent, no longer has spoken language. These afternoons are often convivial and joyful. The atmosphere lightens. There is a palpable sense of presence, with residents reconnecting with themselves and coming together in a powerful way.

Then the music stopped as COVID-19 struck. In March 2020, almost all care homes in the United Kingdom were in crisis. Family visits and social activities ceased immediately as care homes valiantly adapted to the new situation to protect their vulnerable residents. Gary sat at home feeling helpless—thinking about what was happening at Hill House, worrying about the residents he had grown so fond of, and wondering if the situation would spell the end of music therapy sessions there.

Three weeks later, the manager asked if Gary would continue the music sessions by Skype. His first thought was, "This will be impossible!" In those early days of the pandemic, musicians all over the world were rapidly discussing online how to manage music therapy, music teaching, or music performance now. The talk was of synchronous and asynchronous timing—facing the simple fact that on the internet, current technological limitations meant that we see quicker than we hear, so there is a significant time lapse that causes music-making in real time to be challenging and often unsatisfactory. Gary wondered how he could possibly manage this when the people he was making music with also had perceptual and cognitive challenges due to their age or disability.

But he tried. The first week, care workers organized some of the residents in a row in front of the large TV in the living room that was linked up to Skype through a carer's mobile phone, and Gary sat in front of his laptop miles away, singing and playing guitar and piano. The beginning of that first session felt chaotic and hopeless: the signal kept dropping out, and Gary felt he was singing to himself as he watched some of the residents he knew staring at the TV screen in what looked to him like puzzlement. But then a moment later . . . Saul looked up at the TV, moved his arm upward along with the musical phrase, waited, and as Gary sang a downward melody, he gradually lowered his conducting arm along with Gary's voice. Musical connection! The rest of the session was messy, and probably unsatisfactory to everyone, but Gary learned something crucial—it was possible.

In the end, Gary conducted over 100 of these Skype sessions. It has helped him rethink what it can mean to have a—as he understood it—successful session. Frequently, these sessions unfold in a spontaneous and occasionally disordered manner, creating moments of confusion where participants may find themselves uncertain about the proceedings. His vision of the room is limited (mostly he sees just the aspect of the room in front of the camera) and in two dimensions. The internet signal is intermittent. Residents are often sleepy or not feeling up for it—though this is often no different from when music was live.

Despite these challenges, there are moments when it really works, when people seem to look right through the TV, right through the physical distance that separates them. There is mutual learning and support as everyone adapts to the constraints. Residents are singing to each other again. They are pointing to the TV screen, alerting each other to what is going on. Staff are singing with the residents, dancing with them, and dancing with each other. Staff members say that in these tough times when they are stressed and overworked, just five minutes of doing live music with the residents and with each other make all the difference. "It's therapy for us," is what many of them said.

Initially, the concern was about the threat to Music Therapy practice, the core values of traditionally conceived notions like synchronous moments. Then, because the best was the enemy of the good, the practices shifted—away from ideals and preconceived notions of what was absolutely required for, as the team understood it, music therapy to work and toward what was—in a word—practical. From there, new means for establishing co-presence were increasingly discovered and implemented. For example, as we have just described, gesture (and the visual) became increasingly important; moving to music was a way of demonstrating attenuation and connection and the use of props:

> T. who "hands Ed a cuppa" through the TV camera eye . . .
> pointing to Ed on the TV, alerting each other. . . .

In short, the Care for Music project concluded that the adaptations involved in the Zoom format:

> [have] shown up how music-therapeutic presence and the intimacy of musical relationship do not necessarily depend on normal conditions of physical and psychological proximity. Music therapists have discovered how the disruptions of normal practice both make a difference and do not make a difference to the core of their work. (Schmid et al., 2021, p. 317)

Embodiment, under Zoom conditions, was part of this new presence. Analysis of video data from musical events in care settings has shown how embodied musical expression was actually heightened and sometimes exaggerated during online work. The conclusion was that, given the mediated, socially distanced feature of Zoom-music, enhanced musical embodiment is perhaps a natural response to the online situation, compensating for the diminished aural environment by adding more visual cues and expressions alongside the musicking. Indeed, there were some perceived advantages to Zoom; for example, for the members of a hospice choir, meeting on Zoom allowed them, for the first time, to be able to see each other's faces (as opposed to the backs of people's heads). The music therapists in the Care for Music study discovered, through the accidental experiment of social distancing and Zoom, some of the hitherto unnoticed features of what comes to be recognized as a good music therapeutic event—the importance of embodiment, gesture, and visual details, in this case.

Music therapy on Zoom also highlighted the tacit ways that—arguably always—we render spaces intimate, as places of close musicking. For example, during the pandemic:

> The musical-spatial configuration has been both affected and managed by the concerted effort of everyone involved in sessions. Residents have learned to relate to Gary and his musicking in new ways, approaching him physically "at" the TV, talking to him, conducting him (as well as ignoring him!). The care staff have found ways to mediate and link the two spaces (Gary in Norwich, residents and carers in London). Both sides have improvised and developed embodied musicking techniques to help bridge the spatial divide. Music's unique ability to link, merge and transcend space has made the musicking feel close and intimate at times, to everyone's surprise. (Schmid et al., 2021, p. 321)

So, too, time and timing came to be reappraised, such that latency, if not embraced as an actual creative technique, was no longer a "problem":

> Gradually there was clearly a creative learning process (again on both sides) as to how to accommodate the delay—learning what discrepant signals to ignore, and how to anticipate or compensate for asynchrony. The result was often still messy, but it functioned well enough for its purpose. (Schmid et al., 2021, p. 323)

And finally, the hybrid feature of remotely provided music therapy (the music therapist beamed in via the computer and the TV screen, the rest of the group in the care home lounge), highlighted the mediation work done by participants—adapting and assisting each other to enjoy the music, to notice it as an event, and to respond to it, and thus to each other. The accidental experiment therefore brought to the front of the stage many of the otherwise tacit practices that help us attach ourselves to music.

The Care for Music study highlighted the resilience of music and challenged us to open our ears and eyes to many more forms and formats of what might count as music and as musical communication. It also emphasized that many of the impediments to music-making are not in musical circumstances but in our own minds. Moreover, it suggested that these obstacles might just as easily be regarded as creative constraints, contributing to the development of new and interesting musical methods and techniques. Consequently, the study is a broadening of our perceptual and evaluative apparatus, fostering more inclusive definitions of what constitutes an aesthetic experience.

The Care for Music project also underscores the remarkable adaptability of people to be re-socialized, even when deemed "cognitively impaired," showcasing their capacity to learn and engage. They can learn to ignore "noise" and asynchronous events and can learn how to appreciate new sonorities and new modalities of forging relationships and new theatricalities. The project also highlights parallels with traditional musical situations, such as the use of the organ music in cathedrals or Giovanni Gabrieli's antiphonal brass in Basilica San Marco, Venice.[5]

> Maybe the constraints of enforced distanced musicking are helping us notice (and extend) the para-musical features of music. Maybe our already-existing notion of music as Music+ (music is always somewhere, in some context, linked to other things/meanings) is now Music++? In other words, music PLUS all the things that music can be when perfect synchrony is denied are coming to the fore (and this was a key finding in the GIO study): gesture, comportment, words, props, actions, activities, costumes, pictures, people (this list only begins to scratch the surface). . . . Maybe the "latency problem" will lead to a more fully-fledged (or fully acknowledged) notion—following Cook's pioneering work on this topic (Cook 1998)—of music as a multi-media modality, even when we might think we're simply making or listening to "sound"? Maybe, this period of enforced latency will help us to see just what music can do beyond the sonic and the sonic-semiotic. (DeNora, 2020)

New Cultures, New Futures

In summary, this chapter has presented an overview of key issues focused on online virtual collaboration, highlighting the diverse ways in which digitally enhanced group music practices have evolved. The history presented has outlined a narrative that makes it possible to understand how artists, therapists, and communities are exploring and developing practices at the intersection of a growing human-machine world, and has contextualized efforts within the wider health and social impacts that are possible with the advent of the use of these new techno-creative cultures.

With the growing trend of these forms of practice, there are also several concerns regarding the problems and challenges associated with the new medium when the aesthetic priorities associated with synchronous moments are valued and sought to be retained. For example, many artists grapple with the "problem of finding unity" and the desire to create outputs that imitate traditional notions of instrumental balance and mixing techniques. For instance, while groups like Dr. Mesmer's Private Army from New Zealand Group (Mayall, 2021) outline similar discoveries of greater multimedia productions, specifically collaborations with visual artists, they also highlight alternative takes on latency and the difficulties it introduces:

> [It] changes the way we need to think about music, rhythm and playing in time. It also alters our collective understanding of the present moment in the context of mindfulness. We each have an individual present moment that syncs at a fractionally different point. We can remain within an individual mindful improvisational experience but the collective experience is blurred. (Mayall 2021, p. 9)

These aesthetic goals are examples of practice that is attempting to preserve things "as they were" versus willingness to "accept what can be done in simple and low-tech ways." The different values—valuing synchrony rather than welcoming the confusion of latency, for example—are linked to the extent and quality of adaptations being made in and for the event. So, for example, in the case of GIO, the rock 'n' roll music therapists, and at Hill House, what mattered more was the social connection, and what emerged from that value were new aesthetic practices and materials, ones that either compensated for (visual, gestural) or embraced the disruption due to latency and Zoom's speaker selection.

We have seen in this chapter how different adaptive strategies within online improvisation generate adaptive cultures within their work with technologies that reflect each group's unique priorities. The actions of these periods expose implications in thinking about who can do what in creative practice, when, and what counts as "good" music in what kinds of circumstances (and who determines this question).

A wider theme therefore is the consideration of the implications of these practices on lay expertise. Within the digital music settings is a blurred boundary between who counts as a "musician" versus a "client," a musician or a videographer, or even a human or a machine. This shift into uncertainty about identities/roles is further facilitated by a commitment to "simple" tech and a willingness for mutual adaptation rather than a commitment to preexisting or preordained routes of access (complex technology, specialist knowledge, locational or language barriers, etc.). The process is bolstered further by the practices of "deep observing" as well as "deep listening" which abound in these heightened interdisciplinary and audio-visual spaces.

The primary aim of the sessions discussed in this chapter was participation, with the principal process being improvisation. An emphasis on accessibility, participation, and improvisation using Zoom software implicated a number of unique affordances. Of particular importance was the fact that the situation was novel—the vast majority of people involved had no previous experience of improvising online and therefore no preconceived ideas about what an online improvisation should sound like. This perhaps affords a particularly open attitude toward the types of aesthetics that would be produced and a particularly open attitude toward the sort of techniques that could be utilized in order to achieve participation—and it reminds us again of the importance of remaining aware of the politics of experience and the consequences of boundary work. Indeed, it illuminates an important theme within GIO's aesthetics/ethics: lay expertise (discussed further in Chapter 7). What constituted a good online improvisation was not discussed, and there were no particular reference points with which to compare. Unlike traditional settings, there were no canonical works that acted as reference points and no virtuoso online performers whose influence we (GIO) would be expected to, if not follow, certainly integrate into our practice. Over the initial weeks and months, a community of practice developed where new techniques, new aesthetics, and new ways of structuring music and interacting developed.

The particular interdisciplinary crossover from telematic music practice, computer music, new materialist thinking, and therapy/well-being settings is a further exemplar of the unique moment around which these pandemic-related digital creative practices developed. This period has clearly been one of collective adaptation, albeit with unique and bespoke attention to how to develop within these new digital spaces; that is, this book puts forward the notation that by looking at GIO's online practices, we are nevertheless surveying a vast field that developed rapidly over the pandemic period—one which is contending with and contributing toward a future techno-social culture, with great opportunities for positive benefit in attending to existing social struggle and community needs:

As long ago as E M Foster's Howard's End ("only connect") and his dystopian story The Machine Stops, writers have debated technology's dual-edged quality. These debates underscore how, as with music, technology is always technology+. So, maybe creative ways of addressing "the latency problem"—indeed, of embracing latency and working it into the musical system—underscores some of the themes that disability studies have pursued for some long time (Scheer and Groce, 1988), namely that "problems in living" can be transcended if collaborative practices change. (DeNora, 2020)

In other words, disability studies has embraced collaborative and flexible practices as a route to progress for many years and, while engaging with technology presents challenges that cannot be predicted, collaboration and flexibility in how we overcome these challenges provide a pathway for developing new insights. This chapter has highlighted how collaboration and flexibility within telematic music-making can be utilized to enhance health and well-being. In the following chapter, we develop this argument to explore how online music-making facilitates new understandings regarding particular moments in cóllaborative creativity—namely, how improvisations begin.

3
Opening Up Opportunities
The Shape of Things to Come

How and when anything in social life begins can be vitally important for what follows. That importance applies to conversations and how they proceed. It also applies to improvised musical sessions. In this chapter, we consider the new digital creative practice that GIO adopted when it moved online—the opening—the starting point. We also look at how specific sessions themselves opened, and how the novelty of working online posed various challenges and opportunities for the beginnings of improvisations. We consider some of the strategic but often subtly executed, collaborative "decisions" made during the opening moments of improvisations, and we describe the various forms of negotiation (of technical, social, and creative affordances) involved. We suggest that this negotiation served to tap and develop cross-media forms (art, music, language, dance, domestic science, home furnishing, and conversation). We also propose that it is important to consider the genesis and genealogy of the creative, material opening up of possibilities for participants' identities and individual/group narratives. We conclude that, through the ways that the specific constraints (physical distancing, technical limitations) imposed by the online format reduced the possibility of conventional musical interaction, these constraints also provided opportunities for new practices to emerge, in ways that supported and made visible the distributed creativity on which all improvisation ultimately depends. The spontaneous multimodal integration of textual, visual, and audio material within the domestic and virtual environment facilitated a new type of creative collaboration. This creative collaboration was dedicated to drawing out features of social improvisation immediately evident in the distinctive ways that these improvisations started.

New Beginnings

How and when a piece of music, or anything in social life, begins is both interesting and ambiguous. It is interesting because it addresses the question of how creative work takes shape and where ideas come from. It is ambiguous because the question of how, and when, something starts opens up a range of further questions of interdisciplinary interest—practical, sociological, and artistic. Practical questions include how to demarcate the boundary between pre-start and start, and how to explain and identify precedents and possible or putative causes. Sociologically, the topic of beginnings raises questions of attribution: What did the event mean? What was it about? Which were the defining moments and embedded traditions? How was the start negotiated? What was excluded in the way that a piece began, and what became focal points? Artistically, the topic of beginnings raises questions about where materials and ideas came from, how they were mobilized, and why these things were included but not others.

Within GIO, online with Zoom, new questions about openings also emerged. From the start of the online improvisation, there was no precedent for how to begin. The conventional practices for working were no longer at hand. There was a kind of dispossession of the usual ways of working such that working online offered a kind of blank slate. Initially, this blankness puzzled participants but, as the sessions accumulated, it became increasingly reconfigured as interesting and liberating. Over time, problems became resources, opportunities for new forms of creativity, and, perhaps, even an opportunity to express defiance (and thus empowerment) at a time when so many taken-for-granted freedoms were removed (perhaps especially for performing musicians now housebound). Thus, the story of openings online is thus also the story of how GIO members and invited guests discovered new resources for expression, opposition, and with it—empowerment. This chapter, therefore, tells two, and two kinds of, openings stories: first, it considers how actual sessions and pieces began; second, it examines how resources were discovered for music-making *in extremis*. And so, the story of Openings Online is a story of how GIO developed resource-based musical practices: in the face of adversity, new perspectives, attitudes, and empowering practices were located and acted upon by the group (Burke et al., 2023; Rolvsjord, 2010). As such, the story of online openings is also a story of how musicians cultivated a new kind of mutual trust during this challenging time.

Starting Out, Opening Up, and Boundary Objects

GIO's new beginnings were forged in, and because of, its new social setting. That setting was one in which human interaction was heavily dependent upon, and greatly mediated by, technology. Perhaps paradoxically, in light of the social distancing involved, a new kind of intimacy and a new kind of disclosure happened when GIO went online. New features of GIO collaborations, technologically produced, involved a new willingness to disclose vulnerability and personal information. This willingness in turn fostered a new kind of trust. Increasingly, members disclosed personal and extra-musical materials as part of their contributions to the sessions. We understand this process, as Rottle and Reardon-Smith have described it, as "contaminating sounds with personal narratives, [and] contaminating personal narratives" (Rottle and Reardon-Smith, 2023, p. 10).

The process of opening up or "contamination" became evident in how the group managed the beginnings of sessions early on, scaffolded by discussions of the problems of online improvisation. There were many conversations about what kind of algorithm was being employed by Zoom and its preferences. Over time it became clearer that Zoom favored the sound of the human voice and direct input from electronic instruments (those using sound cards or performing live processing in Max, for example). Notably, Zoom always prioritized the visual; as long as cameras were on, the visual was ubiquitous and democratically distributed when in Gallery View. It was evident from the start that the group needed to adapt if a diversity of sounds were to be heard and to work with Zoom, which was now understood to be a new and very powerful and influential participant in the sessions (MacDonald et al., 2021).

Concomitantly, the connection provided by Zoom was all there was: the possibility of an in-person meeting was closed because of the strict COVID-19 stay-at-home restrictions. Thus, there was considerable motivation, on the part of those who joined the online sessions, to make it work and to keep open the possibilities for working online. In the early films, we can see members trying different strategies to make the Zoom sessions viable. One of these involved ambiguity. Members tended to offer ambiguous materials so as not to over-prescribe the direction that any piece might take and to allow others leeway for adaptation and shaping of materials. We understand this process as one of crafting opening "boundary objects" (Burke et al., 2024; DeNora, 2014, pp. 89–90; Star and Greisemer, 1989), that is, offering materials that are capable of holding meaning but that also allow for meaning to float, to be interpreted variously, and to be appropriated in a range of ways while retaining perceived coherence and thus shared meaning. Throughout the sessions, openings reveal a tentativeness and an orientation to motifs and topics that are open-ended. We will see a parallel observation in Chapter 6 when we examine endings, namely, that a motif works best when it is capable of holding multiple, indeed potentially contradictory meanings, when it allows

Figure 3.1. March 24, 2020, first online improvisation.

for many potential moves further along the line and many other potential interpretations.

There was also ambiguity around the question of *when* any one piece actually began—the timeline itself being a boundary object. That ambiguity became an important resource for playing—in all senses of the word—with the improvisation. For example, in more formal in-person sessions the beginnings of improvisations would normally be bounded and started with a ritualistic silence (momentary or longer) after a clear signal from someone in the group. In the online sessions, that rite of passage was never clear. Participants were busy negotiating the new, and still confusing environment of online interactions that included intermittent wifi, domestic interruptions, new sonic landscapes, and adjustments to settings such as volume and microphone. This ambiguity is illustrated clearly in ▶ Film 3.1, the first-ever meeting of GIO in an online setting, March 24, 2020 (see Figure 3.1);

 QR Code: Please follow this QR code to the ▶ companion website to view additional content for Chapter 3. Alternatively, you can access the website using the link provided in the front matter.

Here, participants appear to engage in a somewhat dazed and confused manner, initially disconnected from each other. They express uncertainty about how their sounds will be perceived and are unsure about the sounds they are hearing and how these sounds might come together. Participants begin to question their own agency in this context. Adjusting to this novel environment changed quickly, as we will show. By week three (▶ Film 3.2,

Figure 3.2. April 14, 2020, adjusting to the Zoom setting.

April 14, 2020, Figure 3.2), participants appear to demonstrate that they had learned, or perhaps more accurately, negotiated, how to begin a piece. At this point, interactions exuded confidence, and new "traditions" were beginning to be invented.

By the second month of practice, the group found a working digital structure, one which continued(s) in this form:

- Free improvisation: an open improvisation with no pre-discussed theme;
- Improvisation based on a theme suggested by participants;
- Small groups of 3–4 participants playing free improvisations (alternating players and audiences);
- Free improvisation at the end of each session: an open improvisation with no pre-discussed theme (Argo, 2022).

An important new feature that opened up fairly quickly was the visual which offered the pivot for what we have called the "over-sharing" ethic of the online sessions. That opening of the visual was closely connected to the visual capabilities that Zoom provided. It involved sharing visual features of one's home, family, domestic objects, and, eventually, video material. This addition imbued the sessions with an increasingly cinematic character where themes and motifs (boundary objects) were clarified in multiple directions by visual materials. In turn, the sharing of personal objects and personal visual materials—things that otherwise would not have been seen or known about—led to trust and further disclosure (more over-sharing). One month into online improvisations, this cinematic dimension became overt with the opening of a session being marked by a clap.

The Clap . . . and Cinematic GIO

In ⓟ Film 3.3 (April 28, 2020), we can see how the various new features of online working converged, and how this convergence placed a spotlight on the question of beginnings and new beginnings. For example, there was a negotiation of how and when to press "record," with the further addition of a checking in or reminding people about time syncing. At 00:23, Maggie Nicols asks, "What time is it by your watch in case I am fast or slow?" Importantly, this is the first session in which the group decides to try using a clap to signal the start of a piece. The addition of a viewable and audible hand clap appears as a cinematic convention akin to the clapperboard (see Figure 3.3). It was an innovation that overcame the temporally distributed sound of "let's begin" or "now." It also introduced a new improvisational role: the person hosting the session also becomes the person who does the claps, and says the date and the name of the piece, to signal the nominated or stated "start" of the improvisational time period.

However, the introduction of the clap was not a random development. It coincided with the arrival of artist and filmmaker (author Birrell) to the group, who joined with the intention of documenting the sessions. While the clap was a technical necessity for the editing of audio and visual material (discussed in Chapter 5), it also brought a new clarity to the question of when a piece began. This aspect was subsequently incorporated into improvisations, as described below. Additionally, it overtly emphasized the cinematic features of the group's activities, serving as a reminder that, in online conditions (distanced and latency), the visual held potential.

Figure 3.3. April 28, 2020, the first "clap."

The signaled start clap emerged within GIO culture as a shared reference point. It became something that different hosts played in a variety of ways, and became an amusing reference point for the group (▶ Film 3.4)—"Oh, I've got to clap, don't I?—that's a big responsibility" (March 1, 2022). The clap, and discussion around it, began to offer a platform for thinking and reflexive consideration of framing. It introduced a new feature of GIO culture allowing for the exploration and ability to delineate and play with the differences between social space and playing space. It drew to the fore an awareness of how the latter could also constitute the former, enabling the incorporation of nontraditional instruments, sounds, and nonphysical shared spaces in digital practice. It afforded discussion about this practice which became part of peer-to-peer learning and reflexive play.

In developing this research, the authors have consistently kept the concept of "GIO opening" in mind, emphasizing the notion of a "start" becoming a meta-reference between this research and the sessions on June 15, 2021 (▶ Film 3.5). Author MacDonald suggests, "Shall we make a start?" to which author DeNora replies, "Haven't we already started?," eliciting laughter from the group. At this point, author MacDonald begins miming the clap, to which Maggie Nicols asks, "What is a start?" It becomes clear that many members of the group are already playing with background contributions which can suggest that a performance has started (i.e., sounds that wouldn't be made if the entire group perceived this part of the session as still in discussion). At 40 seconds in, author MacDonald says, "I'm going to clap anyway, I know we have started but I feel the need to clap, but I know we have started," initiating the start "again" with a performative flurry of laughter.

Kinds of Openings

From a general perspective, the beginnings of improvisations can be viewed as the start of a collaborative process. While collaboration is often a stated aim in various creative educational and artistic contexts, it can be difficult to know how to execute productive collaboration. This challenge is especially relevant when considering how a collaboration begins. Who starts? What are the negotiation processes involved, or how do we set up artistic and social conditions that facilitate effective collaboration and cohesive group dynamics? These questions are relevant not only to online improvisational contexts but also, as we said at the start of this chapter, to all collaborative creative activities. In these activities, goals may not be precisely specified, but the process clearly implies a collaborative practice.

That practice is implicitly political, as the way any improvised activity begins—whether talk, music, or dance—establishes potential topics, styles, and a social distribution for activity roles for what can or should happen next. Consequently, the study of openings itself opens up how a "tone" can be set, challenged, negotiated, and changed during improvised activities. There are therefore specific practices that can be employed to close off or open up avenues of participation. This includes the opportunity, and at times the perceived right, to propose a topic, and the chance to develop or alter a topic in the real-time ongoing activity.

Zoom sessions afford unique features that extend musical improvisation into the realm of social improvisation. It is important to note that this is digital conferencing software explicitly designed for human conversation, resulting in the incorporation of numerous spoken elements. Participants are conscious that, unlike a physical room with 20–30 people, side conversations are not possible (except through direct messaging in chat), so all group attention is respectful and directed toward a centralized voice, chosen as the global voice by the software itself. In fact, the blurring of social interaction and musical improvisation has been identified as something expanded and altered in the digital setting in particular. Conceptually, a session always starts with the initiator of a Zoom meeting (a blank digital space) which then becomes populated incrementally by more and more players. An experience on entering the call can matter—Who is there? What is being spoken about? This is in combination with a few hellos, some banter, and the noises of the musicians adjusting their equipment and levels.

For example, global parameters (compositional) can be instituted before an activity of any kind begins ("let's all play quietly"; "only people with purple hair play"; "a 5-minute piece"). More subtly, activities can be framed, early on, or right at the start, through utterances, actions, and specific types of furnishings—in conversation a speaker might choose to use a language or dialect that is not easy for all participants, whereas in a music context, a player might choose to play in a specific style not suited to the entire group. More subtly again, a participant might offer a contribution that runs counter to what has just been offered (asking, implicitly, through the medium of the sonic or visual material to abruptly change the subject).

In an online Zoom improvisation, there are new tools for contributing parameters and feedback during an improvisation, including the use of face-on visual cues (harder to manage in physical spaces because of the greater distance between players and the horseshoe formation GIO takes in person). Zoom also affords the chat feature which can be used to give text-based real-time instructions. For example, a participant might write something in chat, such as, "Let's all play in the lower range of our instruments," or they might hold up signs or hand signals that are easily seen by all members in the call.

In ▶ Film 3.6, an example of the opening of a piece brought to the group by Carl Bergstorem-Nielsen on the subject of "infinity" (February 1, 2022) is exemplified (see Figure 3.4). He introduces the concept as "no limits to the music, a musical space with everything in it, being present in this infinite universe, and what you intend to do is to touch it . . . a hello to infinity!" During his explanation, it is possible to see and hear the interest and agreement from the group, and the idea of infinity itself is taken up and riffed on before the piece even begins (in fact, it takes almost 3 minutes before the piece has its "musical" start). Author MacDonald suggests, "We will keep these short, between 3–5 minutes? We will have to find our way out of infinity in 3–5 minutes!," generating laughter, to which author Birrell proposes that the piece should start with an "infinite silence." The piece then "begins" in a "playing" sense after author MacDonald's clap, at which point he names the piece "a miniature on infinity" (Figure 3.4).

To explore these processes—how new creative opportunities "opened"—we now turn to the question of how pieces began. We will use strategically chosen examples (the first 30–60 seconds of films of selected works presented in the accompanying web page, ▶ Films 3.1–3.8) to illustrate opening strategies and their consequences. Our aim is to illustrate how the notion of "openings" came to be developed and "opened up," that is, made into a reflexive topic for participants in the real-time sessions. We ask the questions: Where did the initial idea come from? How was it initiated? By analyzing the positionality of documented online improvisation, we can identify new understandings of how improvisations are started and what the genealogy of an idea is in this improvisatory setting.

Figure 3.4. February 1, 2022, Miniature on Infinity.

How Shall We Begin?

▶ *Film 3.1: March 24, 2020 (10 players present)*
The very first telematic improvisation conducted by GIO took place the day after the announcement of a nationwide lockdown. In acknowledgment that their monthly rehearsal can no longer take place, as the email in the Preface shows, drummer Stuart Brown suggests the idea of a Zoom session. The very first beginning is a clear one; cellist Jessica Argo whispers, "It's recording," and the beginning of a session of online digital music-making begins. At this early stage, the group is only recording the improvisations when the signal is to "play," with clear delineation of times outside of these "improvising" moments, when the group members are nevertheless still sharing the Zoom call, conversing, sharing thoughts around the uncertainty of the scenario.

In this initial piece, we can clearly see a general testing of the environment, a tentative start: the players look at each other. They seem to be listening, wondering, "How do we do this?" There is a pervading feeling of uncertainty with noticeable space between sounds. This sense of discovery, coupled with the aforementioned "cautiousness," is compounded by the global backdrop of disruption. The film serves as a representation of a resilient community comprising old friends and colleagues who are now navigating a period of great uncertainty. As much as the playing is an opening to a new practice, the setting signifies the beginning of a new way of understanding each other: one shaped by precarity, yet fostering a new form of intimacy.

There is a feeling that, in this first-ever online session, the group is in a kind of "discovery mode," or a heuristic juxtaposition of what is known and what is a "new" understanding of opening an improvisation. This opening does not make use, as later sessions will, of visual props or virtual backdrops. These are yet to be discovered, and yet the domestic setting of the players is prominent. There is a clear reliance on a semi-recreation of the now: a strong reliance on traditional instruments. The sense is that in this first session, participants are trying to make sense of what is happening based on how they "used to" begin an improvisation onsite at the Centre for Contemporary Arts (CCA),[1] with silence in the room, then listening as sounds were initiated.

At this point in the process, we assume (based on the early interviews with members) that the predominant meaning of the meeting was as much for social reasons as for artistic. Indeed, as the group discovered, one of the unique features of online music-making was that the social features were drawn increasingly to the fore as aesthetic resources. In a global sense, these new conference spaces unexpectedly stepped into a totally significant "moment" for humanity to "check in" "reach out," and seek togetherness in a huge migration toward digital social living. As we will observe, the simple feature of hands reaching up toward the camera eye became iconic during this period, both within GIO and more broadly.

Opening of Confidence

▶ *Film 3.7: April 7, 2020 (11 players present)*
Jessica Argo continues to be the host of the session and therefore starts the piece by saying, "Right, it's recording everywhere," but this time with a more confident tone than in the previous session. In this session, we can see more performative movement. Indeed, we believe that movement might be the first "visual" cue to be used in these early online sessions. At the opening of this session, there are still no visual props or virtual backgrounds. But at the end of this piece, author MacDonald and author Sappho use the first visual prompts (see Figure 3.5), a sign held up to signal "the end" and a picture of author Sappho's cat Brutus).

In one very important moment, we see Ken Slaven playing the swanee whistle. It is met by a response from Rick Bamford, who plays the vuvuzela. The focus on winds is further consolidated as author Sappho then picks up and plays the piccolo,[2] deliberately holding it to her left (unconventional compared to the usual right-handed position). She produces a very small, whistle-like sound (Figure 3.6).

We believe that this chain of actions marks the first occasion where it is possible to see members using visual activities as improvisatory moves in an unfolding piece. It is the first time that instruments are "played" without making sound. It is also the first time we see a strategy that became common

Figure 3.5. April 7, 2020, virtual background cat image and "The End" sign.

Figure 3.6. April 7, 2020, piccolo and instrument mirroring.

later—the use of imitation (visual plus sonic) to affirm what someone has done or ventured, in order to validate a musical act. This practice is similar to the mirroring practice in music therapy, where validation as a strategy is often important and where at times mirroring is used to help a client to "see" (perceive) her/himself in the music. This mirroring strategy can be seen to unfold in subsequent sessions as (a) validation and/or support and (b) a way of "dueting" or playing small ensemble pieces (visual/aural) within the wider group improvisation. It is part of how the players recognize the importance of creating value in these crucial opening moments of a session, especially early on, as in this, the second ever session. It is one example of new cultural practices being developed for online work. And it is important that it highlights the discovery of not only "new" working methods, but also new ways to "begin"—to begin each session, and to begin an unfolding history of new practices—a new repertoire of skills and meaningful moves for online working. We are watching culture "in the making here" as participants begin, collectively, to articulate an ethos of online work. Features of that ethos are:

- Familiarity—members know each other—opening to keep it open;
- Opening up improvisation through no prescribed approach to the instrument they are playing;
- Opening to keep it open;
- Finding things in a room and using them (flutes, for example); in the traditional GIO sessions, held at the CCA and with the group sitting in a horseshoe formation, the opportunity to deploy "found objects" or "things lying around the room" was unavailable. And because of that limitation, in a traditional session the ability to mimic or copy others (as a form of validation or support) and to do so both sonically and visually was not available.

- Everyone knows each other and finds ways of getting to know each other, disclosing to each other more (what we later came to understand as the "over-sharing" value of GIO during lockdown and online—the "social improvisatory" feature). In the start of this second session, "finding" things in a room and using them, which is also displaying them, is both "showing" how to continue online and sharing from where a person is. Thus, we believe that what, in later sessions, came to be understood as the "Theater of Home" idea, the mobilization of objects from within the domestic environment that is readily available, can be traced back to these early moments in this session. The opening of this session thus also marks the start of the development of a visual language for GIO online. As such, it is also the tentative production of materials and practices that can, and do, later become shared history.

Community Opening

▶ *Film 3.2: April 14, 2020 (15 players present) and* ▶ *Film 3.8: April 18, 2020 (24 players present)*
Until April 14, 2020, the virtual meetings involve only the regular GIO players who meet monthly at the CCA and make up the traditional ensemble of the band. The only expectation is that author Sappho's flatmates join her Zoom "box" on March 24 but do not return for subsequent sessions. In time the GIO online group, referred to in earlier papers as the "flattening the curve" project (MacDonald et al., 2021), will become a hugely international group of invited artists from the wide web of relationships that players share, but April 14 marks the first meeting where the beginning of this internationality burgeons through an open invitation chain. Anne Pajunen (Finland) joins, a player known to the group from her participation in the 2019 GIO festival, but also present is Dylan DelGiudice (USA) who is recommended to author MacDonald by George Lewis (USA), and Allan Wylie joins the session (a player who will become a staple member of the digital group and later join the physical GIO players in their subsequent festival and performances after lockdown eases).

In this sense, this session is critical, as it marks the emergence of how the group seized new affordances in this developing practice. While the players of GIO are still navigating a creative language and relationship with each other and Zoom, they are now capitalizing on one of the oldest of improvising traditions—relying on the social network. Improvisation is a notoriously cohesive underground and global community. It is, as with many fringe social spaces, galvanized by its ability to sustain and develop DIY and community-organized prerogatives. The network of free improvisers is vast, and one of the scene's most valuable qualities is an openness to sharing contacts, an openness to playing with new people, and a commitment to expand one's own creative network. To this end, the digital means of performance offered a huge opportunity: anyone from anywhere with an internet connection could be invited, and in this session we see the very first kernels of this process take hold.

And yet, while everyone from anywhere (with an internet connection) could join, the group had until this point been meeting on a Tuesday evening at 7 p.m. GMT (the usual day of their in-person workshops); however, differing time zones for artists located further afield would pose a challenge at this hour. As this budding expansion of "who comes to play" begins, this week also marks the first week where the group began their Saturday afternoon sessions (meeting again on April 18), allowing players located further east and west to be able to join at a reasonable hour. The April 18 session was the first week that author Burke joined the sessions, along with Australian musicians Sandy Evans, Peter Knight, Alister Spence, and Tony Gorman (Australian-based Scottish saxophonist).

Figure 3.7 shows the Tuesday, April 14, session screen, full attendance of players, with the three highlighted boxes being players who do not usually work on a regular basis with GIO in person. In contrast, Figure 3.8 shows the Saturday (afternoon), April 18, session, which does not in fact account for all players in attendance as the number was greater than the Zoom screen could

Figure 3.7. Player country locations from April 14, 2020.

Figure 3.8. Player country locations from April 18, 2020.

record on-screen at one time. In this image, 13 out of the 24 people pictured are traditional members of GIO, making the split between invited guests (the beginning of the new band) around 50/50.

Toward a Micro-Historical Perspective on Openings

We have been exploring how people experienced this new set of resources, what they did with it, and how "new beginnings" came to be forged. We suggest that the matter of openings can be fruitfully explored as a matter of micro-cultural history. By "micro-cultural" we mean the study of how, *in real time*, culture is collaboratively and interactively produced and how the unfolding of that production can be traced in terms of its social and aesthetic dynamic and understood phenomenologically as individual participants' lived experiences. Author Burke explains the starting of an improvisation as he experienced that event:

It was 9:58 p.m. AEST (Australian Eastern Standard Time) on a Saturday night—March 2020 in the middle of the first lockdown for Melbourne (256 days). I clicked on my Zoom link ready to join the online session with GIO. Most of the players (approximately 30) were situated in Europe so it was around midday for them. I noticed a few familiar faces from Australia and the USA along with the usual UK and European musicians. There were many faces that I did not know but with the banter, I felt it to be a very welcoming environment. I was excited as I had a compositional idea for the group that involved using the chat function on Zoom which was something that had become useful in meetings and teaching music to students at the university that I work at. It was announced by Raymond MacDonald that I had an idea for a composition by using the chat function as a way for everyone to have input into the direction of the improvisation. I observed that there was banter that exuded positiveness and excitement amongst the background of sounds. From my perspective, I felt that the improvisation started when I first entered the space with the individual sounds of the musicians checking levels, leads, and strings, adding room objects so that they were close at hand, warm-up exercise and of course the banter. Each player, it seemed, was focused on their own singular improvisation and joining into the group's sonic environment when they chose to. I joined in by adding my own contribution to the moment. At this point, the environment felt like what Borgo (2006) terms "swarming": no leadership but a soundscape of improvisation. This banter merged into an official start to the improvisation with my words "have we started yet" and confirmation from performers Raymond MacDonald and Maggie Nicols. We were then into the big idea triggered by the word "Meow" written in the chat—the group as a whole started to make improvisational choices—the improvisation had evolved.

Burke's account points to what were to become important features of any of GIO's improvised online openings: first, how what counts as "the start" is in fact open to interpretation; second, how "the start" involves performative utterances and acts (such as Burke's "Have we started yet," which reflexively highlights that ambiguity); third, the "boundary object" notion that we described at the start of this chapter—the way that opening ideas are deliberately not overly bounded or defined so that they can lend themselves to a wide range of interpretations and renditions. In this case, the word "meow," written in the chat, opened up a veritable barnyard of animal sounds and images, a display of pets, and a general playfulness that lasted several minutes before shifting into a new topic. In a publication linked to this topic, we explore in real-time detail how a particular improvisational opening—the meow opening—took shape, how the space of that session came to be furnished with motifs and materials, and how it shifted over its course (Burke et al., 2024).

Openings Unclosed

In this chapter, we have described how GIO members began to discover new working methods online, and how those methods included new ways for beginning online work. Those methods included attention to open-ended gambits, to, increasingly, the cinematic features of online work, and to the opening up of trust, confidence, and greater sharing of personal materials—objects, talk, and visual presentation. The new openings opened up a space for what we have described as "over-sharing." That space was characterized by a great deal of structure (the clap, the time periods pre-stated) and it allowed for, at any time, a withdrawal to the "backstage" (out of camera eye, turning off the camera, shifting to visuals real and virtual, veiling the camera), which in turn offered a dynamic support for risk-taking through further sharing. The material presented as potential opening material was both bounded, to encourage shared activity and shared meaning, but also open-ended, to afford diverse projections of meaning and pivot possibilities. The new ways of opening were open to the cultural change within GIO—a shift from an ethos grounded in musical/sonic activity to one grounded in social praxis—social improvisation in Nicols's sense (Tonneli, 2015). During the period of social isolation, these new social practices offered company, comfort, and solace. Also, as we shall see in the following chapters, they opened up many new possibilities for GIO members, individually, in terms of new career activities and life changes, and also collectively in terms of GIO's current practices (hybrid, and more visually oriented).

4
Experimentation

Habits, Habituation, Expertise, and Augmentation

Experimentation in improvisation has been cited as a process that can foster, in the appropriate contexts, the habituation of new expertise and creative activities (de Bruin, 2015, 2018; Jordanous and Keller, 2012). In this chapter, through exploration of the lived experiences of players, we describe how online improvisation informed expertise and contributed to the augmentation of virtuosity and performers' habituation as they adapted to online work. That process included challenges to players' expertise and creativity in improvisation and to their instrumental skill sets. We discuss how the process of improvisation and augmentation affected new perceptual and conceptual breakthroughs for practitioners, a critical matter in the relationship between innovation and experimentation.

The Habit[at] . . . uation

As discussed in previous chapters, the GIO online improvisations were conducted within a novel experiential space for many of the performers. These sessions created a virtual habitat that was an intersection of an online non-human environment (the computer, screen, Zoom) and a human environment where each of the actors improvised and experimented in their own creative space. That habitat became and fostered a transdisciplinary practice of experimentation via digital means of furnishing objects including instruments/pets, costume/bodily presentation, makeup, suits, gloves, and so on. Concomitantly, embodied practices (dance, hand presentation, and facial expressions) were now integral to creating new habits that were at the forefront of the assimilation to the new environment, creatively embracing the new creative space and experience (MacDonald et al., 2021). These changed habitats of improvisation engendered new agency for the performers, giving rise to new memories and affective habit ecologies. Dewsbury (2012) characterizes this habitat as an ecological site capable of providing opportunities for both "environmental memory" and "immediate performance" (p. 74). He also suggests that agency within this environment is not discretely distributed between the human and the non-human; instead, it is co-determined, mutually emerging in the immediate material constitution of any experiential encounter. There is, in other words, a co-created, collectively produced matrix of and for agency, a dynamic that is not mechanically negotiated but rather draws all agents, whether human or non-human, into a transformative relationship that exceeds the mere sum of its individual components. The outcome of these recombinant processes is the establishment of new ecologies with fresh relations and renewed participants. This newfound newness presents various opportunities, including participant well-being, at both individual and collective levels.

In 2020, these opportunities were somewhat poignant. The members of GIO were at that time having to contend with other forms of "newness" that were constraining, namely the new, locked-down, performative environmental habitat. That habitat posed dichotomous spaces. The first space was the home, a new space where music-making took place in physical isolation. Home was, circa March 2020, a space central to the process of practice and creativity—its new, and only, location. But it was also, of course, the space where activities beyond music-making happened—namely, living. It was a place of memories and deeply ingrained habits, a place where participants were mostly used to being able to be relaxed and "off-stage."

The second space was online. Online was, initially, both new and very different in ways that disrupted preexisting performing habits and demanded new ones. Online did not have the "traditional" spatial acoustics. Each player's home was a literal space of existence and a space where the players in the Theater of Home embraced and grappled with the challenges and discoveries of new habits through furnishing this digital space. This adjustment included the embodied assimilation of a new material world, appropriating objects that, in earlier times, existed in the background, as part of the furniture, sometimes literally (Barad, 2010; Haraway 2013; Wajcman, 2002). Now, the affordances of this "furniture" were foregrounded; they became a primary resource and the environment of and for the embodied agency in improvisation as players entered into a process of sympoetic entanglement (Haraway, 2016), a commingling of human and non-human in a creative endeavor. For each participant, the new dichotomy of performing space led to unique experiences. It led participants into new performing habits, some of which have lingered, post-pandemic. Author Sappho's further investigations into the triad of human, machine, and fungal co-creative collaborative settings, with a specific focus on exploring mushrooms, mycorrhizal networks, and AI neural networks, aims to discover novel approaches and roles for communication, knowledge sharing, social interaction, and community building (Sappho, 2022, 2023).

Lived Experiences

The new space of online-at-home and its affordances for being, being well, and being/remaining/becoming "a performer" under new and challenging circumstances came to be linked to new habits of improvisation and new habits of perception. It is worth pausing and, in the spirit of GIO, "oversharing" some of that process, initially as some of this book's authors experienced it; to that end, we channel auto-ethnographic approaches and methods (Homan-Jones, 2016, 2018).

A focus on players' lived experience is also a focus on how that experience came to be shaped and scaffolded by the ways that players appropriated new materials for use in sessions. It is possible to trace new habituations as they manifest themselves in daily living and as they developed time-on-time and were transported from the sessions into other realms of daily life. The appropriations in question involved a shift away from foregrounding practices with musical instruments and toward the use of novel materials—domestic objects, visual materials, and spoken/written text. In this process, previous conventions and understandings of what should be allocated to foreground versus background were reconfigured in ways that, in principle, allowed anything to be worthy of the spotlight. That "anything" included features of players' daily lives, their ongoing concerns, and, at times, the quick, almost random adoption of an object-as-instrument. This bricolage and its rearrangement of foreground and background blurred previous preconceptions of what might be included in a piece or a session. And it allowed participants to reimagine sound.

Habits and Habitus

> [A]fter a period of time (1–2 sessions), I started to look beyond my instrument. Being an improviser, I was looking for new ideas to interact—to create ideas. I began looking around my music room to find objects that I could use in the collaborative improvisation. I was inspired and informed by what others were doing in their spaces; the objects and visuals others were using were like an invitation to explore my music room. I was thinking beyond the saxophone. My room had become

my instrument; the objects becoming a bricolage of memories and new identities. I was looking at each artifact from a different perspective and viewing what their possibilities for improvisation were . . . their sounds and how they could visually instigate or stimulate an existing idea. How would they add to the collective idea? I was looking at books in my room. Tapping on them for sound, then opening them up and looking at words and pictures. I was viewing objects through a different lens—how each artifact could be part of my offering to the ensemble. I was triggered by what I was hearing and seeing and then sourcing the room for possibilities. I was making choices of what to add to the collective improvisation outside of just playing my woodwind instruments. Over many sessions, my approach to improvising had changed. I didn't automatically go to my instrument—saxophones, clarinets, etc.—but to artifacts in the room. My improvisatory classification, perception, identity, and general disposition were adapting when playing in this online environment. My habitus, informed by my learned practices and based on experimentation with my learned instrument, had adapted to new approaches to sound and interaction. (author Burke)

The habitus and new habits of experimentation to which author Burke refers can be linked to sociologist Pierre Bourdieu's (1977) notion of "hexis": the tacit and embodied set of a person's feelings and actions that informs their approach to creative work. Rob's creative habitus—his home office/music studio and on-screen space—and his innate approach of being an experimental improviser are imbued through "aesthetically motivated experimentation" (Galenson, 2006, p. 4), welcoming lived and felt experiences and tapping them so as to create possibilities and new habits. This experimentation involves trial and error and produces (musical) causes and effects and asks the question, "What if?" The result is a constantly renewing personal artistic identity (Onsman and Burke, 2018).

Tia's experience was a little different when she observed:

I will never forget, for example, after the first ever GIO session for me (and don't forget, I was a beginner there but made to feel so welcome!), I left Zoom, went down to the kitchen, turned on the water tap (to fill the pasta pot) and was suddenly very "aware" of the sound of water. And I think at the time the key thing was that I found the sound interesting—was definitely more involved with some of the otherwise liminal features of "everyday" life, like the sound of water which in turn sort of recontextualized the activity of filling a pot. (author DeNora)

The use of everyday objects from a home (i.e., household utensils) is not a new idea. John Cage famously composed and performed the compositions utilizing these household objects as affordances for his "Water Walk" in 1959 for the Italian TV program *Lascia o Raddoppia* where he used 24 materials that included a bathtub, toy fish, a pressure cooker, ice cubes (and an electric mixer to crush them), and a rubber duck.[1] The determinate work consisted of organized notations of occurrences centered around the theme of water.[2]

> Two and a half years later those kinds of moments keep happening and in ways that make me think of work by Steven Feld (Feld, 2003), Tina Ramnarine (Ramnarine, 2009) on acoustemology—the ways that environments shape our notions of what music is/can be. For example, the other day I (author DeNora) was on the Isle of Wight for fieldwork and walking with my colleagues through an underground railway tunnel. Somehow we all started to realize how this tunnel had great potential for reverb and then, for the next one hundred meters we were like children shouting out, sounding out the possibilities the tunnel afforded, listening to our "weird" voices as we walked toward where we needed to go. And not simply "diverted" or "enjoying" the sound, but more profoundly, discovering new features of how "sound could sound" and what we could call "singing." Ever since then, as I walk through that same tunnel, I remember this event. And now, often, I take pictures of that tunnel. (author DeNora)

> I think someday when I'm walking through I'm going to make a big sound all on my own, just to sort of "relive" this sounding moment [note from later: she did]. The original moment had an almost immediate (short-history) "afterlife" when we arrived at the venue for that evening's amateur choral concert. How I heard the music that evening was framed in part by the previous memory of the "beauty" of these voices—so when there were, as there always are in amateur concerts (and indeed in professional ones too) the odd glitch, those glitches "had permission" to be "beautiful" rather than "worrying." For example, it was more than OK when somebody momentarily forgot the lyrics to the song they were singing (it was better because it made that performance unique; it also "gave permission" for the audience to support the singing, to imagine what it might be like to be up "on stage"). The particular rendition was, at least for me, even more perfect because it was distinctly "homemade" and also "bespoke"—in the sense that it had all the hallmarks of a uniquely beautiful event and a very human one too. (author DeNora)

So, just as Tia notes that her awareness of the sound of water in the kitchen offered an example of changed habits of listening and observing, so too did the changed context of sound production in the tunnel. In both cases, the threshold of what was possible had new boundaries, which now included a different conception of what artifacts and what affordances were foregrounded; for example, the sound of water filling a pasta pot became foregrounded, whereas previously it might have been so deeply positioned in the background as to have happened unheard and unremarked (unconsciously).

For GIO, the concept of the Theater of Home sparked a reimagination of new possibilities for experimentation in improvisation. This involved leveraging the affordances present, to establish a novel improvisational habitat for the players. In this setting, every object in the room assumed the role of an agent (or potential agent) of action. Each object could contribute to the dynamic and innovative nature of the improvisational experience. Many of these objects held meanings that were personal (memories)—dolls, photos, toys, and souvenirs. At the same time, they had—for the collective—cultural significance (Miyamato et al., 2006); they had a "social imprint" (Dant, 1999, p. 2). In the case of GIO in the online scenario, the boundaries of these objects further evolved in ways that problematized the traditional dichotomy of human/non-human. Each artifact's identities and memories contributed to its agency, which could then be developed to reveal new possibilities. In author DeNora's case, her observation and perception of boiling water transcended the "normal" ways she had previously acknowledged or consciously noticed before. Subsequently, after participating in a GIO online session, she found herself engaged in a domestic task just down the stairs from where the GIO event had unfolded. Associations and habits of attention connected to her study and online experience were transported, literally, to her kitchen sink, over time and space/situation. Consequently, these new ways of engaging with the sink, water, and pot drew her into a state of "being present" in novel ways (and made work at the sink much more enjoyable). That "joy of water" was important to DeNora, especially because swimming was banned during lockdown. In that moment and phase, it contributed absolutely to DeNora's sense of well-being.

That sense of well-being continued to develop each time that author DeNora returned to GIO. DeNora's sense of hearing and vision (and online social skills and improvisatory techniques [see MacDonald and DeNora (forthcoming)] changed. Author DeNora began, increasingly, to notice new things—sounds and sights—that she had encountered in sessions. Outside of sessions, she reheard and resaw those things. Actual causal lines could be traced, from the moment within a given session outward into later times (as in the example above involving the sound of water). Lines could also be traced from things outside the sessions that author DeNora brought into them (or noticed during them). For example, as a beginning flutist, hearing birdsong in the spring of

2021, then connecting it with the sound of members Emma Roche's and Chris Parfitt's flute playing in sessions. These connections helped DeNora to feel part of the group. That sense of inclusion and the sense of coherence, derived from connections between sound worlds, led to author DeNora's developing social resilience, a resilience that grew from feeling included to being able to discover new ways to experience mundane happenings through connections discovered between sounds and sound worlds. This discovery was in some ways similar to the notion of "micro-explorations" advocated during the pandemic—the idea that you can explore your own backyard, street, or neighborhood. Beyond the ways in which the new, GIO-sponsored sensoriality fed into specific "moments" outside of GIO sessions, it also fed into the ways that DeNora thought about ideas for what she might literally bring to GIO sessions. These included such things as kitchen items and, as it later transpired, leaves of a giant species of kale that grows year-round in her garden, which inspired many improvisational ideas. Author DeNora describes the process:

> I would choose either fresh leaves that I later cooked or old, holey, multicolored decaying leaves that I would wear as a face mask with eye holes in the GIO sessions. The look of these leaves pleased me. They seemed to have symbolism (hope, new growth). And I was delighted when Yasuhiro Usui "liked" a picture with one of them in it on Facebook! But they also made a statement about home-grown veg and wabi-sabi beauty (aging beauty perhaps and at a time that I had begun to work on a project around late and end of life, and at a time when I was very aware that I was now also an "older adult") and in those ways, the brandishing of a leaf of kale was also a personal-political act I think. (author DeNora)

So, the water being filled into a pot, to which her attention was called because of what happened in GIO, afforded new identities and prompted memories; it inspired further experimentation (in the kitchen, too, where new kinds of fun with washing dishes happened!) and ideas for improvisation. In sum, DeNora's reflection on the water pouring into the pot became an experience of viewing objects/artifacts through an improvisatory and social lens. That perception furnished her habitat with something new and also added something new to her "habits"—of playing and of perception. The session, the people, what happened, the sounds, the different occasions of GIO and then dinner, the pot, the water—these human and non-human features collided in ways that led to new forms of awareness and—importantly during lockdown—a more cheerful outlook. Reflecting on these events now, while writing this paragraph, DeNora is pleased to think that she was engaged in performing a loosely rendered version, or re-mix, of Cage's "Water Walk."

Augmentation

For author Sappho, the experience of going online allowed her an opportunity to further explore her aims of developing her digital expertise in an improvisational and augmentation context. Author Sappho explains:

> You could say that my practice has been waiting all its life for the switch to digital meetings. That is, I have restless interests that are best suited to spaces of mixed practice and mixed identities. It is in these messy and undefinable realms where I find satisfaction and a voice for my own personal politics. To this end, the outpouring of audio-visual augmentation opportunities in group Zoom sessions fed into my existing interests in three particular ways: centralized the presence of a body (my body) viewed through the unique parameters of the "cyborg gaze," expanded agency in bringing to life "fiction," and afforded the multiplication of "reality," where no one "real" might plausibly be acting alone. (author Sappho)

Software such as Zoom offers complex audio-visual options and an agency for the user experience down to the simplest parameters of how you want to view the ensemble—speaker, gallery, pin view? It is a camera-dependent gaze that is your body, and your space is only "seen" through the limits of your camera lens (lenses). You might, therefore, curate your reality, what you want to show to the other players, but you might also step off screen, face the camera at the wall, or simply turn off your visuals altogether. All actions are almost entirely impossible when in physical stages. And to this end, you are whatever you allow the camera to see, something which in turn you have complete control over as you get to view the results in real time and adjust accordingly—a new kind of cyborg gaze. Like a dancer practicing in a mirror, improvisation might now happen with instant personal reflection and adjustment.

Therefore, with the centrality of a camera in the act of improvisation, we are afforded the opportunity to be and do whatever we want, both reflective and non-reflective of any barriers of the real world. Through the use of curated space, costume, movement, and augmented visual materials, you can, with very little effort, contribute fiction. Fiction in these senses is not merely the contribution of make-believe, but rather is an activation of political storytelling. For example, in her writings, Camille Stories, Donna Haraway invites us to participate in a kind of genre fiction committed to strengthening ways to propose near futures, possible futures, and implausible but real nows (Haraway, 2016, p. 136). The Harawaian notion of a Camille being, therefore, is not merely a story, but rather a narrative in which she can conjure up the pressing questions of her work: living and dying together in the Anthropocene.

As Haraway evokes fiction practices as ways to collectively reimagine new forms of social and collaborative responsibilities, so too do improvisers engage myth-making as a practice to assert, commune, and refract the things that matter, and which are at hand. This is a critical project in expressive art forms like improvisation, and further relationships are also possible to draw between the assertion of these self-stories within the context of making practice from a precarious vantage point. That is, fiction-building creative practices afford artists the ability to assert an agency over a wider sociopolitical reality outwith one's own control, for example, the interstellar mythology of Sun Ra as commentary on the African American experience of "alienation," or the role-play/society-play of gender norms and roles brought to life by the Feminist Improvising Group.

And yet, when technology becomes a central player, the possibilities for storytelling practices are greatly expanded. They bring the body and its context into new unbounded spaces—what Arthur Krokek refers to as "Body drift" (2012). This is an activity that has as much to do with the roles at play in human-machine relations as those that generate new understandings of what we might make of our own human consciousnesses, realities, identities, and histories. These are all parts of the project that contribute new stories made in cyber-futures—by humans and non-humans alike:

> we don't need an artist, we don't need a musician, because all they could give us would be art or music. We need an alien, a revolutionary, a time traveller, a fairy, a future, a madness, a dreamwalker. (Kurunjang, 2007, quoted in Walshe, 2009)

Author Sappho explains:

> I am already performing a politic of an expansion of myself, with new references and idols to stand with me during the performance: augmenting myself to be doubled with Frida Kahlo (Figure 4.1) or Sappho (630 BCE–570 BCE), or pre-recording past versions of myself that make me larger and stranger than life. But then, Tia makes stick figures of the players in the sessions (Figure 4.2) and performs these stick figures of GIO artists during the sessions. That is, she helps us traverse becoming multi-beings in both a digital and analog sense. My stick figure has many arms, as I am apt to often perform—a tentacular being. But other members are present, too; Maggie Nicols holds a spoon aloft, a committed GIO Zoom session cooker. And Tia is performing herself—equipped with her kale leaf, a recognizable feature that the group are attuned to watching her perform with already.

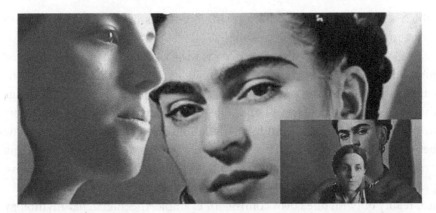

Figure 4.1. May 9, 2020, author Sappho with Frida Kahlo virtual background.

Figure 4.2. Author DeNora GIO stick figures.

In these ways, and so many more, the notion of the improviser, her identity, and her practice becomes so deeply embedded within the group, and in this way, her actions and explorations feed into the shared moment of collectively developing a new form of improvised playing within a group. Just as with the stick figures, one's own new experimental practice gets taken up and cemented within the group, and it is acknowledged and augmented as it expands.

Changing Expertise . . . and Habits

The majority of the players in GIO come from a prescribed approach to learning music, such as taking lessons on their instruments and playing in formalized ensembles. This prescribed learning to play a musical instrument/

voice involves practicing specific techniques and exercises, learning repertoire, improvising, and performing. To reach certain levels of excellence on an instrument involves the well-known 10,000-hour rule, proposed by Malcolm Gladwell in his book *Outliers* (2008), which suggests that it takes approximately 10,000 hours of deliberate practice to achieve expertise in a particular domain, such as playing a musical instrument. That enormity of commitment, along with the disruption of the mode of playing to which it was devoted, helps to contextualize what players were having to change as they moved online.

A GIO player's focus is on experimentation. However, most players in the group are also engaged in highly successful professional music careers that include major orchestras and jazz ensembles. Some are practice-based academics at leading conservatoriums and higher education institutions. Understanding how these players reached such levels of expertise and adapted to the online setting involves serious consideration of the concept of deliberate practice. Deliberate practice involves focused, structured, and goal-oriented efforts, and it plays a pivotal role in attaining expertise and developing new habits (Ericsson and Harwell, 2019). These practice actions are a combination of pedagogical grounding of creating habits and habit formation through regular repetition and are referred to as "practice habits" (McPherson and Davidson, 2006; Miksza, 2007; Vellacott and Ballantyne, 2022). Concomitantly, this theory of practice habits is inclusive of the process of patterns of behavior that are repeated regularly and tend to occur automatically in response to certain stimuli (Orbell and Verplanken, 2010). The longitudinal practice of the online GIO sessions (regular recorded sessions every Tuesday) allowed a gestation period during which players employed a series of repeated actions, gestures, and sounds in their creative process. A space where embodiment, involving the physical, sensory, and cognitive experiences of making music, was developed over time through a process of repetition (Biasutti and Frezza, 2009).

Some players became known for certain visual contributions, and even when their physical human forms were so augmented that they were rendered unrecognizable, their actions were nevertheless known and understood by the group—and were taken up. For example, author MacDonald and Rachel Joy Weiss use the software "Snapcam" in conjunction with Zoom effects, which has developed into distinct uses that are now recognizable. In this example, a certain software combination develops into not only a knowable aesthetic, but also a shared "tool" or language. In Figure 4.3 we see a number of players (author MacDonald, author Sappho, and Rachel Weiss) utilizing a kaleidoscope effect ((▶) Film 4.1).

64 Musical Collaborative Creativity

Figure 4.3. May 4, 2021, kaleidoscope and visual embodied reflections.

 QR Code: Please follow this QR code to the ⓘ companion website to view additional content for Chapter 4. Alternatively, you can access the website using the link provided in the front matter.

Through examples such as these, we can witness the building of a visual language not in fact so different from existing musical techniques and practices. The mimicking of a visual aesthetic technique, or the copying of a bodily movement, might be considered a visual form of a player taking up a melodic line from another musician and playing in "sync." The visual languages and the use of these new formats to contribute ideas appear to have settled easily into the existing language of the group, which already had existing creative alliances (people who often played together in group settings), known group aesthetics (having a reasonable idea of who will be likely to play what at a certain moment), and a knowledge of broader musical parameters (dynamics, textures, colors, tempos).

The habits that musicians develop through their practice routines allow them to perform with a certain level of stability and reliability, even in the unpredictable and dynamic context of improvisation. At the same time, these habits also provide a foundation for innovation, exploration, and flexibility, as experimental improvising musicians are able to depart from their habits and experiment with new sounds, rhythms, and textures. The embodiment of musical habits is also a critical factor in shaping the agency of improvisation in which physical, sensory, and cognitive experiences are integrated and expressed in musical performance (Borgo, 2006). It is the process by which musical habits are enacted and embodied through the body and the instrument; in this case, GIO mediated a new habitat where there was the experiencing of the non-human inclusion of sonic resources and a virtual two-dimensional space: Zoom. The GIO online improvisational experience could be seen as a direct contrast to the experiences and memories of past performances which included new limitations and freedoms through the necessity to discover ways of expressing both new habits singularly, collaboratively, and socially. Moreover, this embodied expression in the online experience introduced discoveries and the development of musical habits through intentionality in this new habitat.

Intentionality in improvisation refers to musical goals performed through their personal style (Onsman and Burke, 2018). From the perspective of jazz improvisers, they practice for many years learning musical patterns which include scales, rhythms, and licks from music that they have analyzed as well as the formation into the action of improvisation (Burke, 2021). For many, the habits of playing in the tradition have inhibited what Bensen describes as levels of improvisation (Benson, 2003), grappling with the paradox of habits, structure, and freedom or "letting go" (Fisher et al., 2021, p. 5). Intentionality guides these formations and expression of musical habits, shaping the improvisation in ways that are meaningful and relevant to the musician. For many musicians, this means improvising within the parameters and, in a sense, sometimes the confines of a canon. For example, the jazz musician's intentionality when improvising over a jazz standard is guided by its structured parameters, such as harmony, melody, rhythm, and historical legacy (Burke, 2021). More broadly, and very much in the case of GIO, improvisation never starts from scratch; there is always some sort of background influence that subconsciously informs the intentionality of the improvisation, whether that is a background of preexisting expertise on their instrument or knowledge/experience of styles as well as memories that inform "anticipations and intuitions" (Angelino, 2019). This could be called an idiosyncratic internal topography (Rojas, 2015) or what Ingrid Monson (2020) describes as the indexicality of styles, which is a qualitative function of how performance histories inform an improvisation. Through these online sessions, the GIO player's indexicality of styles and intentionality were broadened with these new experiences and expertise.

The GIO players experimented with their own expertise on their instrument as a starting point in how they navigated this new environment. Many grappled with a highly developed expertise on an instrument which Tom Davis (2019) describes as disappearing where the relationship between the musical thoughts of the musician and sound produced is one where "[. . .] instrument can be thought of as a direct conveyor of the performer's intentionality" (p. 73).

This notion of intentionality was tested for the GIO player hitherto as the embodied instrument relationship was both challenged and enhanced beyond the traditional improvisational practices. The players had to adapt their expertise to be able to interact with the ensemble. This adaptation took shape in the form of challenges and discoveries, and many musicians grappled with not only how the habits, memories, and intentionality would assimilate into this new experience, but more so how they adapted and creatively embraced the new environment and a new creative practice. In interviews conducted in 2020, many of the musicians stated that they had initial issues with how they interacted in the improvisations and with the effects on how they were able to play their instruments. Bassist Una MacGlone noted, with a hint of ambivalence, how she adapted to this new improvisatory environment. She saw the opportunity to be creative through new discoveries and experimentation, taking on a viewpoint that highlighted the creative possibilities:

> It can't replace that thing of being in a room with someone, but you have this different thing, which is, it has some of the same benefits, well, not all of them. [. . .] I kind of see this is like we're developing a new way of being creative as we're doing it.

For drummer Stuart Brown, the experience was, from his perspective of musical/interactive roles and expertise as a drummer, questioning how his interactive and listening habits have been disrupted and how they triggered solutions:

> [T]he drums are potentially the loudest instrument on stage. And once you start playing, it masks all the other sounds that everyone else is projecting. So it's quite common for me not to be able to hear anything that's being played by a cello player at the very front. And so in that sense, that's another reason that maybe in a weird way, like the Zoom sessions with GIO I actually probably heard more than I normally do in energy or concert—so I had to adapt my playing. Because everyone's audio feed was going directly into my headphones as opposed to the acoustic space just preventing me hearing something.

Here, Maggie Nicols embraces the possibilities of the new environment by describing the experience as a space to elevate themselves through the improvisatory discoveries in their music-making:

[Being] fully present, being in the moment, being able to cope with whatever arises. That's what we're doing. We're actually fully immersed in each moment we're responding to our own impulses, to what, to our environment, to other players, to other musicians. And it's all happening as time unfolds. We're literally in tune with the universe as it's developing and unfolding. We're right there at the cutting edge of life.

Author Burke underwent a transformation in his approach to improvisation and playing the saxophone as a result of the online experience. The following observation, written in 2023, reflects a longitudinal perspective. Author Burke found himself unable to rely solely on his saxophone-playing expertise in an online setting due to sound issues with Zoom. Consequently, he had to shift his focus toward leveraging his improvisatory and experimental skills to assert agency in the online environment. This adjustment was a source of initial struggle for him during the early stages of the GIO experience, prompting him to question his relationship with the saxophone and re-evaluate both his expertise and habits of improvisation:

> It was a 262-day (on and off) lockdown in Melbourne, Australia—the longest lockdown period in the world. I have a very close connection to my saxophone, but during this time we were separated for weeks at a time. No gigs and no incentive to practice. My connection to playing had been an embodiment of me and the saxophone through playing: practice/performances/concerts. This developed over many years through my relationship with the saxophone and the blending of the binary of the hard metal vibrating and connecting with my body. The developing process of improvising using the saxophone as an augmentation of my expression and creativity.
>
> During the GIO sessions, my agency of sometimes being a disruptor on the saxophone through creating ideas, listening, stopping, starting, and trusting changed. My reliance on changing volume, distortion, breath, touch, and the vibration and sometimes wetness on my fingers . . . blending the embodiment of the machine—saxophone and body informing how I interacted in improvisation changed. How I blended this environment to create (and interact with) beauty, tension, distortion, warmth, disruption, hardness, loudness, sadness, and brightness . . . changed. My approach to playing the saxophone in the sessions was completely different. The creation of sound through my saxophone and how that was part of the sonic environment of the past became secondary to my new understanding and contribution to this new creative reality. I felt that improvising on the saxophone was not the centerpiece of my creativity—my place of comfort and expression. I was now extending my expertise on the sax by blending with objects in the Zoom room and

in my room. I was augmenting my saxophone by stuffing objects from my desk and shelves down the bell and around the bell. Using plastic, paper, wooden flutes, pens, cards, CDs, and objects to make a sound. I was playing softer. I did not have the innate power of the saxophone of the past—I had to think differently. (author Burke)

In a separate interview, author MacDonald described a similar experience of adaptation and augmentation, although, as Raymond explains, he has a lot of prior experience in experimenting with his instrument—the saxophone. Along with the inclusion of new visual prompts, the online experience afforded Raymond's new agency in his approach to expertise on the saxophone and more generally in his improvisatory experimentation:

When lockdown started and we moved to online music-making, one of the first observations for me was that my approach to playing the saxophone, my primary instrument, started to change. I found that if I played "full tone," that is, blowing my instrument in the usual way, I couldn't hear the other instruments in the Zoom session. While it would have been relatively straightforward to adapt my technology, perhaps using a combination of headphones and enhanced computer software, I chose to adapt my playing technique to suit the technology that I had immediately available—laptop computer and headphones. I began to experiment with smaller sounds that I could embed within the sonic array I could hear in the Zoom session. These small sounds included very quiet, conventionally played tones on the saxophone, key clicks and percussive sounds from the saxophone, and breath sounds, in other words, sounds that might otherwise be considered artifacts of normal playing. I also started using many other instruments that were available in my studio/study and also deploying any other sound-making devices available and objects that I could place into the visual array that I felt were making a contribution to the overall improvisatory landscape. This has clear links to the Theater of Home topic discussed in previous chapters.

This approach to playing the saxophone was not new for me, and I am frequently experimenting with trying to find new sounds using what might be called extended techniques, but the context was completely new, and the resultant explorations also felt new and exhilarating. Playing online and trying to hear what others were playing online and trying to respond, support, complement, and integrate with what others were doing was unquestionably new for me. Not only was this new but it was really exciting, I found I was enjoying the challenge and the new explorations I seemed to be making, or should I say discovering new ways of making sounds and interacting with others online. (author MacDonald)

In summary, during the COVID-19 period, humans became much more reliant on technology to live their lives in a non-human approach to communicating and doing. What we have discovered in this collaborative online period with GIO is that human and artificial agents developed and entered into an augmented reality. In doing so, new understandings of human augmentation, such as the experiences of authors Burke, DeNora, Sappho, and MacDonald, demonstrate that the combination of human and artificial collaboration creates new capabilities and potentialities. An augmented reality that further develops, or augments, humans. Through regular GIO playing sessions and the augmentation of both habitats and players, novel identities and habituations emerged, blending the human and non-human elements. This transformation within the ensemble and among the players led to the creation of new virtuosities.

5
Virtual Foam

Performing, Recording, and Remixing Ensemble Improvisation in the *Zumwelt*

Improvisation Within a Mise-en-Scène of Constraints

> *If gender is a kind of a doing, ... it is a practice of improvisation within a scene of constraint.*
>
> —Judith Butler (2004, p. 1)

Judith Butler's rendering of gender as a performative improvisation within the parameters of symbolic social constraints provides a useful parallel on a range of levels—musical, social, technological, aesthetic—for our reading of the recorded weekly online ensemble improvisations which GIO hosted via Zoom during lockdown. Importantly, Butler reminds us that we do not produce our author identities or artworks autonomously, in that identity emerges in "a complex interaction between individual doing and societal constraints" (Landgraf, 2011, p. 16). In short, the individual is always already enmeshed in an "ensemble of social relations" (Marx, 1975, p. 423). As Henri Lefebvre also reminds us, "[t]he spontaneous is already part of the social" (Lefebvre, 2014, p. 513). As Elizabeth Hallam and Tim Ingold elucidate: "There is no script for cultural and social life. People have to work it out as they go along. In a word, they have to *improvise*" (Hallam and Ingold, 2007, p. 1).

From such perspectives, spontaneity and improvisation are fundamental and integral methods for producing the social fabric of everyday life. This is perhaps how we should understand the role of improvisation in Butler's reading of gender. For Butler, the emancipation of collective and individual bodies consists of the formation of new assemblages of situated gendered identities navigating a series of sedimented and shifting layers of political, economic, legal, social, technological, and cultural contingencies. In short, identity as performative performs an improvisation amid a mise-en-scène of everyday social constraints. As Edgar Landgraf notes in *Improvisation as Art*:

Likening the construction of gender to improvisation, Butler conceives of gender—and by extension, the construction of the most fundamental tenets of a person's identity, his or her being-in-the-world, the way you relate to yourself and your environment—as resulting from a continuing and continually changing performance. (Landgraf, 2011, p. 16)

The combined notions of performative identities, sociocultural contingencies, and digital technology (the screen "interface" of contemporary social relations), then, provide the theoretical framing for our understanding of improvisation within a "mise-en-scène of constraints."

This view of subjectivity as collectively formed and emerging from the ensemble of social relations introduces a spatial dimension to identity, understood as a relational and improvised "being-in-the-world" (Heidegger, 1962). Perhaps the most influential spatial terms for critical theory in the past decades derive from the thought of Deleuze and Guattari in their discussion of the "rhizome" and "rhizomatic" network structures. In the age of digital connectivity and the multiplicity of lines of communication and interaction, of network and flow, we might assume that the potent deterritorialization of the rhizome structure would provide a fertile spatial model for understanding the agency of emergent collaborations and free improvisations. In the context of ensemble improvisations, however, a more productive spatial term might be the related term "assemblage," advanced by Deleuze and developed by Manuel DeLanda (2016), which we will draw upon below. For Peter Sloterdijk, however, the spatial metaphor that best describes the topologies of contemporary social life takes a slightly different turn. In what appears to be a ludic extension of Jürgen Habermas's (1989) notion of the "public sphere," Sloterdijk understands the morphology of the social as a multiplicity of spheres, as manifest in various globes, bubbles, and foams. Like Butler's mise-en-scène of constraints, Sloterdijk's foams and bubbles are social spheres founded upon coexistence. As Iwona Janicka writes: "[Sloterdijk's] assumption is that human beings start as a co-existence, rather than a metaphysical autonomous one ... it is co-subjectivity that is a basis for subjectivity ... being is always primarily being-with" (Janicka, 2016, p. 65). As an innovative conceptualization of Heidegger's "being-in-the-world" as a form of "dwelling," it is Sloterdijk's spatial morphologies of bubbles and foam that accord most with the immunological conditions of online ensemble improvisations.

The lockdown measures and social distancing guidelines implemented to combat the spread of the global COVID-19 pandemic, therefore, represent the first level of the "mise-en-scène of constraints" within which the GIO ensemble improvisations were performed. The term "mise-en-scène" adopted here follows Antonin Artaud's usage in '"Mise-en-scène" and Metaphysics' whereby conventions of stagecraft become an "active" and "concrete language" of his "theatre of cruelty" (Schumacher, 1989, pp. 92–97; see also Artaud, 1958). The social constraints of lockdown, under which entire populations were commanded that they "must stay at home," formed, therefore, not simply an exterior sociocultural backdrop against which GIO sessions took place, nor merely a conventionally static proscenium arch frame within which gestures of communality were enacted: differing and shifting state immunological strategies formed a variable parameter of the project. The second variable parameter of this mise-en-scène was, of course, our use of the digital communication platform Zoom.

While the sessions began with the aim of maintaining an established musical and social community, they quickly developed into a means of producing new and interesting work. The latency attached to all internet conferencing software did not hamper the interactions, as it was incorporated as an emergent feature of the improvisation. Another feature of Zoom software restricts what can be heard, with only a limited number of sound sources being audible at any one time. This has significant implications for larger ensembles attempting to use Zoom. However, rather than regarding this "thinning out" process as a limitation of the medium, an unwelcome impedance or interruption, GIO incorporated it as an active agency of the improvisation. In a similar fashion, the viewing options of Zoom were incorporated into the recording and video editing. In this way, the algorithms and affordances of Zoom formed part of the process and final recording—a live *Zoom* recording as distinct from a pre-recorded *room* recording.

During our experience of using Zoom as an "agential interface" for ensemble improvisations, we encountered a similar level of what might be regarded as the usual combination of technical obstacles (latency) and creative opportunities (collaboration) as identified by previous "Networked Music Performance" (NMP) research projects.[1] The issue of audio latency is perhaps most often cited by musicians working with online networks, and its effects have been measured across a range of digital communication platforms.[2] Variable internet speeds and computer-processing speeds, for example, have been said to lead to the problem of "undesired audio dropouts" (Renaud et al., 2012, p. 2). There have been attempts to alleviate both of these perceived creative constraints and contingencies. For example, in 2014–2016, Falmouth University conducted an Arts and Humanities Research Council (AHRC) funded research project led by Michael Rofe, who asked how networked digital technologies might enable musicians living in remote communities to access similar opportunities for ensemble and orchestral performance as their more urban dwelling counterparts.[3] A key outcome of the Falmouth Online Orchestra project of 2014–2016 was enhancing access to a connected community of musicians and the ability to overcome distance and maintain a musical community (also a notable feature and outcome of the GIO sessions initiated during lockdown). However, the approach and structure of the research project differ significantly from those adopted by GIO Zoom sessions during the pandemic. First, the Falmouth project involved the prearrangement of superfast broadband access in Truro Cathedral and the Isles of Scilly for participating groups of musicians. In contrast, during lockdown conditions, GIO online sessions were remotely accessed in domestic situations with variable equipment, setups, and connectivity. Second, the Online Orchestra's approach to telematic performance was to adopt a "bespoke latency-control programme" to construct a low-latency environment (Prior et al., 2017, pp. 185–196). In the process of seeking to maximize affordances associated with NMP, the Falmouth Online Orchestra project effectively attempts to engineer out and eradicate contingencies.[4] In contrast, the GIO project might be said to have adopted a "Latency Accepting Approach" (LAA), which regarded the technical constraints of the platform as integral to the process of improvisation.

The implications of adopting such an "open" approach to telematic music performance are not merely technical but philosophical. From the outset, the framing mise-en-scène of constraints—both social and technological—were, to borrow the words of Ernest Becker, "part of the intellectual and editorial fabric of the work itself."[5] In methodological terms, GIO adopts an approach to ensemble performance that is grounded in what other thinkers have described as the "radical acceptance of contingency" (Lewis and Piekut 2016, p. 228). The radical acceptance or "emancipation of contingency" in "situated" improvisational performances (in the here-and-now) is a feature that commentators such as Timothy Hampton, Davide Sparti, and Gary Peters (following Niklas Luhmann) ascribe to the practice of improvisation.[6] Such an acceptance and emancipation of contingency as the basis for ensemble improvisation as a manifesto in the online collaborations of GIO recall Husserl's grounding principle for a pure phenomenology: "Individual existence of every sort is, quite universally speaking, '*contingent*.' It is thus; in respect of its nature it could be otherwise" (Husserl, 1983, p. 7).[7]

This (ethic of) openness to contingency extends to both beings and objects, recalling R. Murray Schafer's description of the musician of the contemporary soundscape as "anyone and anything that sounds!" (Schafer, 1994, p. 5), and characterizes GIO's experiments with the affordances of the apparatus of

Zoom. To borrow the words of Hazel Smith and Roger Dean, GIO approached Zoom as an experimental 'improviser-computer interface' (Smith and Dean, 1997, pp. 250–251), whereby the software 'interface is the feature which dictates the utility to improvisers of a particular medium' (Smith and Dean, 1997, p. 251). It is here that the emancipation of contingency meets the contingency of emancipation. In short, in situated Zoom improvisation sessions, GIO enacts the emancipation of contingency and the contingency of emancipation in online Zoom performances and (as we shall see) adopts a recording process "attuned to the entanglement of the apparatuses of production" (Barad, 2007, pp. 29–30). We will follow here Foucault's notion of "apparatus" as a "network" or "formation" (Agamben, 2009, p. 2) established between elements of power, discourses, or technologies to the extent that it connects with Manovich's description of the "cultural interfaces" of new media and Galloway's concept of the "interface effect." In the process, we approach the notion of "interface" not as a technical prosthesis for expanding the practice of improvisation (as traced by Smith and Dean, 1997) but as an *environment*.

Improvisation-as-Bricolage: The "Prop-Being" of "Whatever Is at Hand"

If we accept Gary Peters's (2009) claim that improvisation is the emancipation of contingency, then it might be useful to pause here for a moment to consider, however briefly, Claude Lévi-Strauss's reading of contingency in the context of artistic creation as embodied in the cultural practice of "bricolage" (1966). As a "science of the concrete," the practice of the bricoleur (one who practices bricolage) offers an interesting model for approaching the improvisational odd kinship between musical instruments and household objects, which in turn offers a further kinship to the recording and remixing process (as "extensions"). For Lévi-Strauss (1966), contingencies are sets of cultural and concrete "pre-constraints" that affect artistic creation, which can be both "intrinsic" and "extrinsic": "extrinsic" contingencies are the concrete social and intellectual contexts and situations which frame the production and reception (posterior or anterior contingencies) of the creative act; "intrinsic" contingencies are those which pertain to the process of execution of the work as manifest in the direct encounter with concrete materiality in the process of its being transformed:

> the size or shape of the piece of wood the sculptor lays hands on, in the direction and quality of its grain, in the imperfections of his tools, in the resistance which his

materials or project offer to the work in the course of its accomplishment, in the unforeseeable incidents arising during work. (Lévi-Strauss, 1966, p. 27)

The creative artist responds to these material and cultural pre-constraints via a particular form of improvisation, which he terms "bricolage," after his reading of indigenous cultural practices. Lévi-Strauss writes:

> The "bricoleur" is adept at performing a large number of diverse tasks; but, unlike the engineer, he does not subordinate each of them to the availability of raw materials and tools conceived and procured for the purpose of the project. His universe of instruments is closed and the rules of his game are always to *make do with "whatever is at hand,"* that is to say with a set of tools and materials which is always finite and is also heterogeneous because what it contains bears no relation to the current project, or indeed to any particular project, but is the contingent result of all the occasions there have been to renew or enrich the stock or to maintain it with the remains of previous constructions or destructions. (Lévi-Strauss, 1966, p. 17)

As a bricoleur, the improviser's task in making sound or images is a makeshift "make do with 'whatever is at hand.'" In this context, all objects, whether ornament or implement, working or broken, are explored and exploited for their affordances as noise-making implements: wind-up toys, kitchen utensils, glasses of water, rubber gloves, empty beer can. As Anna Dezeuze succinctly puts it: "the bricoleur speaks through things, as well as with them" (Dezeuze, 2008, p. 31). A feature that distinguishes improvisation-as-bricolage from other forms of musical "free improvisation" (e.g., free jazz) is that objects used are those

> which are already there, which had not been specially conceived with an eye to the operation for which they are to be used and to which one tries by trial and error to adapt them, not hesitating to change them whenever it appears necessary, or to try several of them at once, even if their form and their origin are heterogenous—and so forth. (Derrida, 1978, p. 285)

In the ad hoc world of improvisation-as-bricolage, "making do" becomes a symbiotic method of "being-with" the world. Making do and being with "whatever is at hand" suggest that all objects, regardless of origin or material or intended purpose, can become noise-making instruments: there is no hierarchy in the flat ontology of noise.

As a defining feature of the combination of "making do" and "making with" in terms of the role of objects in GIO's improvisation in the context of lockdown and "Theater of Home," it might be said that the improviser enters, in the words of Iwona Janicka's reading of Sloterdijk's "spherology," into a "symbiosis with the apartment, becoming one with one's immediate environment . . . made up of links with inanimate objects and the environment in which humans are placed" (Janicka, 2016, p. 67). To put it another way: "to achieve being-at-homeness-in-the-world you have to begin from your own dwelling-place" (Bate, 2000, p. 109–110).

We dwell on the role of bricolage here not simply because it was a key feature in the experimental Theater of Home of GIO online improvisations, as a playful and expedient method of making noises, but as a method of artistic research. As a method of creative inquiry, bricolage critically interrogates and undermines notions of scientific method and disciplinary discourse formation. As Derrida noted, "it has even been said that bricolage is critical language itself" (Derrida, 1978, p. 285). As a critical language, bricolage decodes not only our dwelling place but the very "tools" of cultural practices. As a non-hierarchical approach to things in the world, the practice of bricolage rebounds upon and perhaps ultimately undermines the ontological status of the category of "musical" instruments in general. For example, we might consider the use of a domestic implement, such as a kitchen utensil, for its noise-making capacities, a process which we might regard as unveiling the "expanded affordance" of the object, a process which interrupts or redirects (detours) its prior ready-to-hand status, or the tool-being of the object as intended conduit for a set of prescribed functions. In this situation of free play, formerly circumscribed capacities or anticipated affordances are expanded in unanticipated and manifold directions. In this way, objects at hand are considered not as tools (ready-to-hand) or as means to an end, but as conspicuous objects (present-at-hand) in a "democracy of objects." Nevertheless, improvisation-as-bricolage does not ultimately reside in the interaction of emancipated objects but dwells in an effervescent assemblage of relations, in the molecular "frenzy of agitation" of interface effects. For reasons that will become apparent below, we will call this effervescent frenzy "virtual foam."

Umwelt as Bubble

As will have become clear from our discussion in previous chapters, the adoption of Zoom software in GIO ensemble improvisations is not to be apprehended as an *extrinsic* contingency alongside the social context of lockdown conditions. Rather, the use of Zoom and its recording settings are *intrinsic* contingencies, subject to similar bricolage methods (remixing the reality of the virtual) in the production of poly-ontic improvisational assemblages. As an intrinsic contingency, therefore, Zoom software is not simply a "medium" *through* which musicians perform in order to evaluate the efficacy of the software as a means of musical improvisation. Zoom is an environment in which new improvisation formations (or *foam*ations) emerge. Nevertheless, it is certainly a familiar aspect of the (initial) experience of online ensemble improvisations for musicians to evaluate whether Zoom is a suitable medium *through* which an ensemble might perform improvised music, whether it is an adequate or inadequate tool for such a task, and so on. And, if found "wanting," then the onus is to seek to mitigate or eradicate perceived impediments and glitches. It is perhaps inevitable that a degree of this perspective on telematic music performance will persist, particularly in the wake of a welcome return to live music performance in a "post-pandemic" world. Such approaches to online performance contexts, however, overlook the essential entanglement of performer and platform in an interface of unpredictable assemblage formations which might be termed *relational* in not only Nicolas Bourriaud's sense of relational *art* "taking as its theoretical horizon the realm of human interactions and its social context" (Bourriaud, 2002, p. 14) but also John Dewey's earlier sense of relational *form* as "something direct and active, something dynamic and energetic" (Dewey, 1958, p. 134). In this sense, GIO's online improvisations might also be considered *environmental* improvisations in which GIO adopted an "environmental aesthetic" (Berleant, 1992) approach to online improvisation where there was "no outside" to the software, where the improviser is acknowledged as continuous with the digital environment.

As has been said above, Zoom is not so much a medium *through which* performances are enabled to take place (during lockdown conditions or otherwise), but an interface of new formations *in which* such separations of performer and platform, of viewer and listener, sound and image, of *glitch* and *ground*, begin to break down. As such, Zoom is not simply experienced as a *surrounding* (*Umbegung*) in which one might perform—but an *environment* (*Umwelt*) produced via a process of activity and creative *intra*-actions. We might be tempted, then, to describe the environment of Zoom as a *Zumwelt* (pronounced Zoom-welt).[8]

In this context, it is important to note that Jakob von Uexküll's influential 1933 work, *A Foray into the Worlds of Animals and Humans*, in which he coins the term *Umwelt*, or environment, not only rests upon a musical analogy of harmony and counterpoint as a way to understand the symbiotic relations of human and animals, of hosts and parasites, in the collective production of the "score of Nature." Uexküll also employs the metaphor of the ecosystem as consisting of individual and ephemeral "bubbles" from which interconnections and new worlds might arise:

> We begin such a stroll on a sunny day before a flowering meadow in which insects buzz and butterflies flutter, and we make a bubble around each of the animals living in the meadow. The bubble represents each animal's environment and contains all the features accessible to the subject. As soon as we enter into one such bubble, the previous surroundings of the subject are completely reconfigured. Many qualities of the colorful meadow vanish completely, others lose their coherence with one another, and new connections are created. A new world arises in each bubble. (Uexküll, 2010, p. 43)[9]

Uexküll's visualization of the ecosystem as a morphology of interacting bubbles is an important point of reference for Sloterdijk's study of globes, bubbles, and "social foam" (Janicka, 2016, p. 76). In the context of state immunological conditions of COVID-19 lockdowns and government guidance on "social distancing" and the formation of isolated social "bubbles," it is to Sloterdijk's spatial morphology of foam as "the theory of co-fragile systems" and "an interactive network based on the principle of co-isolation" that we will turn to consider the "multi-celled chaos" of GIO's ensemble Zoom improvisations as the performative (dis)embodiment of virtual foam (Sloterdijk, 2016, pp. 38, 56, 48).[10]

Forays in the *Zumwelt*: The Three Ecologies of Attunement

Amidst the discussion of the Theater of Home and mise-en-scène of constraints, we might recall that Lev Manovich, in his groundbreaking study of *The Language of New Media*, exploring the human-computer interface, affords a central position to cinema, its camera techniques, and its theoretical vocabulary. This discussion revolves around the dominant condition whereby "reality is cut by the rectangle of a screen" (Manovich, 2001, p. 104). For Manovich, it is cinema that provides the dominant measure by which we understand the relationship between the viewer and the screen—the "viewing regime"—of the human-computer interface (Manovich, 2001, p. 96):

> Dynamic, real-time, and interactive, a screen is still a screen. Interactivity, simulation, and telepresence: As was the case centuries ago, we are still looking at a flat, rectangular surface, existing in the space of our body and acting as a window into another space. We still have not left the era of the screen. (Manovich 2001, p. 115)

Performing Through, To, and With

If we have not yet left the era of the screen interface, an understanding of the dominant patterns of engagement with the screen interface in GIO's Zoom improvisations might provide some insights into the different "ecologies of attunement" at play in the intra-actions. In general terms, these interactions and intra-actions fell into three broad categories: those who performed *through* the screen (as if the assemblage of software-camera-computer screen were a transparent medium facilitating remote musical interactions); those who performed *to* the camera, foregrounding the framework of the computer camera and incorporating and interacting with the Zoom virtual background and applying online filters as an integral component of the improvisation (conscious of the camera as a framing a visual performance[11]); and there were participants of the ensemble who performed "with" the screen (using the visual affordances of the computer camera or other lenses and settings as an integral component of the performance). At times, there were performances that utilized additional cameras or used a mobile phone as a roaming camera device in planes, trains, and public streets when lockdowns eased (which combined elements of performing "through," "to," and "with"). The differing incorporations of the camera in improvised performance, each with different approaches to interaction/intra-action within and with the apparatus, might be thought of as different "ecological assemblages" in Haraway's notion of "sympoiesis" ("sympoietic arrangements . . . otherwise known as cells, organisms, and ecological assemblages") (Haraway, 2016, p. 58). Further, performing *through*, *to*, and *with* the sympoietic assemblage of computer-camera-screen interface might help us navigate the "unfolding," "overlapping," and "intersecting" lines of what might be called, following Guattari (1995), the three ecologies of the virtual (which for Guattari are psychological, social, and environmental). These might, in turn, map onto our own "ecologies of attunement": "enfolding," "enframing," and "entanglement":

- "Enfolding": performing "through" the camera communication network; Zoom is a means to an end (as if the camera were a transparent window); exploring the affordances of the software as a means of communication in a manner that prioritizes musical questions and considerations; although exploring audio contingencies (latency), visual affordances of the interface are less important.
- "Enframing": performing "to" the camera, taking into consideration framing, lighting conditions, body position, costume, and so on, the affordances of the interface of the computer camera and related settings, including virtual background; and exploring audio and visual contingencies of the computer interface.

- "Entanglement": performing "with" the camera and settings as a "dynamic screen" (Manovich); manipulating virtual background (e.g., in a manner that disintegrates the distinction between background and foreground, body and image), applying app filters, employing multiple cameras, different types of lens, and so on, exploring affordances of the computer as "performative" interface; characterized by playful experimentation with the mediatized audio-visual conditions of Zoom improvisation.

The three ecologies of attunement to Zoom improvisation of performing "through," "to," and "with" the interface, which might be said to accord with conditions of enfolding, "enframing," and "entanglement" with the apparatus, simultaneously coexist in GIO's Zoom improvisations.[12] There are also areas of overlap (e.g., between performing *to* and *with* virtual background), and the different approaches are frequently interchangeable by individuals from week to week, or even within individual sessions. They should not be understood, therefore, as a form of aesthetic teleology, whereby musicians gradually evolve from an expedient performing "through" a technology that enfolds the improvisation toward a complex state of entanglement in "performing with." The ensemble is an assemblage of these individual (and interchangeable) approaches. They are individual attunements to the apparatus. They are simultaneously subjective and intersubjective, independent and interdependent, different, divergent, incoherent, but above all collective (an ensemble as an inoperative community in perpetual re-formation). In GIO, there is no hierarchical or prioritized approach, and there is no pressure to conform to any single approach. Any such pressure would burst the bubble of respect for individual differences. In their interaction, combination, and relation lies the interface effect. It is the coexistence of these individual bubbles, performing an effervescent ever-transforming assemblage of difference in multiplicity, an inoperative community, that produces the condition and experience of virtual foam.

Gallery View, Active Speaker View, and Pin View

We might extend this analysis of the screen interface further by exploring the interface effects of the salient viewer settings of Zoom: Gallery View, Active Speaker View, and Pin View. We might also draw upon some of the thinking of cinema to help us navigate the distinctly different experience of the visual afforded in Zoom in the two automated settings of Gallery View and Speaker View. The names of these settings would suggest that the former foregrounds the opticality and visuality of framing participants, and the latter is activated acoustically by the sound of a participant's voice or the sounds of a musical instrument or noise-making implement. Evoking Deleuze's reading of cinema, it could be argued that each of these viewer settings foregrounds different cinematic axes, with Gallery View foregrounding a movement-image (space) and Speaker View presenting a time-image (time).

Gallery View

In Gallery View, participants appear in a grid of individual and identically scaled rectangular windows. This arrangement mirrors the computer interface itself, whereby the user's screen is "ruled by straight lines and rectangular windows" which themselves contain smaller rectangles of "individual files arranged in a grid" (Manovich, 2001, p. 63). In Gallery View, there is the paradoxical illusion of a community gathering who are nevertheless subject to rigid partitioning. There is also the appearance of a spatial democracy, whereby each segment of digital space affords equal visual access to all the others on the screen (although depending upon the number of participants and the configuration of the settings, there may be more than one screen of grids to parse). There is nobody sitting in front of you who is taller or wearing a hat obstructing your vision. In the interface, everyone is the same size and an equal distance away. This digital democracy witnesses the flattening out of the curvature of ensemble improvisational space-time. Simultaneously, the scopic regime of Gallery View induces a sense of disembodied overview, as if consulting a map of a city or regarding a collection of curios, a cabinet of curiosities—a digital *Wunderkammer*.

The "host" is normally anchored in the top left-hand corner of the screen, and each viewer sees themselves as positioned next in line to the host horizontally. (We will discuss the presence of the "parasite" below.) This means that for each participant in the online ensemble, the arrangement of the assemblage of gridded screens is slightly different. Nevertheless, there is no linear direction in which to read the interconnections between performers. In contrast, as with Landow's reading of the electronic cultural interface of hypermedia and hypertext, Gallery View is "experienced as nonlinear, or, more properly, multilinear or multisequential . . . [where] . . . new rules and new experience apply" (Landow, 1997, p. 4).[13]

During the ensemble performance, sound and movement flow across the surface of the screen, but not in a ring of concentric circles like ripples from a stone cast in a pond, but in erratic veerings and scatterings, like cracks in ice. At times there is sonic confusion, a multidirectional cacophony of activity, and a hubbub of instruments, implements, voices, and gestures. In the words of the art critic Leo Steinberg, writing on the photo-silkscreen works of Robert Rauschenberg, "intimations of spatial meaning [are] forever cancelling out to subside in a kind of optical noise" (Harrison and Wood, 1992, p. 951). For all the rigidity of its enframing, Gallery View remains fundamentally unstable. The experience of GIO improvisations in Gallery View is to witness (in the words of Sloterdijk) a series of "constant leaps, redistributions and reformattings occurring inside the multi-celled chaos" (Sloterdijk, 2016, p. 48).

But if Gallery View does not render improvisation liquid like water in a pond, it is not solid either. Perhaps it is a kind of volatile gas. Or perhaps it is some kind of combination of the solid and liquid states. Maybe the screen is a volatile *glass*. With the détournement of everyday objects, the improvising bricoleur constructs sonic assemblages and visual performances, which in Gallery View resemble a Situationist stained-glass window—Gallery View as optical noise. The composer Olivier Messiaen may have attributed bedazzlement to the stained-glass window effect of his compositions, as the highest form of (religious) music (see Messiaen, 2001 [1978]). In contrast, free improvisations might be said to be the highest "bedevilment" of music-as-noise. The word "bedevil" here is not used in the sense of "bad" or "evil" but in terms of noise being ontologically and epistemologically "troublesome." Free improvisation is a way of *staying with the trouble* of the emancipated contingencies of art.

Sometimes gestures and sounds appear momentarily coordinated or mirrored; at other times, they appear incoherent. There are individual moments of quietude against a background of collective disquiet. It is a collectivity in which any equilibrium is constantly collapsing into disequilibrium, and structure is lost in the effervescent clamor of being. In short, Gallery View manifests GIO's ensemble improvisations as audio-visual polyphony ("it's like cocaine for the eyes"). One might be tempted to describe the regimentation of the grid-like structure of Gallery View as a rigid frame trying to contain chaos unleashed from within the medium itself, that the ensemble improvisation takes on the character of a chemical reaction gone wrong, and some new species of ever-expanding foam is about to escape from the confines of the lockdown laboratory. This chemical metaphor suggests a molecularity of the image, of Gallery View enframing an uncontrolled chemical or alchemical chain reaction of images "intercepted in full flight, caught bubbling over, held seething [... and ...] hurled one against the other in an inconceivable riot" (Artaud on "Alchemical Theatre" in Schumacher, 1989, pp. 100, 116).[14] In Zoom, Gallery View enacts a "molecular theatre" (Birrell in Home, 1997, pp. 22–24). But this *molecular mise-en-scène* does not in the end frame a chaotic alchemical *mess*. Rather, it weaves a *mesh*—it generates a new spatiotemporal fabric of improvisational space-time. We must recall that Zoom is not simply a medium but an environment. The meshwork that Gallery View innovates is the interlaced and interwoven fabric of new performative virtualities, a porous and foam-like structure of the audio-visual multiverse. The *Wunderkammer* meets the Open.

Meshwork and Meadow

Despite all this effervescent clamor and interaction, there remains a fragile isolation, with each member of the ensemble cocooned in their own screen bubble. As Uexküll writes of insects populating a meadow:

> We must... imagine all the animals that animate Nature around us, be they beetles, butterflies, gnats, or dragonflies who populate a meadow, as having a soap bubble around them, closed on all sides, which closes off their visual space and in which everything visible for the subject is also enclosed. Each bubble shelters other places, and in each are also found the directional planes of effective space, which give a solid scaffolding to space. The birds that flutter about, the squirrels hopping from branch to branch, or the cows grazing in the meadow, all remain permanently enclosed in the bubble that encloses their space. (Uexküll, 2010, p. 69)

We might imagine that for Sloterdijk, Uexküll's image of the ecology of the meadow would represent a being-in-foam, producing "an interactive network based on the principle of co-isolation" (Sloterdijk, 2016, p. 56). This sense of collectivity as co-isolation carries through in the audio recording settings of Zoom, where it is possible to select a separate audio stem recording for each participant in addition to the collective audio track. If we follow the trajectory and paths of these butterflies and beetles, their bubbles might describe arcs and lines that are not parallel but randomly overlap and interact, but which nevertheless preserve this sense of an "interactive network of co-isolation." Alternatively, Tim Ingold might describe the interface effect of Gallery View as a "meshwork":

> the pathways or trajectories along which improvisatory practice unfolds are not connections, nor do they describe relations between one thing and another. They are rather lines along which things continually come into being. Thus when I speak of the entanglement of things I mean this literally and precisely: not a network

of connections but a meshwork of interwoven lines of growth and movement. (Ingold, 2010, p. 3)

Where Ingold talks of meshwork, Uexküll might talk of "webs." In his contrapuntal ecology, the forms of web and bubble are complementary terms. Webs enclose gaps, and bubbles require a boundary. As Geoffrey Winthrop-Young notes, "bubbles are connected and woven together into a web" (Uexküll, 2010, p. 214).[15] Sloterdijk's term for such a weaving together of co-isolated bubbles is "foam."

The overriding visual interface of Gallery View remains the rectangular grid and suggests a rectilinear morphology of transparency and screens and windows. They might be considered as opening onto or unveiling individuated worlds, or alternatively, revealing the confinement of lockdown in our separate domestic cells. Either way, the viewer surveys the mise-en-scène with an all-seeing voyeuristic eye. Gallery View is part panorama, part panopticon. Nevertheless, what is witnessed in the ensemble improvisations is a "constellation of moments" that erupt and evaporate, appear and disappear, expand and implode. The visual polyphony of the performance suggests an altogether more organic metaphor; one of molecularity, of the biotic interactions of "vibrant matter," of chemical reaction and effervescence. Screens become cells, bubbles become foam. The morphological analogy of the bubble and foam brings us back to the immunological context of COVID-19 lockdowns from which we embarked upon our discussion of GIO's transition to performing with Zoom software to maintain its practice of ensemble improvisations.

Speaker View ("Active Speaker View")

If Gallery View is an interface whose visual regime is predominantly spatial, then the modality of Speaker View is predominantly temporal. As a setting designed to respond to the speaking voice during video conferencing and to orient the audience to a person speaking at that moment, when adopted as an interface for ensemble improvisation, Speaker View offers a fundamentally fragmented and disorienting spatiotemporal experience, preventing the viewer or participant from obtaining a coherent overview of the ensemble and who is playing what when, or who else is even participating. The participant is subjected to an overwhelming onslaught of sound and image, an endless succession of an apparently disconnected (often ludic-comedic) "constellation of moments" (Lefebvre, 2014, pp. 634–652): discontinuity, incoherence, and fragmentation reign supreme in this digital condition. In Speaker View, there is a constant (incessant) interruption. The timing is always slightly too late, and the apparatus is subject to the latency of audio-visual and internet connection speeds. It also has a tendency to "jump cut" to a different player in the middle of a movement. In its "processual dynamic," Speaker View is, therefore, the combination of—or rather the tension between—two different temporalities: the "too late" and the "too early." Speaker View thereby establishes its own distinctive groove. As an unstable aesthetic of interruption, it is the digitally embodied performance of the dialectic of glitch and groove.[16]

Although formally titled "Active Speaker View," this setting is actually "reactive" and cannot anticipate a musician about to perform (e.g., raising a trumpet to lips, etc.). As the emphasis of the function title suggests, Speaker View does not respond to elements of visual performance or actions which might be occurring on screen, as the setting is activated by acoustic signals. The engaged listener is also frequently overlooked. In this respect, the ensemble and partial view are further fragmented. Speaker View amounts to an unstable enframing (or bracketing) of performances, in a succession of apparently autonomous moments, disparate and disconnected, but which are ultimately heteronomous, subject to the contingencies and clamor of the ensemble, competing noises, and the fleeting image as yet or forever unseen.

As with Lefebvre's "theory of moments," the "narrow and limited" lens of Speaker View brackets and fragments the implications of ensemble interactions. Each moment, characterized by discontinuous activity and interrupted duration, nevertheless "exhaust[s] itself in the act of being lived" (Lefebvre, 2014, pp. 638, 642). This reactive bracketing offers a momentary and fragmented virtual phenomenology, but just as we are about to apprehend the activity, the scene shifts to another world in the process of its unfolding. In fact, Speaker View could be said to consist only of discontinuity and disparate unfoldings; it offers only a succession of folds—"pli selon pli"—pleats in the curvature of improvisational space-time. There may be arresting images, but there is no time for rest. There are multiple new shoots but no soil from which to grow an organic hermeneutics as the seeds of any emergent description are wildly dispersed and lost. Speaker View is not drifting with the flow of the river of time, it is more like shooting the rapids, as it "dislocates the linear order of presents." At an experiential level as a viewer/listener, what might be said to be standard across Gallery View and Speaker View is an effervescent "visual polyphony," the "optical noise" of the clamor of being.

Working with the automated functions of Gallery View and Speaker View in recorded improvisations, the software effectively became, in Bruno Latour's terms, a "non-human collaborator" and equal "actant" in the production of the final recordings (Latour, 1999, pp. 174–215). In both these settings, the recordings that documented the improvisations were effectively "surrendered to artefacts or algorithms" of contemporary communication software (Serres, 2008, p. 344). In filmic terms, we might consider Zoom as a "new automatism" (Cavell, 1979, pp. 101–108), with perhaps the disorienting "medium" of Speaker View as a manifestation of the "psychic automatism" of the apparatus (Krauss, 1999, pp. 5–7):

> What "automatism" thrusts into the foreground of [the] traditional definition of "medium" is the concept of improvisation, of the need to take chances in the face of a medium now cut free from the guarantees of artistic tradition. It is this sense of the improvisatory that welcomes the word's associations with "psychic automatism"; but the automatic reflex here is not so much an unconscious one as it is something like the expressive freedom that improvisation always contained, as the relation between the technical ground of a genre and its given conventions opened up as a space for release—the way the fugue makes it possible, for example, to *improvise* complex marriages between its voices. (Krauss, 1999, pp. 5–6)

In this sense, we might suggest that Speaker View as "non-human collaborator" is also improvising. For Michel Serres, the settings of Gallery View and Speaker View might represent "the given" of Zoom software. More precisely, however, following Gary Peters's distinction, we might consider the automated settings of Gallery View and Speaker View to be "the there" (the earth), and the performative intra-actions which take place "with" the software as shaping "the given" (the world) of the recording sessions. In Heidegger's terms, respectively these might reflect the "earth" and the "world" of the *Zumwelt*. But there is a further recording view option that affected the production of archival recordings and to which we will now turn: the altogether more interactive and controllable Pin View.

Pin View

As its name suggests, in Pin View, you are able to maintain the camera on a selected participant's screen. The host or co-host may also have the option of pinning more than one participant at a time. In this respect, the viewer chooses the participant who will occupy the frame of their screen. In this way, they are actively curating the visual recording of the session. With Pin View, the viewer takes on a form of directorial or authorial control to the viewing experience, which has been likened to the "live editing" process associated with VJ-ing or editing live TV broadcasts. Pin View editing decisions during ensemble performances often take place at a feverish pace, "at an unprecedented rhythm, in quasi-instantaneous fashion" (Derrida, 1995, p. 17), mirroring and tracking the improvisations they record. However, with respect to the recording and documenting of the Zoom improvisation sessions to produce an archive, Pin View recordings do not simply document the past but actively shape that which is recorded. As a result, when conducted via Pin View, the process of "archivisation produces as much as it records the event" (Derrida, 1995, p. 17). In addition, at the recording stage, these "live editing" decisions made during performances and events remain subject to the parameters of Zoom as the "instrumental possibility of production" and, as such, are "codetermined by the structure that archives" (Derrida, 1995, p. 18).

The notion of pinning also implies a physical act within a virtual context. It brings to mind the act of pinning down a butterfly in a display case, or in a more everyday context, of pinning a memo, a postcard, or a snapshot to a noticeboard. In Pin View, the screen effectively becomes a virtual noticeboard. It might be interesting here to return to the art critic Leo Steinberg's contribution to the understanding of the collage process of Robert Rauschenberg's photo-silkscreens from the 1960s, in which the artist collaged and combined images culled from newspapers and magazines, the media of everyday life, and often extended these into three-dimensional object assemblages or "combines," a practice which has many resonances with our earlier discussion of improvisation-as-bricolage. With respect to the photo-silkscreen works, Steinberg considers that Rauschenberg makes a pivotal maneuver in the visual field from the vertical pictorial field addressed to the standing viewer, which dominated the history of painting since the Renaissance, to the horizontal "Flatbed Picture Plane" more familiar to the context of the printing press (Harrison and Wood, 1992, pp. 948–953, 949–951).

The bricolage of the artist-as-transformer, sampling and remixing the archive of the everyday experience of being-in-the-image-world, and the improviser-as-bricoleur extend to the editing process of Zoom recording itself. Editing in Pin View is a form of audio-visual bricolage. The film remixes developed from the archival recordings produced via Gallery View, Speaker View, and Pin View—our "Theater of Home Movies"—are multilayered audio-visual assemblages which might be said to be manifestations of an "archive fever."

Archival recordings which utilize Gallery View as the primary mode of the Zoom interface have been frequently referred to as the basis of our session analysis in previous chapters. Parallel to the combination of Gallery View and Speaker View as default mode for host recordings, we created an archive which was based upon a "live edit" of Pin View recordings of audio-visual

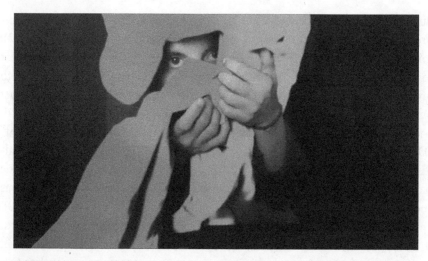

Figure 5.1. Ross Birrell & Glasgow Improvisers Orchestra, *A-111* (2020), video still.

Figure 5.2. Ross Birrell & Glasgow Improvisers Orchestra, *Kokoro* (2021), video still.

improvisations, often working with up to six laptops for each session with individual "audio stems" for each participant (i.e., one per device). From this combined archive of Gallery View, Speaker View, and Pin View of the same session, it was possible to develop a series of audio-visual remixes which combined footage from different improvisations within the same session or from across different sessions entirely. The short remix films *A-111* (2020) (Figure 5.1) and *Kokoro* (2021) (Figure 5.2), for example, are assemblages of edited and post-produced fragments drawn from Pin View recordings and remixes of individual improvisations or sessions and related individual audio tracks.

In the process, the remixed and post-produced films begin to move beyond the (all too) familiar audio-visual interface of Zoom (see ⊙ Film 5.1, Ross Birrell & Glasgow Improvisers Orchestra, *A-111,* 2020, dur. 9 min., 29 sec.; and ⊙ Film 5.2, Ross Birrell & Glasgow Improvisers Orchestra, *Kokoro*, 2021, dur. 9 min., 55 sec.).

 QR Code: Please follow this QR code to the ⊙ companion website to view additional content for Chapter 5. Alternatively, you can access the website using the link provided in the front matter.

By way of contrast, the short film *Archive Fever* (2022) (Figure 5.3) returns us to the more familiar visual territory of a Gallery View recording. However, this 20-minute film actually consists of 36 edited individual Speaker View recordings, all of which are from the year 2021, of the opening 20-minute "free" improvisations which feature at the start of the GIO Zoom sessions. As a contribution to the ongoing and developing archive of "Theater of Home Movies," this short film is akin to an archive on steroids and offers an audio-visual "information overload." The recording becomes increasingly spatially and temporally disorienting as the multiple layers of improvisations progress and the same performers appear multiple times across the screen (often playing different instruments or in different clothes, in different locations, and at different times of year). *Archive Fever* also contains a ludic structural

Figure 5.3. Ross Birrell & Glasgow Improvisers Orchestra, *Archive Fever* (2022), video still.

inversion whereby the customary opening "clap" intended to synchronize audio and visual recordings familiar to filmmakers—and which had become an integral part of GIO's Zoom improvisations (see discussion in Chapter 3)—appears as a fragmented refrain throughout, appearing in isolation or in repeated groups, eventually synchronizing in all 36 sequences to bring the chaos and cacophony of the approximately 12 hours of audio-visual improvisations it contains to an emphatic close (see ▶ Film 5.3, Ross Birrell & Glasgow Improvisers Orchestra, *Archive Fever*, 2022, dur. 20 min.).[17]

Amidst this discussion of the varying perspectives and affordances of Gallery View, Speaker View, and Pin View, we might note that there remains an important perspective, or "angle," to consider in the Zoom interface and which returns us to the distinction that Steinberg has drawn between the vertical and horizontal picture planes, associated with our relationship, respectively, with Nature and Culture: the *angle* of the computer screen itself. The angle of the computer screen is more often tilted and sitting at a diagonal angle between the vertical and the horizontal. In this respect, it reflects the hybridity of contemporary "nature-cultures" and "cyborg" identities (see Haraway, 2003 and 1991). We might call this angle the "tilt of the virtual," and this diagonal plane forms the raked stage upon which the improvisations, archiving, and remixing are virtually performed.

Culture of Remixing

More recently, such a sampling and remixing approach to creative practices has become known as the art of "post-production." Following the "relational art" practices of a generation of post-conceptual artists who emerged in the 1990s, the curator Nicolas Bourriaud describes "post-production" as "a culture of the use of forms' which he associates with the contemporary music culture of the DJ and the programmer" (Bourriaud, 2002, p. 17). For Legacy Russell, the cultural practice of sampling and remixing might be exemplified in artistic practices and in the digital domain, but it ultimately extends beyond them, remixing identity in life AFK (away from keyboard). In "Glitch Feminism: A Manifesto," Russell writes: "To remix is to rearrange, to add to, an original recording. The spirit of remixing is about finding ways to innovate with what's been given, creating something new from something already there" (Russell, 2020, p. 133). For Russell, remixing is a tactic of resistance—predominantly of Black, queer, and feminist identities—against normative white male cultural encodings. In a manner that echoes our earlier discussion of Judith Butler and gender identity as an act of improvisation within a "mise-en-scène of constraints," Russell advances the emancipatory effect of a culture of remix:

> We are faced with the reality that we will never be given the keys to a utopia architected by hegemony. Instead, we have been tasked with building the world(s) we want to live in, a most difficult yet most urgent blueprint to realize. If we see culture, society, and, by extension, gender as material to remix, we can acknowledge these things as "original recordings" that were not created to liberate us. Still, they are materials that can be reclaimed, rearranged, repurposed, and rebirthed toward an emancipatory enterprise, creating new "records" through radical action. Remixing is an act of self-determination; it is a technology of survival. (Russell, 2020, p. 133)

Both Bourriaud and Russell situate the tactic of remixing as playing with "original records" or previously existing objects, codes, or cultural forms. However, remixing is an integral component of the archival recording process of GIO Zoom improvisations; hence, subsequent editing and post-production of new moving images and audio works tend to be remixes of remixes.

Host and Parasite

What agency performs the recording and remixing in the contrapuntal ecology of the *Zumwelt*? What is the identity of the post-producer? If every Zoom meeting has a "host," then it also has a "parasite." In ecological terms, the parasite is a symbiont species that lives alongside and feeds off the host species; in some scenarios, the parasite eventually kills its host. In cultural terms, there are many pejorative examples of the use of labeling a person a parasite, from cultural critics to curators and art dealers feeding off the creativity of artists. Yet, in the context of literary criticism, J. Hillis Miller asks, "can host and parasite live happily together, in the domicile of the same text, feeding each other or sharing the food?" (Hillis Miller, 1977, p. 439). The symbiont relation is an ecology of interdependence:

> "Parasite" is one of those words which calls up its apparent "opposite." It has no meaning without that counterpart. There is no parasite without its host. At the same time both word and counterword subdivide and reveal themselves each to be fissured already within themselves and to be, like Unheimlich, unheimlich, an example of a double antithetical word. (Hillis Miller, 1977, p. 441)

It is curious that Miller draws upon a domestic context to stage his symbiont discourse. The Theater of Home ultimately becomes *unhomely*, an uncanny digital twin in the virtual universe of the remix. For Michel Serres, the parasite is also translated as noise and interruption in the flow of the communication system (Serres, 2008). The parasite is the ecology of glitch.

Virtual Foam

The virtual is fully real in so far as it is virtual.
—Deleuze (1994, p. 208)

We conclude this chapter with a reflection on the presence of the virtual. In the context of GIO's Zoom improvisations, this would most commonly be encountered in the use of the "Virtual Background." For example, some participants would use this setting to interact with uploaded images or moving images or employ visual filters from other applications. In these performances, the body of the performer appears to disperse and disintegrate as it merges with the virtual image, a kind of immersive being-in-the-virtual-world. Such visual performances appear to *foreground* the virtual as a contemporary condition rather than consign it to an optional background option. Nor should this suggest that a performative interaction with the virtual is restricted to those performers experimenting with the aesthetic and affective affordances of the Virtual Background. Paradoxically, the presence of the virtual has become the ground of the actual.

As outlined above, GIO's Zoom improvisations are characterized by an effervescent clamor of images and a multiplicity of simultaneous performative intra-actions. They perform a "musica energeia" which unfolds across the "dynamic screen," enacting a virtual ecology—a "chaosmosis"—with the potential to engender new formations (or "foamations") of ethical interrelations and ensemble subjectivities: "virtual ecology will not simply attempt to preserve the endangered species of cultural life but equally to engender conditions for the creation and development of unprecedented formations of subjectivity that have never been seen and never felt" (Guattari, 1995, p. 91).

If we follow the divergent lines of Deleuze and Guattari with their reality of virtual ecologies on the one hand, and Sloterdijk's recasting of Heidegger's "being-in-the world" to be socially understood as "being-in-foam" (Sloterdijk, 2016, p. 59) on the other, then our ensemble being-in-the-virtual-world today must entail our becoming virtual foam.

6
"I Love Lemons"
Negotiating Endings

In this chapter, we explore how improvised endings are affected and how that topic is important for matters further afield from musical improvisation. Those matters include how to keep a topic (verbal or musical) open even while ending a particular communicative event. We analyze one specific case in which a difficult event was under development in which the serious topic of endings, including the end of life, was broached and explored. We show how the skill demonstrated in improvisation includes the cultivation of a light touch for heavy topics. That touch involves knowing how to remain open-ended and how to avoid imposing any single set of meanings or any single definitive conclusion. It allows the materials that are deployed to retain multiple possibilities and to remain open-ended to future work. We effect our own ending of the chapter by describing some of the transferable lessons for communication gleaned from close observation of GIO's techniques.

Good Endings?

We have noticed, as we watched the film footage, that there is almost always a high degree of attentiveness from each player in GIO when an ending is at hand, and each online session within GIO offers variants on the manifestation of this attentiveness. How an online group of sometimes 30+ players, displayed across more than one screen, manages to achieve what comes to be recognized as closure is complicated, especially if members seek to achieve what they consider to be a good (e.g., graceful or satisfying or artful) ending.

Various tactics are used by GIO members to end improvisations. They include becoming silent, switching off the camera and/or mic, use of the chat facility to remind participants of the proposed time finish of a given piece or to give instructions such as "play for 20 minutes," using specific music motifs or museums (Tagg, 1979) or taps, slowing down, speeding up, getting increasingly louder and more energetic or vice versa, and many other piece-specific techniques. Despite these conventions, within GIO, and within improvised music more generally, players do not know, in advance, just how or when a piece will end. This process takes attunement, negotiation, and drawing on past experiences with the ability to improvise with an overarching compositional lens. However, it also includes times when the move to closure is disrupted—playfully, inadvertently, and/or deliberately (Burke et al., 2023).

Indeed, as many observers and critics have commented, GIO is renowned for its distinctive, uncanny, and collective sense of how to end an improvisation. So how are these endings achieved? In what sense is an ending a resource for a future beginning (and beginning of what)? To explore these questions, we focus on one ending—what we term the "lemons" ending—an ending that demanded considerable skill and subtlety to navigate and address a challenging topic, while also necessitating a delicate touch in handling that subject. First, we set the scene by examining GIO endings more generally and considering the broader topic of endings in other communicative arts.

Why Improvised Endings Are Important in Music and Elsewhere

Improvised musical endings (of improvised musical pieces) share some of the features of ordinary conversation. There, in talk, material is produced in real time; what is said can take any number of directions, speakers constantly work to sustain the conversation and shifts, and topic changes and endings are locally negotiated, dependent upon careful and subtle use of signals of intent to close. In essence, insights from the field of socio-linguistics, particularly conversation analysis, offer valuable lessons for examining the collaborative construction of endings in improvised music. Conversely, the unique characteristics of improvised music, distinct from conversation understood as information exchange, provide lessons for the analysis and practice of verbal conversation. The focus on musically improvised endings thus holds great potential for the study of communication processes writ large.

Endings are important for various reasons, not least because every ending is, potentially, a starting point for a subsequent new beginning. "We quarreled when we parted last time," or "it was such a good way to end a meeting—when you said. . . ." The ending, last time around, can feed into and frame a new beginning. Endings nourish the genealogy of efforts next-time-round. The framing work that endings do for new beginnings is brought to the fore, especially when, in crafting an ending, there is something important "at stake"—a social issue or relationship, for example (how we say "goodbye" before a major parting, for example). So, too, an ending can be especially important when a communicative event involves something socially, culturally, or psychologically "sensitive" and when the pathway to closure potentially affects a future relationship and future communication. On that topic, as we will describe, there is much to be learned from close observation of GIO endings. To that end, in this chapter, one of the key aims will be to enrich current approaches in conversation analysis devoted to endings with an examination of what GIO endings add to the general topic of "difficult" communication.

"Terminal Exchanges" in and Beyond Conversations

In a pioneering 1973 article entitled "Opening Up Closings," the conversation analysts Emmanuel Schegloff and Harvey Sacks observed that conversations do not "simply end" but rather are "brought to a close" (1973, p. 290). Using recorded data from telephone conversations between two speakers, the authors described the micro-procedures whereby speakers indicate a desire for closure and employ linguistic and paralinguistic strategies to achieve "an ending" in a single conversation. As they rightly observe, not all conversations are easily demarcated as "single" (we might be talking about a topic time after time as we meet and converse—so the idea of an ending as a resolution and completion is different from the idea of an ending as a need to stop in time). They also highlight how closings are affected, how a closing may involve a series of strategies such as "pre-closing" utterances ("we-ll" or "so-oo" with a downward moving pitch), which may or may not be matched with a returning acknowledgment of the move toward closure. If it is, then a move to close can be achieved. There are various other techniques, such as establishing that all has now been said—"okay?"—or producing a summation utterance, often with a moral tone—"Well, things always work out for the best" (Schegloff and Sacks, 1973, p. 303). Pre-closing strategies when successful produce a "warrant" for an ending. Failing these techniques, an "announcement" can be offered—"I gotta go" and "okay."

Schegloff and Sacks not only focused on two-party conversations, but also examined communicative events characterized by a system of turn-taking (one, then the next unless interrupted, and so forth), including "adjacency pairs," where two turns at talk form a cluster (e.g., "Hello, how are you" and "I'm fine, thanks"). Additionally, their analysis extended to communicative events taking place over the phone, emphasizing, for example, that talk in the living room of a house, where people may be moving in and out, usually does not require formal endings such as these. In GIO, however, as in many musical improvisations, these features not only do not apply: they are irrelevant. In GIO, moreover, a ground rule is typically established for when a communicative event (improvisation) will end: "Shall we play then for 30 minutes? So, end at 7.15?" In GIO, any number of speakers (i.e., performers) can be making sound simultaneously; there is no system for turn-taking unless specified as a condition of the piece being played. So the question of how, with or without a pre-specified time frame, a GIO closing will occur, is interesting, not only in terms of the mechanics of closure (Schegloff and Sack's concern) but also in terms of the qualitative content of that closure (the audio-visual materials and their arrangement).

As Schegloff and Sacks themselves concluded, the study of how endings are affected is germane to a wide range of social topics and social problems. A good ending may be essential to the continued quality of a social relationship. A good ending satisfies insofar as it can help participants in a conversation or communicative event to feel that what transpired was also good, and the devices and means for achieving "good" events involve complicated signaling and, at times, the use of ritual and conventional procedures and practices. An example offered by Schegloff and Sacks is the offering of a snack at a social event that signals that event's terminal phase (often the question, at the end of a dinner party, "Would anyone like more coffee?" is not literal but symbolic and the—socially—correct answer has less to do with a desire for a beverage and more to do with signaling that the hearer understands this as a cue for ending the evening: "No thank you, I guess we'd better get going").

The expression "all's well that ends well" summarizes aptly just what is at stake in the crafting of an ending: the quality of an ending will impact the assessment of all that came before it. This is precisely why the question of "who gets the last word" can carry significant weight. In the art and science of diplomacy, endings are critical. Exploring how endings can be crafted so all parties present believe that the meaning of the ending is satisfactory and satisfying is a topic of great interest. Crafting a definitive ending might still afford multiple interpretations; indeed, one might ask if the last word really is the last word, considering that the conversation continues across various venues and times. As we will show, effecting an ending under online conditions presented new challenges for all the participants. The types of nonverbal cues—such as eye contact, body movements, hand gestures, subtle musical signals, and others—that are used in face-to-face improvising were absent, and therefore the group had to achieve a successful ending in a new context without the regular set of social and musical cues and interactions we would normally use. What developed was a series of spontaneous signals, sometimes very straightforward—"let's finish this piece on the hour" (many musicians were in different time zones); sometimes the chat channel would be used to signal the end, for example, "find an ending in your own time." Sometimes text would be written and shown to the screen ("stop now"); sometimes hand gestures could be used, and in one piece people gradually held their hands up to the screen and that became a cue for the piece to draw to an end. What is important is that strategies evolved over the weeks and months, and the group developed a repertoire of social musical approaches that helped to facilitate satisfying improvisatory endings.

Last Words, and When Does an Ending End?

Performing participants of GIO often take the memories of the improvisational experience away with themselves, to relive the moments and think about those ephemeral moments—those ideas that had an impact. These experiences and memories are part of the process that informs the next improvisation (Berliner, 1984; Pressing, 1998). In the case of GIO online, this process was amplified through the experiences of new discoveries in our "laboratory" of weekly sessions, listening to films of the performances, and group analysis of the films. The online intimacy of the Theater of Home allowed the participants to express elements of what their lived experiences and current stories were week to week. In the next sections of this chapter we present our case study, the "lemons" ending. We present this case study in real-time detail in order to convey the intimacy and flow of how the ending transpired.

The "Lemons" Ending

At the start of this piece, the group had been instructed by author MacDonald (henceforth Raymond throughout this chapter) to finish at a designated point in time (see ▶ Film 6.1 for the full version of this piece).

QR Code: Please follow this QR code to the ▶ companion website to view additional content for Chapter 6. Alternatively, you can access the website using the link provided in the front matter.

As the ending time drew near, hints of an ending emerged with comments (in the chat function of Zoom). For example, author Burke (henceforth Rob throughout this chapter) wrote in the chat function that participants should "play themselves out in an orderly way. George Lewis then added an electronic voice that said, in a mechanical manner, as if speaking about a GIS route or a stopped piece of machinery, "Unable to continue." Rob followed that with one word in chat, which could be read as a commentary on his previous "instruction": "Un-orderly." "Unable to continue" was then developed as a theme. It is a theme that can be read, given what the group already knew, as meaningful on at least two levels—it is, in other words, a boundary object. First, it is a joke, since it references the need to wind up the session. Second, it is a theme about not being able to go on, and as such it is a theme that was attended to in that way, we think, by at least some of the participants as a reference to one of the most serious and pressing matters within the group— the imminent death of John Russell (who died six months later). In what follows we present sections of the session transcript, along with headings to cover the *time, speaker/spoken text*, what appeared in the *chat text*, the *visual* features of the ongoing action, *sounds*, and our interpretive and contextualizing *commentary*.

The Transcript

* *Transcript times refer to the internal timer within the accompanying* ▶ *Film 6.2 (ending of chat piece selection).*

> *Time*: 30:37
>
> *Speaker/Spoken Text*: George Lewis: Unable to continue [electronics]
>
> *Chat text*: From author Burke: Un-orderly
>
> *Visuals*: Author MacDonald continues to deal playing cards. He deals the cards with a "poker face"—looks perhaps even slightly somber (Figure 6.1).
>
> *Sounds*: Author MacDonald did not know it at the time, the cards hit his laptop and thus make a definite clicking sound.
>
> *Commentary*: There is, or could be, at this stage a message about "things being dealt" cards (fate, being dealt a hand). However, at this stage, that is only a *potential* message. That is to say that, at this stage in the "now" of the unfolding ending, the "message" has not been underlined by subsequent acts that might further clarify it. However, read in the context of author MacDonald's repeated "dealing of cards," the two acts can also be read as offering an opportunity to develop a "serious" line of thought around the theme of being able to continue (or not), endings, and what "is dealt."

Figure 6.1. May 9, 2020, chat piece, author MacDonald dealing cards.

At this point (30:59 into the piece), it is of course still unclear where this is going, and what kind of ending (in terms of its content) will transpire. This real-time ambiguity highlights one of the key features of a "good" improvised ending: its polysemic potential, that is, its open-endedness to continuing possibilities for development and for definition. Thus, there is a paradox around crafting an ending—a "good ending" needs attention and needs to be open-ended in terms of what is unfolding within it, and what might unfold after it—the next time around, in the future, elsewhere.

Thinking about how an ending can offer, down the timeline, new beginnings highlights the historiographical quality of endings—their historical production and significance. For example, each ending may employ material from, or otherwise take account of, previous events and shared history. That history may be endogenous (from within the unfolding improvisation, such as in this case that the session was organized around text and chat) or exogenous features (such as knowledge about performers' knowledge of previous sessions).

At the point when George Lewis contributes the "unable to continue," there is a kind of stepping back on the part of most of the other participants, a kind of watching and waiting, a kind of physical "falling silent." The music therapists Katharina Fuchs and Wolfgang Schmid have described how falling silent or being silent is by no means equivalent to "doing nothing" (Schmid and Fuchs, 2022, p. 6). The active value of silence can be seen here in how the group stepped back at this point. That retreat can be read as a (possibly unconscious, collectively unconscious) strategy that supports, without steering, the situation that is seemingly developing—"It affords space for a kind of not knowing, and for listening" (Schmid and Fuchs, 2022, p. 7). In this sense, the participants are doing what we described at the start of this chapter: showing attentiveness to what is assumed to be an imminent (and potentially important, socially speaking) ending (we say important socially because at this stage the unfolding action might become connected to something that is known to part of the group—the situation around John Russell's illness and impending death). This moment within the session is therefore not only important; it also highlights how important matters that are outside the unfolding improvisation but part of the group knowledge of participants may also serve as anchors for how participants make sense of ongoing action. By anchors, we mean that they are things that can come to stabilize meanings within the real-time, unfolding communicative event, and give those meanings and meaningful communications a particular slant. They can come to cluster actions and actors around specific semiotic points and keep actions/actors fixed, fast around those points.

That particular inflection of "unable to continue," then, was linked to the relatively recent knowledge some of the group had of John Russell's condition, and perhaps as anticipatory grieving because of John's illness, the phrase came to be anchored (by those events) and then came to anchor what happened in the improvisation at this point. It gained gravity and significance; thus, we believe that at this moment in the developing ending, there was a collective sense of "something important and something somber, serious unfolding." That sense, we think, led to a corresponding attempt, by most participants, to "give space" for that unfolding.

That "space-giving" can be seen in the film recording. It is indicated through various unobtrusive sounds associated with waiting. For example, author Sappho sighs. There is a very quiet piano/synth music-box melody. There is the sound of rustling. It is significant here that, so far, no single participant or sound can be said to be coming to the forefront. Then Maggie Nicols says:

31:03
Speaker/spoken text: Maggie Nicols: As long as we are alive we continue, eh?
Visuals: Everyone continues to watch, Raymond continue to throw, or deal, cards toward the screen, roughly at one per second. They fall below camera level onto the laptop keyboard.
Sounds: Raymond cards hitting the mic on his laptop. These sounds punctuate the sound of a small music-box-like melody, small mumblings and agreements.

Commentary: The sound of a click (from the cards) in the context of the need to end (time getting on) can be read as implying time ticking. The group has already spoken about needing to end and everyone knows, or might remember, that the improvisation has now been running for nearly all of its predetermined time. The authors asked Raymond whether he had any notion at the time that the cards could be heard/seen as like the second hand of a clock. He replied:

Yeah that is what I was thinking at time—very rhythmic—one a second—I didn't know where the mic was on my computer (still don't) but I was hoping it would make a percussive rhythmic sound—I have a sort of stupid idiotic poker face too while doing it—was trying to afford some sort of "role."

(We suggested to Raymond that his "poker face" was of course in keeping with the "role" of a card player; the notion of what the cards might deal a particular player further enhanced the emerging sense of how this "ending" was also addressing the topic of "ultimate" endings.)

The next utterance to be offered came, in fact, from John Russell himself, who picks up the theme of "ticking" or moving incrementally along and says:

31:21
Speaker/spoken text: John Russell: One foot after the other.
Visuals: Raymond continues gambling, smiles from Rob, Yasuhiro, Neko.
Sounds: The melody continues with the rhythmic fall of the cards.
Commentary: The notion of cards being dealt, one at a time, and at the tempo of a clock ticking might have primed this utterance. The fact that it came from John Russell himself led to a kind of large collective smile—the group seemed to understand the reference.

The theme of time is then made explicitly by Maggie Nicols:

Time: 31:26
Speaker/spoken text: Maggie Nicols: A new shared time, someone said.
Sounds: Melody continues. Rustling, Yasuhiro Usui puts down guitar (acknowledging close to end?).
Visuals: Yasuko Kaneko leans forward, Rob continues to smile, and Allan Wylie and his son are close to the camera, they look like they are chatting.
Commentary: Following this, John Russell then utters what, if the group had been unaware of the "sensitive" situation, might have seemed like a non sequitur,

but in fact, obliquely addresses the theme of time moving on, one step at a time (a faint echo perhaps of "one foot in the grave"? Or not? At this stage in the evolving, emerging web of meaning-making, one might not be too sure.... Or perhaps, that ambiguity is one of the many resources available precisely for rich meaning-making?) and he says:

Time: 31:35

Speaker/text: John Russell: If you've only got lemons, make lemonade.

Visuals: Author MacDonald throwing cards continues. Peaceful faces still watching. Rob is still smiling. Yasuhiro Usui goes off screen.

Sounds: Melody continues. Rustling. Maggie Nicols agrees.

Commentary: John had used the "lemons" metaphor earlier, when he was interviewed for the GIO research project (MacDonald et al., 2021). At that time, though, John Russell was commenting on the adaptation and use of new technologies during the pandemic:

I mean the technology we're working with at the moment—let's face it—isn't good enough but you know, but when you when you're given lemons, you make lemonade, really.

In this GIO session, however, and in the context of themes about "not able to continue," "one foot in front of the other" (was this by any chance an echo of the expression "one foot in the grave"?), the phrase "if you've only got lemons . . ." takes on a plangent and existential tone. When the authors watched this section (and indeed this was the reason for choosing this section), we all knew what it was "really" about. But the handling of this sensitive topic was as quicksilver—just as it arrived, it glided off into a lighter mood, led by Maggie Nicols, who says:

Time: 31:39

Speaker/spoken text: Maggie Nicols: I love lemons, oh I love lemons.

Sounds: Melody continues. Sounds lower. Slower. Rhythm of cards still. General rustling sounds.

Visuals: Cards continue. Author Burke still smiling. In Steve Beresford's square it appears he is smiling.

Commentary: After this, a lighter, culinary theme is developed, led by John Russell:

Time: 31:49

Speaker/spoken text: John Russell: Oh lemon cheesecake.

Visuals: Gerry Rossi is rolling a roll of tape (a metaphor for "winding things up"?). Raymond is still throwing, or dealing, cards. Suzie, a dancer, is low on screen and we see only the top of head. Yasuhiro Usui is still off screen. Allan Wylie and son are close together and close to the camera.
Sounds: Cello note from Jessica Argo. Low resonant. Melody appears to have stopped. Sounds of cards. Rustling.
Commentary: The general soundscape remains hushed, plangent, restrained.

Time: 31:55
Speaker/spoken text: John Russell: Persevered lemons in the tagine.
Visuals: Yasuhrio Usui back on screen. Christine off screen. Cards still being thrown. Allan and son still close to camera.
Sounds: Faint background singing. Cello sounds. Rustling and cards.

Time: 32:02
Speaker/spoken text: John Russell: We're gonna do an eating piece next week.
Visuals: Cards still being thrown. Allan Wylie and son close to camera. Allan Wylie whispers in his son's ear.
Sounds: Faint singing. Rustling.
Commentary: The general form of activity involves minimalism, deference, quiet (whispering, Suzi Cunningham's head down, time "ticking" from the sound of the cards) set against the "cheerful" discussion seemingly about food that can be made with lemons.

Time: 32:08
Speaker/spoken text: John Russell: Yeaaah [to Maggie] could that include recipes?
Visuals: Cards continue. Jessica Argo smiles. Yasuhiro Usui smiles. Maggie Nicols smiles. Thomas Rohrer smiles. Author Burke puts the saxophone in his mouth. Allan Wylie's son smiles. Gerry Rossi rubs together hands. Christine Kazarian re-enters screen with the dog. Jessica is plucking the cello. Rob is very close to the camera.
Sounds: Cello notes. Rustling. Cards. Distant high arpeggio. Few saxophone notes? Allan Wylie's son speaking to him faintly? Author Burke begins a two-note repeat on the saxophone. High synth-music box melody returns. Maggie Nicols hums a little and, very gently, reminds people of "the time" which is a cue around the topic of the need for an ending.

We now pull out key moments in this process to show the interactive development of the theme:

32:31

Speaker/spoken text: Maggie Nicols: Ach no, it's 14, on my iPad it says 14 . . . 52, because I cannae read very well because of the sun, which is why I was a bit slow on the uptake of some of the directions, because I had to go into the chat function, to read a wee bit.

Visuals: Cards continue, then stop at 32:50, Raymond folds hands in front of him. Rob playing saxophone. Christine Kazarian holding a dog. Allan's son blows into some kind of pipe. Dmitry Shubin is playing inside the piano (his hands are plucking strings inside the body of piano and not playing the keys conventionally). Allan Wylie and his son move further away from the camera.

Sounds: Saxophone melody, two notes from Rob. Distant electronics. Piano synth in dialogue with saxophone.

Commentary: A sense of quiet, minimalism, things closing, folding. Maggie Nicols reminds people of the need for an ending.

32:48

Speaker/text: Maggie Nicols: What's it say, it says 14:50 . . . something.

Chat text: From Rachel Weiss: 52.

A more precise time-telling here.

Visuals: Participants closing their eyes. Jessica Argo's eyes closed, listening. Author MacDonald picked up many cards and showed them to the camera.

Sounds: Low electronics, underwater sounding. Allan Wylie's son "papa," John Russell, "ahh." Further references to the time (and thus to the need to end) from John Russell:

32:58

Speaker/text: John: Uhh I can't find me watch, ah well any way [shows watch].

Chat text: From Rachel Weiss: 2.

Visuals: Raymond holding up many cards. Allan Wylie's son off left screen. Jessica Argo and author Burke continue to keep eyes closed. Christine Kazarian puts the camera down to show the dog. John Russell shows his watch.

Sounds: Low electronics intensified, more arpeggios are present. Rustling.

Commentary: Visual display of "closing" (eyes, gathering up the thrown cards, pointing to the time) with further reminders of time running out.

33:18

Speaker/text: John Russell: 14:52 it says here, it's Maggie, look [here John Russell is speaking to his partner, Joanna].

Visuals: Joanna is briefly seen in John's window. Fergus Kerr is drinking something. Author Burke's eyes are still closed. Jessica Argo's eyes still closed. Author Raymond is showing fewer cards, only two cards now. Maggie Nicols is drinking something.

Sounds: Melody electronics.

33:23

Speaker/text: Joanna: Hello Maggie.

Visuals: Maggie Nicols smiles. Joanna is seen briefly. Rob eyes remain closed. Jessica Argo's eyes open. Raymond folds hands in front of him. Jessica smiles.

Sounds: Synth melody continues. Quieter.

33:24

Speaker/text: John Russell: Joanna is saying hi, Maggie.

33:27

Speaker/text: Maggie Nicols: Joanna, I love you. Joanna how lovely to see Joanna, you are the precious one, you are precious Joanna, precious, precious precious! I love that woman.

Visuals: Author Burke's eyes closed, then he goes off screen. Jessica Argo smiles. Yasuhiro Usui is smiling. Rachel Weiss is smiling.

Sounds: Quiet synth sounds.

33:48

Speaker/text: Joanna: Yeah, gunna sit outside and read, thank you.

Visuals: Maggie Nicols is smiling. Thomas Rohrer is playing. Allan Wylie is holding his trumpet. Jessica Argo is smiling. Yasuhiro Usui is smiling. Fergus Kerr is clasping his hands.

Sounds: Faint melody still. Plucked sound from Thomas Rohrer.

33:52

Speaker/text: Maggie Nichols: [hums] It's all mingled in, that's how I love it really, all the different, fascinating shape-shifting, and twists, and turns, and sublime and chaos, and space and density, a bit of rabbit, a bit of conversation, a bit of all mingled in.

Commentary: Maggie Nicols observes the quicksilver, ambiguous, floating character of this "difficult" or "sensitive" topic and its handling. She reintroduces the theme that the serious, the humorous, the mundane, and the sacred can intermingle here, in this communal, improvisatory space. She does this in a way that, virtuosically, simultaneously both opens up that space and prepares it for its (necessary, due to time of day) closure, while (with the word "rabbit," keeping it light [earlier in this session animal noises had been explored]). But the closing here can also be read as an opening for future communication. Nicols is, as it were, tilling the communicative ground for a next-time-through return to the topic (which in fact did occur, as we describe below). Additionally, Nicols's utterance sparks an animated conversation on the nature of matter, astrophysics, existence, matter, and connection in what we might call *community philosophy* in the making and, we believe, philosophy in the service of making sense of life and death issues.

34:15
Speaker/text: Maggie Nicols: And this is the way I want to live, really....
Visuals: Allan Wylie is putting down the trumpet. Everyone is watching, attentive. Fergus Kerr smiles. Yasuhiro Usui nods to Maggie Nicols. Gerry Rossi stretches his neck.
Sounds: Melody faint. Scratchy sound, like a frog.

The conversation continues, becoming more explicitly serious, using the discussion of the "darker" things in human existence:

34:18
Speaker/text: John Russell: Apparently if you get all the um, all the parts of the ... atoms that make up the entire human race and take all the space out in between its the size of a sugar cube. That's the whole of humanity.

34:32
Speaker/text: John Russell: So um, we've got a few cubes here, but we would be sort of nothing without the stuff in-between, you know?

34:39
Speaker/text: Maggie Nicols: Aye

34:40 Simultaneously:
Speaker/text: Maggie Nicols: And I also....
Speaker/text: John Russell: And that's great....

34:43
Speaker/text: Maggie Nicols: Sorry, John, you go on.

34:44

Speaker/text: John Russell: I'm so pleased we've got the stuff in-between, you know it's. . . .

34:47
Speaker/text: Maggie Nicols: Oh aye!
Visuals: Sandy Evans is smiling. Rachel Weiss is smiling. Stuart Brown is smiling. Jessica Argo smiles. Christine Kazarian has a dog on lap. Yasuhiro Usui gets his cat to show.
Sounds: Faint melody continues. Only music sounds besides the conversation. Then quick saxophone notes?

34:50
Speaker/text: John Russell: Bit of stuff in-between is jolly good! [laughs]
Visuals: Maria's hand in front of camera. Jessica Argo is smiling. Rachel Weiss is smiling. Stuart Brown is smiling.
Sounds: Faint melody.

34:53
Speaker/text: Maggie Nicols: It is [sings] it is, and I read too because I am writing a book about the sacred dark because I hate the way the dark is demonized and used as a metaphor for everything that is ignorant and evil when we need it if I don't . . . I have too much light, too much bloody screen, and not enough rest in the dark, not enough sleep, but I read scientists say that without dark energy which is the majority of space, there would be no galaxy! The lovely sparkly galaxy would fall apart.
Visuals: Author Burke's hand is close to the camera. Jessica Argo is smiling. Allan Wylie's son comes back on screen with mugs. Everyone watching and listening.
Sounds: Melody stops. Only conversation sounds.
Commentary: John Russell and Maggie Nicols are now "soloists" discussing the sacred dark in a serious/funny way that alludes to "darker" and "serious" matters that are just beneath the surface here:

35:20
Speaker/text: John Russell: Where would you be without a galaxy?!

35:22
Speaker/text: Maggie Nicols: Exactly, and the dark energy is holding the galaxies together, now how kind of demeaned and misunderstood and sort of OHHH it drives me nuts, I must . . . you see I am a bit partisan about that [growl].

Visuals: Raymond smiling. Sandy Evans smiling. Jessica Argo smiling (putting down her bow). Author Burke smiling. Yasuhiro Usui smiling. John Russell smiling. Stuart Brown smiling. Fergus Kerr smiling. Neko Kaneko smiling. Rob's fingers are close to the camera.
Sounds: Voices.

35:37
Speaker/text: John Russell: [laughs].

35:40
Speaker/text: Maggie Nicols: [laughs].

35:40
Speaker/text: John Russell: Oh that will, cut that into a nice ending. I am a bit partisan about that [growl, laughs].
Visuals: Author MacDonald smiles, Neko Kaneko smiles, Jessica Argo smiles, Stuart Brown smiles, Furgus Kerr smiles (laughter). Author Sappho's fingers are close to the camera.
Sounds: Just conversation.

35:48
Speaker/text: Maggie Nicols: It's often an allowed . . . (acceptance?) [laughs].
Visuals: Smiles, moving about.
Sounds: Someone puts something down? Resonant boom.

35:53
Speaker/text: John Russell :Are we getting un-orderly enough? [laughs].
Visuals: Fergus Kerr smiles, a Raymond smiles, Neko Kaneko smiles, Jessica Argo smiles, Robert Henderson leans into camera, and Stuart Brown smiles.

36:00
Speaker/text: Maggie Nicols: [laughs] Yeah, are you and me at it again, John?

36:04
Speaker/text: John Russell: I know.
Maggie Nicols: Where's Raymond? I'm looking for Raymond. Raymond, Raymond, where are you?

36:07
Speaker/text: John Russell: He's down there in the bottom corner.

Visuals: Raymond waves, Jessica Argo smiles, Rob, Rachel Weiss smiles. Rob is off-screen. Robert smiles, Yasuhiro smiles, Thomas smiles.

Sounds: Voices.

Commentary: The group is shifting now, away from the serious/not-serious talk about dark things, lemons, one foot in front of the next, away from visually featuring tokens of sacred moments such as closed eyes, folded hands, silence. Now there is a return to the pragmatic world of online improvising, the achievement of the end of the session. The group ventured into the "sacred dark" and is now emerging back out into the light of the session and what they are doing and have just done.

Talking About but Not Talking About, Finding a Way to End Serious Talk Gracefully

Music therapists have occasionally noted that topics and issues that are difficult to address directly in talk are more easily addressed as part of song material. There are various reasons that songs make it easier to broach difficult topics. As all creators of libretti—and anyone who has listened to different settings of the seemingly same text—will know, the musical features of a song can accentuate or draw out particular moods and textual meanings (and they can also suppress, or background, other moods and meanings). Because textual meaning can be hyper-explicated or underscored by music in ways that can shift or enhance meanings (Kassabian, 2001), music has the power to effectively reposition a topic, give it a tilt, spin, or new semiotic charge. For example, Rolvsjord (2010) and Lewis (2017) both describe how the specific ways in which songs are crafted can, for the songwriter and their experience of previous events, restructure memory, indeed, give difficult issues a new tilt, reposition them further in the background, or foreground, or otherwise reappropriate past experience.

Songwriting is, therefore, a rich and useful way of framing and processing events, whether done by and for oneself, performed to others (Lewis, 2017), or from within a music-therapeutic process (Baker, 2005; Rolvsjord, 2010, 2010; Tamplin et al., 2016). So, too, singing songs and listening to songs whether together or alone, allow for different forms of emotional "work" and emotion regulation (Ansdell and DeNora, 2016; DeNora, 2000, 2013) and discussion of a topic. That discussion may take place within the song—the lyrics being proxy for conversational description—and it may take place around a song—before, after, or during the song's audition. Songs are also resourceful for airing issues for the reason that they are songs—a different modality. One can sing a song and thus air an issue as if allowing the lyrics to stand in for one's own views, experience, or desire for something to be conveyed to an audience or listeners—as with conversation. But, unlike conversation, songs can be, at any time, redefined as if they are only, or merely, songs (i.e., not literal or really about an issue)—as a different medium. One can say, "Oh, that was only a song but not what I 'really' think." This ambiguity by design is, in other words, a major communicative resource, holding open interpretive flexibility while also opening a space for sharing meanings and experience (while, seemingly, not—really—talking about it; Ansdell and DeNora, 2016).

So, too, here, in this song—this improvised musical/textual piece by GIO as we watch two masters of improvisation talking together as part of producing an ending—it may seem impossible to decide whether the talk here is, or is not, about mortality, and indeed, John Russell's illness and impending death. This ambiguity and the space that ambiguity creates for multiple but shared meanings is, we propose, exactly what makes GIO sessions so useful socially, and for well-being (as described in MacDonald et al., 2021)—the format allows for things to be simultaneously real and imaginary, literal and figurative, serious and light. With categories frustrated, with the waters murky (or "dark," as Maggie Nicols describes [Nicols herself runs mental health improvisation groups, The Gathering], the "sacred dark" where things are "all mingled in"), deep matters can be glimpsed and considered in ways that allow participants to feel safe. At the same time—and expressly because of the deliberately oblique treatment, such matters are prevented from becoming trivialized or overstated/over-specified, or from falling into preexisting, potentially overly conventional formats or tropes. In the "lemons" example, we saw music, understood as improvised audio/visual/textual activity, offering a resource for drawing experience into shared categories of meaning. The virtuosity of the "lemons" example lies, we think, in how a topic was skirted in ways that people recognized and behaved toward with visual and audible respect, but did not attempt to overly define.

The "lemons" topic, and its related topics of the sacred dark and endings, remained open-ended. It became part of GIO's material and topical history and as such was available for subsequent employment. The theme of "lemons" was invoked again, one week after this first "lemons" session. And it was invoked by John Russell himself, in conversation with Corey Mwamba. John Russell, talking on screen with Mwamba, tells the orchestra about his health—what had been known or suspected by some (Maggie Nicols, author MacDonald, Jessica Argo, and others who were prominent in the previous week's "lemons" session) is now fully aired. The lemons motif, in other words, and the gentle, open-ended manner of airing the topic, glancing to and away from its gravity, from ticking time and one foot in front of the other, and life giving you lemons to lemons in the tagine, to community philosophy and the importance of embracing "the sacred dark," the protagonists found a way to open up a difficult topic and to allow it, gently, to enter the orchestra's general collective knowledge. This way was forged by tapping back into the motif and allowing it to travel into more explicit discussions of John and his illness. And so GIO offers us, in and through its improvisational materials and their handling, lessons in how to hold a conversation about the difficult matter of grave illness and impending death.

The ending of the lemons piece, facilitated by Maggie Nicols, allowed for profound and important matters to be witnessed, touched on glancingly but repeatedly, but in a light enough manner that they could be displayed from many angles, refracted from adjunct discussions of food, cosmic philosophy, and humor. The ending, as it was ultimately produced, emerged from within the endogenous context of specific GIO conventions, forms of knowledge, and skills, combined with a shared awareness that an ending was, increasingly, required due to time constraints. Thus, the crafting of a musical piece, and in particular its ending, is also a way of crafting shared knowledge about impending endings in other realms, indeed, in relation to a life itself. In commenting on this chapter, palliative care music therapist Wolfgang Schmid observed that in his work with severely ill patients, he observes mutual awareness of how the joint musical situation is also a situation for reflecting upon loss and in some cases irretrievable health. For example, Schmid (2017) described how, in an improvisation with Marc, a patient who had experienced severe brain injury, it was

> almost that we have built the repertoire for the end already on the way. And while in the beginning, it was somehow my gut feeling that made me confident that we were doing "this" together, that I should continue. His [Marc's] initiative for the end [of music, but also of music as a metaphor or proxy subject for life itself] was a clear sign for his presence and co-musicianship that led to it.

So, too, here, each unfolding moment of this—remarkable—GIO ending offered resources and building materials for what happened next as these virtuoso musicians themselves took the role of co-therapists, or expert social listeners and improvisers. Each moment, we hope we have demonstrated, offered anchoring materials for how to develop what became a theme and for a way of drawing in important group knowledge and concerns as a focal point for meditation and airing, in this case, an amalgam of cosmology, philosophy, lemons, cooking, recipes... and death.

7
New Virtuosities
This Is Our Music

New "arts" practices inevitably transform the process of making music together. The question, always, is how and with what consequences. This chapter considers the transformations that occurred after GIO went online. It describes how these transformations came to be linked to new conceptions of virtuosity and new routes into music-making associated with new pathways for making music accessible. Examining these new pathways, in turn, underscores the limitations of conventional notions of virtuosity. These traditional views, often grounded in specific understandings of what counts as skill (instrumental technique, sight reading, knowledge of conventional improvisational practices), are musically and socially restrictive. During lockdown, the skill set of GIO widened, as we have described in previous chapters. That widening facilitated a reimagining and reconfiguration of aesthetic priorities. It led to a shift in ways that repositioned creative agency as a collective, rather than individual, skill, and as a skill that included much more than virtuosic musical techniques. With this repositioning came new possibilities for how creativity and skill came to be viewed, both within GIO and, potentially, for music-making in other settings.

This chapter also explores the novel virtuosities that emerged when GIO went online. We will use this exploration to consider the concept of musicality and to broaden that concept in ways that illuminate frequently overlooked or undervalued social and cultural practices that are part of what being musical means. To that end, we will present extracts from the online interactions that draw out a notion of new virtuosity/virtuosities and in particular as these new virtuosities are facilitated by new technologies and new uses of technology. Additionally, we consider some of the consequences of these new virtuosities, in particular in relation to the question of how music is, or is not, accessible. We shine a spotlight on enhanced agencies as evidenced in video recordings and reported by performers, facilitated by the online environment. Then, looking to the future, we discuss how the forms of enhancement we describe hold potential for performers working in online, non-virtual, and hybrid contexts. We consider how those contexts support new thinking about

New Directions in Musical Collaborative Creativity. Raymond MacDonald, Tia DeNora, Maria Sappho, Robert Burke, and Ross Birrell, Oxford University Press. © Oxford University Press 2025. DOI: 10.1093/oso/9780197752838.003.0007

technology, instruments, and instrumentation, as well as forms of interaction, identity relations, and aesthetic inclusion. New virtuosity, in other words, promotes new ways of imagining music and new ways of valuing what counts as creative practice.

New Musical Virtuosities

Idealist notions of an expert or virtuoso musician typically emphasize technical mastery and perfection (Devenish et al., 2023; Ginsborg, 2018), developing from years of study and regular practice (see Chapter 4). This dedication culminates in an advanced instrumental technique with these virtuoso performers then entering an elite echelon of society. They are (with a capital M) Musicians and Professional Musicians (Bennett, 2008; Burland, 2005). Possibly, underpinning this type of musicality are restrictive definitions of what we might term *musical virtuosity*, with an emphasis on technical instrumental and vocal skills (Bernstein, 1998; Burnard, 2012; O'Dea, 2000). Within our conception of new virtuosity, the fundamentals of music focus more on the social-interactive, creative, and self-expressive affordances that music serves, while the technical qualities represent a more surface-level approach.

There is a place for extant practices of virtuosities that are fundamental to historical documentation and social and cultural contexts, and this again is not to say that the technical virtuosity of musicality is not important for music-making. However, perhaps there is a need to reimagine conventional ideas of musicianship and musical virtuosity, with one of the aims being a more inclusive definition of what is viewed as musicality. Adopting a more holistic and inclusive understanding of musicality, rethinking what virtuosity can mean and how it can be valued, can, moreover, be of tremendous benefit; it can open the imagination to how otherwise excluded individuals and groups might be able to be equal partners in musical activity—as opposed to being construed as beginners versus advanced players. In short, we propose that virtual music is, in other words, both a tool for enhancing these areas and a practice for widening the horizons of what and how musicking is and can be. In other disciplines and arenas, many traditional notions of virtuosity have already been challenged. In the visual arts, for example, the shift away from purely craft-based notions of mastery has been long underway. In this context, conceptual and critical thinking are key components of an artist's skill set (Devenish et al., 2023). Virtuosity is no longer defined by mastery of traditional skills, such as being able to draw a perfect circle, but encompasses arrangement, framing, and curation (Acord, 2010). Likewise in music therapy, virtuosity extends to the skills of facilitating inclusive musical interaction and supporting others (Pavlicevic and Ansdell, 2004; Procter, 2011).

Similarly, GIO's emergent virtuosity underscores social and interactive forms of musical engagement emphasizing skilled decision-making. This shift highlights decision-making related to planning and strategy, extending beyond considerations solely related to the playing of sonic materials. While that decision-making may pertain to what happens next within a given improvised piece, its aims are both artistic and social. For example, Sawyer (2006) has suggested that collaboration in the broadest sense of the word is a key skill that musicians, regardless of genre, are required to develop. By that logic, expert musicians should be considered to be virtuoso collaborators. At the heart of musicality and collaboration lies decision-making. For GIO, both online and in hybrid contexts, this decision-making involves considerations about the social possibilities that might emerge from different musical configurations. Resonating with this approach is a growing body of research that emphasizes social, improvisatory, and collaborative aspects of creative engagement as fundamental to musical development (Randles and Burnard, 2022). Within this research is a new emphasis on the social and collaborative aspects of musicality and virtuosity (MacDonald and Saarakallio, 2024).

This body of research has shed light on the multifaceted nature of musicality, revealing that it encompasses not only the development and integration of what is traditionally considered a "musical" idea—such as the handling of sonorities, communicating emotions, valuing/responding to the moment (Cross, 2008; Devenish et al., 2023; Hallam, 2010)—but also involves important social and cultural practices. Indeed, sophisticated knowledge of these social and cultural practices and knowing how to deploy them in creative contexts is, arguably, an increasingly important component of musical engagement and musical skill.

Though improvisatory music may have been slow to join the movement toward musical/social skill, there have been precedents and pioneers. Most notable is Maggie Nicols. Nicols, throughout her long career, has advocated and exemplified an approach to improvisation that includes and recognizes social settings and contextual factors (in other words, many of the things that are otherwise backstage or offstage during more conventional improvisations). For Nicols, the "skill" of improvisation is to find ways of drawing these marginalized sonic/social materials into the ongoing flux. Nicols calls this practice "social virtuosity" (Nicols, 2023; MacDonald and Wilson, 2020; Siljamäki, 2022; Tonelli, 2015). Within GIO, online and hybrid, this approach to "social virtuosities" found its way to the core of the group's virtuosic practices and values. We illustrate what this virtuosity looked like and how it developed in the following sections to show how the group forged new ways of working together that exemplified "social improvisation."

Virtuosity is not only a contextually dependent series of perceived attributes but also a contested set of competencies, since what is socially constructed as virtuosic emphasizes what is viewed as an essential repertoire of domain-specific skills. Thus, over time, behaviors that are highly valued (precise reproductions of well-known material, in any genre, supported by appropriate nonverbal communication—facial expressions, dramatic gestures, authentic clothes, etc.) are normalized to become clear markers of virtuosity, signaling membership in an elite group (Davidson and MacArhur, 2021). One impact of the development of these types of socially constructed music virtuosities is that through these processes of normalization, people wishing to engage in musical activities who do not meet these expectations and parameters may feel "unmusical". Thus the emergence of a cultural elite (i.e., those who can display these specific types of virtuosities) produces a socially constructed sociocultural underbelly (i.e., those who see themselves as unmusical). For reasons that usually include an economic, cultural, and political positioning, this sociocultural underbelly of non-musical people is essential in order for the sociocultural elite (i.e., "musical virtuosi") to exist and thrive. These feelings of unmusicality inhibit musical engagement of any type, whether it be in the setting of informal singing with family, to engagement in more public activities such as singing in a choir or learning an instrument. Interrogating existing virtuosities and reimagining new musical virtuosities, therefore, become important, not only in terms of promoting new ways to be collaboratively creative, but also in helping to break down barriers and increasing access to musical engagement across all sections of society, particularly for those from disadvantaged backgrounds and those who view themselves as "unmusical."

The social and cultural development around narratives of virtuosity is also intertwined with technology and technology-related skills. For example, historically, pianists would have been able to tune their own instruments, and the choice of their tuning systems would have been (as with other instrumentalists of the time) highly customized and personalized (Duffin, 2008). Tuning was, arguably, a form of virtuosity in its own right, a form of virtuosity subsequently lost as pianos became common household items. Huang (2022) identifies this loss as an example of how musical labor became "deskilled." That deskilling impoverished the general skill set of keyboard players who collectively forgot how to tune an entire piano and how to tune a piano to alternate tuning systems as well as to equal temperament.

However, the equation shifted again with the advent of electric keyboards, synths, and midi, none of which require physical tuning. These advancements created possibilities for broader access to complex and variable tuning systems. It is now possible to download and apply a host of world tuning systems and composer-specific tuning systems easily on a keyboard. Consequently, the tuning and sound of an instrument as it develops and the roles that coalesce around being able to achieve these different sonic aesthetics illuminate the ways that skills and aesthetics come to be valued differently over time. As a result, the concept of virtuosity is revealed to be culturally specific, ascribed, emergent, and linked to culturally variable notions of musical complexity and rigor. These tangled sets of relationships involve roles, skills, assistive technological developments, and associated narratives that shape our understanding of aesthetic value and the concept of virtuosity.

What we draw from this case study of keyboard tuning, and its connection then disconnection to virtuosity, are broader lessons around the question of how we "notice" virtuosity developing. What we come to hail as "virtuosity" will vary widely over time and space. There will be forms of virtuosity that are in plain sight/hearing and others not, or perhaps hiding in plain sight/hearing. There are yet others that may be emerging, still in liminal positions where they are occasionally glimpsed as, perhaps, something "special." The question, then, of how liminal, half-recognized, or potential virtuosic practices come to assume the limelight is an important empirical question, the answers to which can illuminate the politics of how musical skill is debated and determined. Over the centuries, even with a canonic composer such as Beethoven, what came to count as "skillful" was a matter of contention and cultural entrepreneurship (DeNora, 1995). When something is deemed as a "type of virtuosity," it becomes imbued with "virtue," becoming a valuable entity to a particular community. The establishment and dissemination of these values, which are supported and cultivated, are fundamentally social processes. Virtuosity, in other words, is always a social, technical, and cultural/practical assemblage. It is intricately involved in the ongoing processes of developing virtuosities, societies, and technologies.

GIO: New Virtuosity Communities

In our practice and our research, we noticed that new ideas around virtuosity took shape as GIO players gradually discovered new possibilities where the Theater of Home, both as the site of performance and the medium of performance practices, shifted from "home" literally to anywhere that the players happened to be in the course of their everyday lives. With it, virtuosity became, within GIO, increasingly about showcasing and mobilizing social, spatial, and material environments—sharing materials and features of the settings where participants *are*. Thus, increasingly, the "theater" as displayed from within individual Zoom boxes expanded from kitchens, studies, bedrooms, and lounges to include airports, buses, and outdoor natural settings such as mountains, beaches, and gardens.

Integrating Sound and Vision: A New Practice Emerges

After two months of weekly sessions (May 2, 2020), the players/participants were beginning to draw on and introduce approaches and tactics of improvisation that they had employed in in-person sessions prior to lockdown. After a few weeks of online sessions, four members had begun to experiment with virtual backgrounds (visual material, photos, videos, distortions).

We can see the incorporation of old, in-person practices and new virtual backgrounds with their emphasis on visual material in the May 2 session. The session includes a composition based on a virtual background. That background is used to convey specific instructions to the participants (▶ Film 7.1). These instructions were written on paper and then incorporated into the virtual background. They included instructions such as long notes, only voice, please stop, short sounds, and loud/noisy

QR Code: Please follow this QR code to the ▶ companion website to view additional content for Chapter 7. Alternatively, you can access the website using the link provided in the front matter.

These written instructions were supplemented with specific hand gestures used to develop the piece. In this example (Figure 7.1), we see author MacDonald employing conduction text backdrops to mimic classic improvisation text scores often used by players—this time in a live "conduction"-like setting.

Neither conduction nor the use of visual prompts was new to the group, which had been using these techniques since shortly after the group's inception in 2002. Performing this conduction piece online, however, allowed the players to explore the new, online space and its related affordances. So, the grounding structure of the improvisation might have been already "known"

Figure 7.1. May 2, 2020, improvisation with hand and virtual background conduction.

to the group, but the experiments in responding to the improvised composition instructions were very different from those that had previously transpired when conduction and visual cues had been employed in an in-person session. For example, at 01:23 (▶ Film 7.1, Figure 7.2), trumpet player Robert Henderson uses the flashlight feature of his mobile phone to contribute to the improvisation where the specific instruction had been to use "only voice"—the phone light came to afford a visual notion of a "voice" within this new Zoom frame.

Robert Henderson, who had performed in GIO for 20 years, had only ever improvised/experimented on his trumpet. Here, however, he uses the flashlight on his phone as his improvising instrument, producing light rather

Figure 7.2. May 2, 2020, Robert Henderson improvising with light.

than notes ("only voice"). The torch as an improvising instrument/affordance made its debut in this session (it later made reappearances and was used by others). Henderson's action here therefore shines a light on how members were beginning to incorporate and showcase objects in their rooms within online sessions and pieces. It highlights how the specific affordances within a participant's room could be utilized to facilitate the development of a piece. Moreover, it highlights how the specific technological features of the Zoomesphere—specifically the video—enable experimentation and creative developments. For Robert Henderson, the use of the flashlight represents a shift in the way he engaged in improvisation: the agency and the choices he makes, and a new approach to the expressive and embodied nature of his artistic participation.

At this time, the group also developed into an international ensemble with over seven countries and four continents represented in the sessions: the local community had become a global community and, significantly, the group now found a global perspective that affected how, collectively, it understood and discussed virtuosities. There were now many cultures that were introduced, as well as many approaches to improvising, including visual and musical approaches that were culturally specific and novel to the Glasgow members.

Toys and Cooking: Themes for a New Modality

On May 9, 2020 (▶ Film 7.2), the ensemble created an improvisation using a suggested theme of "toys" (Figure 7.3). During this session, a number of important moments highlight the creative introductions of household objects and, in particular, toys. Toys were a definite extension of the evolving history of tapping the improvisational affordances of domestic objects and using them in tandem with musical instruments. Their unconventional use here served to further blur the boundaries between the formal performance environment and the informal domestic environment. As such, the use of toys heralded one of the central features of the Theater of Home.

This blurring of the domestic and the formal also facilitated another noteworthy feature of this improvisation, the appearance of family members (children) of one of the performers (Fergus Kerr). The section of the session where the family made their first appearance is worth highlighting. It involves the appearance of a young girl (Fergus Kerr's daughter) fully engaged in improvisation (▶ Film 7.2, 12:33). Kerr's daughter (Nancy) actively contributes to the improvisation through her visual and musical performance. She not only mimics her father's creative actions but also adds her own playful

Figure 7.3. May 9, 2020, toys piece.

interpretations and input to the performance, utilizing various toy instruments that both father and daughter play. The dynamic interaction between parent and child adds a layer of creativity and spontaneity to the improvised session. Nancy's playful interpretation of toys in their homes influences many players, impacting the emerging shape of the improvisation. Her contributions add to the collaborative and responsive nature of the music-making process, showcasing the interconnectedness of individual expressions within the collective improvisational space. This playful moment serves as an important signifier of the emerging forms of virtuosity: a pathway of inclusion where the category of "virtuoso" is not dependent upon extant understandings of "how to play" or getting notes "right" but is, rather, about engaging in playful expression with a focus extending beyond musical notes.

Virtuosity, in this context, also foregrounds the actions of Nancy, emphasizing her engagement rather than solely focusing on her technical competency as an instrumentalist or a singer. It shifts the focus from individual expertise to a collective approach, offering an example of inclusive improvisation that celebrates diverse abilities and emphasizes an aesthetic based on the collective agency and the context of the improvisation. This marks an important milestone in GIO's history, as a "newly virtuosic" aesthetic emerged from playful interactions between parents and children. This "playful" aesthetic not only influenced other performers but also prompted the children to adapt and experiment with their performances in response to the ensemble's reactions.

This dynamic interaction established a reflexive circuit and solidified the children's sense of belonging to the ensemble. The result was the development of a social, inclusive, explicitly playful form of musical expression.

In the same piece (Figure 7.4, for example, players initiated a reciprocal showing of toys, puppets, and soft furry animals on screen that are featured throughout the session. This type of improvisational interaction bears clear links to music therapy practices, particularly in its mirroring and imitation aspects which validate a client's gesture so as to offer empathy and "synchronizing" (Wigram, 2017, p. 82). Wigram describes this synchronizing as "signals to the client that the therapist is listening and present and that the client will see their own behaviour in the therapist's behaviour" (p. 82). We believe that this reciprocal synchronizing, exemplified here by the showing of toys in this context, serves an important function of what Wigram refers to as "fused" and "symbiotic" music-making (p. 82). It is noteworthy that this interpersonal validation in music occurred during a time of uncertainty and anxiety in the early phase of the pandemic.

The choice of introducing a theme of toys opened up new possibilities in the Theater of Home. It signaled to the group what is possible and defined what constitutes a "toy." In some instances, we see the use of "toy" pianos across players, while others engage in a "playful" exploration of more "everyday" household objects. Some players utilize their virtual backgrounds to expand the possible toys and children's references that they can bring in visually, while others bring in toys that are quite literally toys from their children. For instance, Maggie Nicols holds up a kids' writing/drawing pad device

Figure 7.4. May 9, 2020, toys piece—family play.

(etch-a-sketch) adding a further interesting meta-ability to convey "thoughts" to the screen in a playful way (neither spoken, drawn on paper, nor typed in the chat piece on which she writes "Hyfred Iausn!" ("very good" in Welsh) (see Figure 7.5).

An interesting point in the use of "toys" is that akin to children, the act of showing one's toys and granting permission to allow others to play with them signifies willingness to share and trust one another as custodians or perhaps brokers of imaginary worlds. Further, the use of toys thus opened up pathways as a possibility to the notion of "over-sharing" as not simply acceptable within the online GIO sessions, but interestingly, becoming a modality of and for new virtuosities.

Maggie Nicols reflects on the "toy"-themed session where she contemplates "playful" improvising with "fun" and "frivolous" objects. She notes:

> Lovely. It had so many different twists and turns in it, you know. It was play, it was sound, it (had) brought out deeper meaning for me. I just thought of the Kindertransport with Paddington . . . [Kindertransport was a method of moving children from Germany to Britain, 1938–1939]. Suddenly I remembered Paddington Bear and how everybody—everybody—wanted a Paddington Bear and none of the shops had it. It was Christmas and Aura [daughter] desperately wanted a Paddington Bear. I went through every single shop in London and had to get a cab in the end go to bloody Harrods. That was the only Paddington Bear I could get. So Paddington is very special. And then I found out that it was very much about, the you know, the Kindertransport. It was a symbol of the children, you know, refugee

Figure 7.5. May 9, 2020, toys piece, central player holding up Welsh sign written on children's toy.

children. So that just all came up. You know, so lovely, Paddington Bear, eh? (Nicols, May 9, 2020, internal recording).

Similar themes of experimentation with non-human and new-musical objects are evident in the following week on May 16, 2020 (▶ Film 7.3), where the group improvises around a theme of "cooking." The playful experimentation continues, where some players are performing "real" cooking, while others are utilizing the tools of cooking in creative ways, for example, whisks being used, pasta thrown around, bags being rustled, and bottles being shaken. The exploration of toys and cooking is by no means made in isolation. That is, in many instances the group's themes of play explore a deeper relationship that might be had with non-human and objects at hand. In this vein, the theme of cooking becomes a powerful reference point, and later returns for the group's hybrid performance at the AJIRN (Australasian Jazz and Improvisation Research Network) conference (2022, ▶ Film 7.15), as discussed below. As the weeks progress, the group explores specific objects and non-human elements as themes, including items such as cards, plants, pets, books, and more.

The food theme serves as an example of how the themes are triggered as an improvisation evolves and as an expression of social virtuosity. In the cooking improvisation (Figure 7.6), player Maggie Nicols breaks into a song monologue surrounding her current thinking on food politics:

> Well, I was aware that I was cooking and eating and a lot of these things. But I've also been fascinated by it. Well, no, it's very important. I've got a few friends, who I don't see now at the minute. But we're very, very concerned with things like food security, and how we share food and growing food and resisting the

Figure 7.6. May 16, 2020, cooking piece.

destruction of biodiversity. So I'm feeling quite passionate about it at the moment, and how agribusiness can sort of take over and pretend that they want to feed the world, but can seduce people into—farmers into buying lots of pesticides and they're not let[ting] them share seeds. There's lots of stuff around who owns food, you know, at a local level or is it global? [vocal musical interlude] sharing food, sharing land—that's important—obviously different local environment issues but the same issue that everybody needs to eat and the healthier we eat. So these things are important. Seen loads of brilliant ideas and . . . stuff about greening the cities as well which is really exciting. Culture all these different things you know. Oh working with nature, learning from nature. And nature's about diversity and free improvisation is about diversity. (Nicols, May 16, 2020, internal recording)

A lively conversation continues after the official improvisation is over; three players, Jessica Argo, Maggie Nicols, and John Russell, discuss the primacy of thinking about food during the pandemic and the evolving cultural and social meaning of "eating together," with broader reflections on food accessibility, security, and the future of humanity (▶ Film 7.3 at 34:34). Through the medium of toys and play, GIO has initiated a platform for serious political commentary.

Conducting Improvisations

The May 9, 2020, "chat piece" (▶ Film 6.1, discussed in Chapter 6) offers another example of a new use of a feature of Zoom technology—the chat box—to develop a new working practice. This can be seen conceptually as a continuation of the initial background "conduction" works discussed previously (May 2, 2020, in ▶ Film 7.1), which might then be seen to emerge strongly as a solid working practice in the expanded possible forms of "conduction" that are seen a repeated practice of "hand conduction" signs made by author MacDonald (e.g., March 2, 2021, ▶ Film 7.4 and Figure 7.7). In these pieces, which were often repeated by the ensemble in various rehearsal and performance settings, MacDonald's floating and disembodied hand performs what is known as signed hand conduction (Morris, 2017). In these films, players follow author MacDonald's hand to traditional conduction signs. The players tried this piece twice in rehearsal.

Players also experimented with using their bodies for visual conduction. For example, on March 2, 2021, the group were paired up in a way that one player performed visual conduction, and another player translated that visual

Figure 7.7. March 2, 2021, hand conduction example.

Figure 7.8. March 2, 2021, paired players—visual conduction and sonic interpretation.

conduction into sound. In ▶ Film 7.5 and Figure 7.8, one player conducts with "air piano" gestures, which a second player translates into actual piano sounds.

A second example (▶ Film 7.6) involves one player holding up a number of fingers to indicate how many people should be playing at once—players must self-direct how they can adhere to the held-up ensemble player number (Figure 7.9).

These examples, both from March 2, 2021, highlight the development of using bodily movements as a "score," where players contribute "without sound." This concept is further explored in the sessions where players engage

New Virtuosities   127

Figure 7.9. March 2, 2021, numbers conduction.

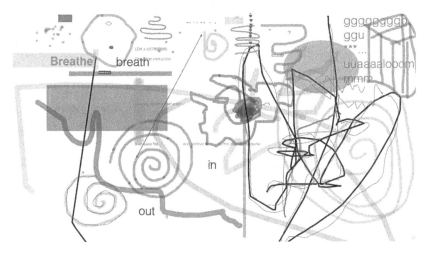

Figure 7.10. March 1, 2022, live collective graphic score.

in non-conventional musical activities (sonic, instruments, notes being played). For example, on March 1, 2022, players create a live graphic score collectively while playing together (▶ Film 7.7 and Figure 7.10). Additionally, in the goodbye piece (▶ Film 7.8 and Figure 7.11), players improvise by waving goodbye and turning cameras on and off to mark the passage of two years under lockdown (March 22, 2022). This was a particularly poignant moment in the group's online work together.

By this point, the group members have significantly expanded their use of "conduction" techniques to include visual, text, embodied, and sonic

Figure 7.11. March 22, 2022, two years in lockdown "goodbye!"

elements. While GIO's activities during the two-year period of 2020–2022 are clearly anchored in this history, drawing inspiration from works such as John Zorn's "Cobra," Butch Morris and Walter Thomson's hand conduction signs, and beyond, there is a crucial novel aspect, namely, the use of technology to facilitate social improvisation interactions. This practice, largely unexplored outside of pandemic-related works, stands out for its integration of technology into the creative process. Notable exceptions in this domain include works that engage in-person players with live text-based and social interactions, such as "Joy Against the Machine" (2021) by Libero Mureddu, where a machine is live-feeding instructions to a band on stage, influencing their actions (both sonically and visually),[1] and Brice Catherin's "Symphonie pour une Femme Seule" (2018), which instructs the players to communicate through a WhatsApp chat on stage to mediate the performance internally.[2]

Expansion of Spaces and Development of New Realms

During the lockdown periods, a new phenomenon related to location and place emerged in the GIO session that sowed the seed of a more hybrid approach to new virtuosities in the way that improvisation was conducted. Players began to venture outside of their homes, practice rooms, and bedrooms, taking their artistic contributions to their backyards, parks, and social places to contribute to the online sessions. The first to do this in the early sessions was Maggie Nicols (on May 2, 2020), who would then regularly be outside her house on her iPad, contributing by singing, talking, and showing the space outside her house or on trains in the middle of her commute. This was followed by author Sappho, who on May 19 went for a trampoline jump at the end of an improvisation (Figure 7.12), which began an example of a practice for experimenting with the body outdoors and with movable cameras. For example, on May 30, 2020 in ▶ Film 7.9, author Sappho joins the session from her garden, experimenting with virtual backgrounds on her body while playing with a pot. In ▶ Film 7.10, Figure 7.13, she explores a moving camera outdoors during the "card piece"

Figure 7.12. May 19, 2020, jumping on trampoline.

Figure 7.13. May 30, 2020, experiments with body, virtual backgrounds, and sunlight.

Figure 7.14. May 30, 2020, card piece, movable camera, and virtual backgrounds.

Figure 7.15. June 6, 2020, Estonian forest through a movable camera and translucent fabric.

(Figure 7.14). Olenka Bulavina, a participant based in Estonia, also engaged with her camera in an innovative way on June 6, 2020, treating her camera as an explorative object while interacting with a light translucent fabric, offering others a small glimpse of a forest scene (▶ Film 7.11, Figure 7.15). By September 2, 2020, Faradina Afifi and Marion Tremby were both performing outdoors, while author Sappho took the group on a guided close-up phone tour of the garden and neighborhood (▶ Film 7.12, Figure 7.16).

Figure 7.16. September 29, 2020, Marion and Fara outdoors, and exploring the garden with Tammy the dog.

Figure 7.17. May 18, 2021, Thomas Rohrer takes the orchestra on a train ride through the Italian alps.

Theater of Home+

All of these examples illustrate players challenging and disrupting the concept of space within these new improvisatory spaces. As the lockdown period eased and greater freedom of movement became possible, music-making expanded to mixed public spaces with players performing from street corners, trains, planes, cars, bikes, and engaging in holiday activities. Figures 7.17–7.24, depict a range of "Theater of Home+" settings across the easing of lockdown in

132   Musical Collaborative Creativity

Figure 7.18. June 1, 2021, Maggie Nicols train improvisations mid-commute (Wales).

Figure 7.19. August 24, 2021, Peter Nicholson brings the group to a swim on a loch (Scottish Highlands).

Figure 7.20. August 31, 2021, author MacDonald travels by plane to Germany.

Figure 7.21. September 14, 2021, author Sappho "breaks in" to author MacDonald's apartment.

Figure 7.22. September 21, 2021, performance to the sunset at Broughty Ferry (Scotland).

2021. The ability to carry technology in one's pocket with an internet connection (phone) allowed the sharing of space and place with the blending of the physical and digital realms. We propose that, at this point, a form of augmented sociality has emerged. This sociality involves re-specifying the social sphere as a blended sphere, possibly constituting a hybrid human-cyborgian community.

Examples of this "expanded sphere" abound in the later recordings, highlighting the ways in which Home+ evolved. For instance, orchestra members joined sessions from seemingly incongruous places, such as a trip

Figure 7.23. October 5, 2021, a cupcake riding a bike through the Scottish Highland with David Robertson.

Figure 7.24. December 14, 2021, GIO's post-lockdown monthly workshops at the CCA.

through the Italian Alps with Thomas Rohrer, commutes with Maggie Nicols, and author MacDonald's journey through an airport (Figure 7.20), including landing in a plane, going through customs, and taking a taxi ride home as part of his contribution to one session (December 7, 2021, ▶ Film 7.13). In response, GIO players respond to author MacDonald's surroundings, and in turn, MacDonald incorporates both visuals and sounds—some inadvertently part of his traveling environment, and others deliberately chosen and included on camera, as well as the sounds he makes when he speaks.

Other examples of the expansion of places in which a member might bring the group during a session include tranquil views of a Scottish lake with Peter Nicholson, a beach with author DeNora at Broughty Ferry, and a bike ride through the Scottish highlands with David Robertson. The necessity for this new blended practice continued to arise throughout the easing of lockdowns. This is best exemplified on one memorable occasion when author Sappho takes the group on a train ride with the secret (and pre-arranged) intention of "breaking into" author MacDonald's house. A playful idea generated by the pair developed into a meta experience that brought the group to the "command deck," which was author MacDonald's office: a familiar image on his screen during the improvisatory sessions.

These moments of rekindling in person and also playing alongside the now-established digital practice continued to emerge as members who could meet up and join sessions together in person developed new ensembles to join sessions. Eventually, this practice evolved to become a staple in merging the digital and in-person sessions of the orchestra upon the resumption of live sessions and festivals at the CCA. This integration primarily involved the Scottish contingent of the group, while concurrently sustaining collaborative engagements with digital and global members of the band.

In 2021, the expanded Theater of Home practice reached a significant milestone with the inaugural GIO digital hybrid performance. On May 4, 2021 (aptly coinciding with Star Wars day), GIO performed as part of an art exhibition at Annalix Forever, an art gallery in Geneva, Switzerland. This marked the first time the group had attempted to integrate live performers in one location with an online group of musicians performing via Zoom.

The structure of the hybrid performance was organized as follows:

1. Ensemble members performed in person in the gallery before a small audience.
2. Simultaneously, an online group of musicians performed on Zoom. The integration of the Zoom performance and the live performance was achieved through a combination of screens and speakers strategically positioned in the gallery.
3. A virtual audience had the opportunity to view the entire performance via a broadcast on YouTube.
4. The audience in the gallery was also able to hear/see the performers on Zoom via the screens and monitors installed in the gallery, while the Zoom audience could watch and hear the live performers in the gallery since they performed in front of computer screens connected to Zoom.

In response to the hybrid format, players were quick to embrace its novel features. For example, at 12:02 (▶ Film 7.14), author MacDonald positions his saxophone very close to the camera on his computer. Meanwhile, he utilizes a virtual background, as well as making small clicking sounds with the keys of his saxophone. For the audience on Zoom, the imagery was ambiguous—a blurred image of a saxophone merging into a grainy virtual background. For the audience in the gallery, the imagery was different. They could choose to watch the screens and see the digital version of the performer, or watch the actual performer in the space, or a combination of both.

In a sense, this digital music practice merged the traditions of "busking" and gallery/concert hall performance. It extended what Keith Sawyer terms "collaborative emergence" (2000) or a development linked to group interaction, as well as textual and historical matters. In the case of GIO, group interaction encompasses the ongoing improvisation; the textual dimension involves the visual developments of onscreen experimentation, including technology, spaces, and places. The historical development pertains to how the social contexts around GIO shifted over time, transitioning from in-person sessions within a specific room to augmented reality with an impetus toward social connectivity via the Theater of Home and Home+.

In 2022, at the AJIRN conference, a collaborative improvisation involved the development of a score that centered around the theme of "cooking" (▶ Film 7.15). What resulted was a convergence of spaces from around the world that included 25 players in an auditorium at Griffith University in Brisbane (Australia), as well as players in the United Kingdom, Japan, and Australia interacting from their music online spaces as well as cooking food in their kitchens, explaining their recipes and processes and discussing their successes and failures. This session encapsulated the themes explored in this chapter and in a way showcased how GIO's Theater of Home has developed and evolved into Home+. Players were seen eating with their families (lunch), walking through the streets of their neighborhoods, and interacting with visuals of food spaces. The composition and improvisation artfully incorporated elements of daily routines, food, eating, and global and cross-cultural variations, all infused with playfulness, sociability, text, and the inclusion of multiple objects and virtual backgrounds. Figure 7.25 shows on the left the main onsite room (to the right there is a glimpse of the screen).

Figure 7.25. Cooking in the Theater of Home at the AJIRN conference, 2022.

Creative Developments, New Virtuosities, and New Virtualities

In this chapter, we have highlighted how the specific social and technological environment in which the Glasgow Improvisers Orchestra was meeting facilitated new creative and social developments, shaping an alternate notion of virtuosity. This notion involved incorporating domestic objects for creating sound and involved a series of decisions and judgments about how to integrate these objects into a creative context. The sessions also involved moments where technology was employed specifically to create new types of audio-visual compositions, contributing to the emergence of new virtualities. Hybrid identities and digital versions of the self were intricately woven into the performances, evolving over a number of weeks or months. These new hybrid digital identities transformed the embodied nature of the musical experience for both performers and the audience. The working context of GIO facilitated the engagement of people not previously involved in such activities, including family members and colleagues. The Zoom environment enabled unique types of socio-artistic interactions as showcased in this chapter, which would not have happened without the unique circumstances facilitating them. These interactions and objects described herein would not have happened had the pandemic online situation not arisen.

In order to acknowledge the significance of this artistic process, we propose that the repertoire of skills that are valued within musical participation needs to be expanded to include these types of socio-artistic interactions. The specific moments highlighted in this chapter that took place during the improvised activities are contextualized within a broader discussion regarding the types of musical activities valued as important by society in general. Those musical activities valued as important become seen as characteristic of advanced and successful musicians, often referred to as virtuosi. Thus, as suggested above, musical virtuosity is defined by a series of socially constructed musical skills. If the scope of valued skills remains limited to technical instrumental proficiency alone, numerous creative and musically significant activities may be overlooked or marginalized. Therefore, there is a need to expand our definition of what types of musical skills are seen as important. We thus propose a broadening of the definition of what musical virtuosity constitutes.

The accessibility of an arts practice that offers creative engagement at any level of virtuosity can have a transformative effect on music education and the ways we feel about making music in our everyday lives. The location of creative agency within a group (online or otherwise), rather than within an individual, has significant implications for how we view creativity. These issues, other aspects of the online environment, along with suggestions made by the authors for new directions in studying, making, or researching music and other improvisatory arts in years to come, are proposed in the following chapters.

The activities outlined in this chapter demonstrate particular types of virtuosity in terms of being able to make spontaneous decisions about how to develop a new piece of music creatively and how to integrate gestures, objects, spaces, places, and social contexts into an ongoing musical improvisation. We propose that these types of activities should be valued within broader discussions around what is musical and what is artistic and that these types of activities could contribute toward what we value as being exemplars of musical and artistic virtuosity. In the next two chapters, we discuss the implications of valuing these types of contexts and decision-making interactions. We explore the educational, clinical, cultural, and social implications of these findings. These ideas are proposed in order to highlight how the specific artistic and social developments made during these sessions link to wider cultural issues, contributing to our understanding of how collaborative creative activities develop over the coming years.

8
An Improvising Life
Implications for Identity, Education, Therapy, and Beyond

The previous chapter concentrated on recent innovations in improvisational practice. We now build on that discussion. We connect it to themes around health and well-being. For more than two years, weekly improvised sessions revealed numerous examples of health- and well-being-related practices related to identity formation and community resilience. These examples highlight how GIO's online collaborations came to foster empowerment, supporting individuals to navigate the then-ongoing pandemic as well as ongoing challenging issues in their personal lives.

In the interviews conducted by this research team, and in more informal conversations, many participants explicitly stated that the sessions enhanced their sense of health and well-being. We explore this theme here because it also allows us to consider how the distinctive creative environment may not only support health and well-being but also have broader implications for online community practices—in education and therapeutic areas, for example. In relation to education, we describe how the practices we observed within GIO have transferable lessons for the design of teaching and learning spaces and how they might be used to enhance educational experiences.

Identity: Agency and Performativity

Literature on music, health, and well-being often note that well-being can be derived from empowerment and agency—in music and in life. In modern times, and in particular, as so-called lifestyle issues have come to the fore, and as issues surrounding identity have increasingly been thrown into flux, to be able to assert and develop self and group identity—and more broadly to be able to participate in identifying people and things in a shared world—is to have a degree of empowerment. For these reasons, identity has, in modern times, become integral to health and well-being (DeNora, 2013; Giddens, 1991; MacDonald et al., 2017;). Being able to engage, collaborate, and create new work is part of the process of identity formation. Being creative can enhance feelings of agency, self-esteem, and broader communication skills. These psychological constructs—agency, self-esteem, and communicative skill—serve, in turn, as important markers of identity. And they enhance well-being, especially during challenging times, on a day-to-day basis.

During the pandemic, when individuals were not able to take part in ordinary and everyday interactions or to play the roles they had otherwise played routinely in their daily lives, the sources and resources for individual members' identity work were imperiled and identity was problematized. Quickly, however, we saw GIO members developing adaptive strategies that were pressed into use to maintain and develop identity—individual and collective. That work was helped in great part by the new, overtly multimedia features of online working, first and foremost by the opportunity that weekly, and later twice-weekly, online improvisation afforded for remaining connected to colleagues, friends, and collaborators. Exploring how those connections were retained, and indeed enhanced, also highlights in a grounded way what it means to speak of health as a performative concept and the performance of health as intrinsically linked to the ability to take identity stances within a given field, setting, scene, or world. The mechanism for that performative well-being is, as we will now describe, improvisatory agency.

Improvisatory Agency

In GIO online, that agency developed and was scaffolded by an expanding repertoire of practices and a diverse set of props, materials, and techniques that became resources for the promotion of well-being. Chief among these, as reported in interview settings, was the altered and expanded set of possibilities in digital practice for experimenting with and exploring new frontiers for self-presentational strategies.

Participants experimented with how they appeared online through decisions about where to be positioned, how to dress, do hair, or paint the face, and what instrument(s) to play on, or off, camera. Some experimented with makeup. Some experimented with "setting a scene" in the room from which they Zoomed. Some experimented with color with virtual backgrounds and with new instrumental techniques that might have been inappropriate or, if visually based, not visible in a live performance. So, while the lockdown period brought loneliness, anxiety, uncertainty, and loss, it also brought opportunities for experimentation of and with self and self in relation to others. It was a time for "trying out" new identities and self-presentational strategies in a "safe" haven, in a place where, for example, lighting and camera angles could be controlled, where, if the situation became difficult, one could simply leave the meeting or mute or go off-camera or switch to a virtual background, a video, or a filter over the camera (real or digital). So, too, because of the vagaries of Zoom and its selection algorithms, combined with the sheer number of individual screens and mics, one could experiment with new sounds knowing that they might, in fact, never be noticed or heard. And when others did hear or see and validate or endorse (e.g., through flanking, echoing, borrowing, etc.) one could experience immediate validation of one's tentative techniques of self-identity experimentation.

Experimental music, in other words, became, in the Zoomesphere, simultaneously, experimental theater and experimental social relations. The Zoomesphere also became a site for resource-based health promotion where things that might otherwise have remained on the margins, in the background, or behind the curtain were drawn out and placed in, or closer to, the spotlight. In short, the empowerment that the sessions afforded, the ways that they allowed participants to experiment with self-presentation and even "reinvent" themselves, was an unanticipated consequence of improvisation during lockdown. When we interviewed people about the health benefits or health-linked effects of online sessions, they acknowledged these points, underscoring how the performative features of self-presentation and mutual self-validation were important to their well-being:

> And so yeah, psychologically, it was: It was a benefit, I would say it was beneficial to my mental health during the lockdown, for sure. (Stuart Brown)

> GIO has been a very important part of nourishing me in a way that is, you know, lifting my spirits enough that I don't default to addiction. (Maggie Nicols)

> They give me something to do. And they give me something to look forward to. And they give me goals. (Steve Beresford)

Being and Sharing: Health and Identity

> One of the things I like is that—you're in your living room, you can get away with blue murder sort of thing. So it's a completely different vibe, but you're sharing it, you know, which is, which is fine. It's just very open. And it's just great fun to do. So it takes you to different spaces. You know, I've got this wretched—obviously called shielding. So, it looks like I'm not going to be able to go outside the front door except

to go to the hospital until they find a vaccine! You know, so I'm kind of locked down in like (it's a very nice prison), but . . . so it's great to see you people and be with you and, and share the lunacy of my isolation chamber. (John Russell, May 9, 2020)

Although John was confined to his home during this period and "shielding" for health reasons as a result of a cancer diagnosis, he still felt he could "be with" other people with the improvisatory regular interactions of GIO, facilitating a sense of togetherness and community. John's case was extreme, but it serves to highlight how for many other GIO members the online sessions heightened a sense of connection and belonging. These types of collective/interactive musical experiences, while "shielding," highlight the importance of both listening and practical activities in developing communication and inclusion for the disabled and marginalized (Kotarba, 2023; McFerran et al., 2022). We now turn to a series of case studies to illustrate some of the ways that members used music during the pandemic as a technology of self (DeNora, 2000)—a means of identity-care and social support during a period of isolation and challenging circumstances.

Participation in music is a foundation of equity and inclusivity, especially health and well-being during COVID-19 (MacDonald and Wilson, 2014; Reason, 2023). What GIO members achieved, individually and collectively through their activities, was significant and tied to equally significant changes in identity. We believe that these effects are derived from improvisation. Improvised music is a medium that allows the priorities of the moment to shape and be acted upon as part of interaction processes (Kamoche et al., 2003). These processes in turn can be used to express and demonstrate (consciously and unconsciously) specific concerns. John Russell's words, quoted above, illustrate how an individual's personal concerns and worries are aired in the context of a group session—placed as it were into the frame of what might be improvised on—in music, but also in talk—and thus drawn into the fold of group concerns. These processes include asserting agency—helping to furnish the collective "basket" of topics and helping to steer attention to things that matter (to John, to the group).

Here, improvisation can be seen to offer a means for individuals to express feelings while being with others *in the moment* (MacDonald and Wilson, 2020). As such, improvisation can be understood as a technology of well-being, a way of focusing group attention (on things that matter) and thus for the generation and deployment of agency (Ruud, 2022). This generation and the group focus, as observed by John Russell, in turn helps people to feel connected at a time of domestic sequestration. It is a way of airing and sharing serious health matters.

The musical context or GIO themes, such as hands, cooking, and others, as mentioned in previous chapters, also allow these feelings to be expressed without words—materially and sensorially. This expression was important because many of the interviewees were experiencing health and psychological issues related to the pandemic.

Projecting Images of What It Might Mean to Be Well-in-Illness or Well Under Duress

> It's about sharing, and it's about fun. And it's about a kind of lack of commodification. You know we are sharing things as the planet falls apart. We have to learn to share things. And we have to share with nature [. . .] and let's keep in touch. One of the reasons for making Mopomoso TV is that it represents a point of contact and a point of sharing around the world. [. . .] it's probably the—I was going to say the only hope we have—but let's be hopeful. (John Russell on Mopomoso TV, October 2020)

John Russell made a significant contribution as a long-standing pioneer in the "free improvisation" community and was at the forefront of the practice in the UK, European, and Japanese scenes in both performing and curating concerts. To this end, he ran numerous festivals and concert series, including the founding of the Mopomoso concert series, considered the longest-running event for improvised music in the United Kingdom. Russell ran Mopomoso until his death, often conducting the team of volunteers from his hospital bed.

During COVID-19, the Mopomoso TV series aired a monthly improvisation concert in place of the in-person gigs at the prestigious Vortex jazz club in London. The online concerts presented about an hour's worth of improvised music films (pre-recorded and organized by the team) of pieces up to five minutes in length, showcasing the GIO online sessions on several occasions. Even though the works were recorded, the show was shown to an active online audience who experienced the event as a form of shared liveness from real-time viewing and interactive use of YouTube's live chat and "première" function. This experience was enhanced by the Mopomoso team, who made bespoke introductions that addressed the imagined audience and contributed toward this program's unique form of oral history. These introductions provided another opportunity for John to connect and communicate with the outside world, and as the monthly MC (master of ceremonies), John would appear in colorful themed suits and outfits (see Figure 8.1). Despite his

144 Musical Collaborative Creativity

Figure 8.1. John Russell in Mopomoso TV episode 2, July 2020.

declining health, the premieres of the Mopomoso series now archive a luminous view into the "Theater of John"—a home packed with guitars, a lovingly looked-after garden, and a wealth of recorded and priceless stories, anecdotes, and jokes alongside the promotion of this music, championed in John's inimitable way.

Advancing Communicative Practices

John's situation has shed light on the issues associated with the advancing of communicative practices for "difficult" or "tense" situations/topics, as described in Chapter 6. It has brought attention to the implications for developing vocabularies and cultural practices in support of things such as how to talk about dis/ability, death, dying, and bereavement (Wildfeuer, 2015), which encompass the connection to specific practices and how they rest on improvisatory capacities (Tsiris et al., 2022). These implications are conspicuous since conversations about death and loss are not only difficult but are often seen as taboo, leaving individuals often unprepared to navigate the topic of death in group communication (Kirshbaum et al., 2011). By contrast, in GIO, we found that the often oblique or liminal nature of text or talk, as part of the improvisation, was conducive to the notion of "over-sharing." Topics that might have been difficult or impossible to mention in ordinary conversation could become "material" for the improvisation. This process thus opens up a space for airing and sharing, specifically, a safe, bounded, quasi-theatrical or fictional space. Within this setting, it then becomes possible at any moment, and it could be implied or overtly declared that this was "only" an improvisation and that it was a theatrical exploration of "material" rather than an attempt to communicate about, for example, loneliness, illness, or loss.

Incorporating visual and theatrical material into the otherwise "musical" improvisations, and its development over time as "Theater of Home," moreover allowed participants to express meanings on multiple levels, that is, to both be "talking about" something and yet not. This ambiguity itself became a resource for "over-sharing," and thus, within the group, improvisations became at times quasi-therapeutic, but in a peer-to-peer way where anything, in principle, and everything could be interesting and "okay" as a topic for sharing and as a topic for improvisation. Examples include a participant saying they had not been kissed since lockdown as part of the over-sharing; and, as discussed in Chapter 6 and above, the discussion around the impending death and the loss of a group member and how it could be explored, gently, and under the rubric of "when life gives you lemons." Here, we can see the facilitative role of "boundary objects" foregrounded: a topic could "mean" many things to many people all at once, and in ways that would allow each person to, as it were, find their own depth in relation to that topic. So, as in the case of the "lemons" session described in Chapter 6, the talk could be understood as "only" about recipes or as "really" about death and loss, or indeed as about how all of these things are, in Maggie Nicols's words, "mingled together" in an inclusive, and accepting, holding form; one that is capable both of holding on to the complexity of meanings and of holding together a diverse group.

While the example of how the group handled John Russell's impending death, and John's own willingness to share that journey during his final months of life stands out as a vitally important case in point, there were also many other examples of group sharing and airing and identity maintenance/development. For example, in an interview conducted by Jessica Argo for the GIOfest XIV, one member (Laura Cavanaugh) recounts the importance of Russell in their memory with a reflection that exposes a much wider impact of the understanding of the human practice that was developed during this new digital way of working. This serves as a poignant example of the novel affordances, glimpses into each other's lives, and memories that can be acquired by a practice that connects innovative connections. The Theater of Home intertwines intimate and yet globally resonant practices, creating a platform for shared experiences that transcend traditional boundaries.

Laura Cavanaugh:

> One moment that sticks out for me, because it's inclusive of the sort of river of life and, you know, things flow and John Russell was with us for a long time. And then, and then he passed on, you know, and, but one day, he had this wonderful card behind him with this lovely bear on it. And I said, "What a lovely card." And so he picked it off the shelf, and he proceeded to read it to me. And it was a young person. And they proceeded to say that they're very sorry that he wasn't feeling well, and everything, and they were really missing him. But he said [the card writer] "Nobody understands me, and nobody listens to me, like you. And I'm really missing you."

And I thought that was a really wonderful, delightful kind of window into the beauty of the practice of art and the practice of life. And that's a moment that sort of sticks out for me.

Jessica Argo:

And a lot of the most meaningful moments, I think, from working with GIO online over the last year and a half have just been so many philosophical insights from John, but also just beautiful, hilarious moments as well—he brought a lot of love to the session. So yeah. And he had a lot of friends around him too. One of my favorite memories is just wondering what John was going to wear to a session one day. I loved the surprise of is it going to be like, like your hat? Is it going to be bright orange? Is it going to be a gold sparkly suit? He just brought so much light to the sessions. And that was yeah, that's how I met him. I've never met him in person. But he was such a big part of my life for several months. So yeah, we've done quite a bit of work for well, in remembering John as well. We made some pieces specifically for John. I think there's still an archive of a special Mopomoso session dedicated to him available online. If anyone's interested. He made a lovely film for us last year as well. I think that was one of the climaxes of one of the evenings—referring to a film for GIOfest XII.

Laura Cavanaugh:

Well, I think that's the thing is everybody is allowed to show up as their own tremendously unique human beings, and everybody seems to show up their best human being, you know, they show up with their best, their best spirit, and it's very inspiring.[1] (quoted in Argo, 2022, n.p.)

The examples above highlight how the specific context of the online creative activities helped facilitate communication developments in both artistic work and in terms of personal communication. Key features of this context include an emphasis on improvisation, process (as opposed to outputs), non-specific goals, and socio-artistic processes that are flexible. These features combine with a supportive social environment to create a unique experience for the participants. This socio-artistic environment with specific technological, creative, and social affordances, which we call the *Zoomesphere*, helps facilitate these new communicative practices. We now move on to discuss the ways in which engagement with these activities influenced the identity process related to a sense of empowerment for participants.

Empowerment

The performative exploration of self-presentational strategies assumed many forms, and yet paramount to most of these identity expressions was the heightened presence of the "self" in the face-on, camera-oriented, audio-visual setting. The presentation of the physical "self" in improvisatory music is relatively new; more common is for a musical body to "disappear" behind technique and "mastery" (e.g., the traditional, if now outmoded, wearing of a black "uniform" when performing classical music, the requirement of audience members to be utterly still and silent). Typically, when bodies are noticed in music, it is for their "otherness"; indeed, almost all discussions of the visual presentation or visual aspects of bodies in improvised practice are made more in relation to gendered (Smith, 2001) or racial stereotypes (Mwamba and Johansen, 2021). However, in the GIO environment, there was an abrupt shift in favor of the visually present and presented body. This shift quickly eclipsed existing traditions for improvisational noticing and interaction with its focus on sound, instrument, or disembodied actions such as breathing techniques, hand movements, and eye contact in favor of performing bodies/performing selves. Time and time again, players reported how they not only tried to push themselves to experiment with and invent new creative practices that involved their bodies, as we have discussed in earlier chapters, but they also described how they contended with broader, personal, and underlying experiences and relationships with their bodies, their potential identities, and the possibilities for visual power.

For example, Jessica Argo describes her actions during a themed piece on "color" that the group performed in 2020. In an interview, she describes a particularly unique element of online working practices, highlighting the felt "privacy" of experimenting with vulnerable subjects. In this case, she had the confidence to explore her visual image within the broader context of her experiences within the music industry toward deconstructing the perceived judgement surrounding her day-to-day use of makeup and the reception of her femininity.

> I've never used makeup in improvisers' performances before.... I thought this, this actually feels kind of safe. To try this. Cause it's just, it's just one thing in many.... I didn't overtly sort of share an artist statement about it or anything, but I felt like it was quite exhilarating for me to do that well, because I was, deconstructing a lot of, sort of worries that I have about my visual as a woman in the music industry or in probably more in sound and kind of digital technology kind of profession that I'm

in. You know, makeup is something that, and color and clothes, it's something that I love, but it's something, I feel like I'm not really taken seriously if I wear too much of it or, or yeah well I have actually had comments about, you know, if I do my hair differently and things like that. So yeah. It was just, it was, you know, for me it felt quite kind of political and quite powerful, what I was doing it. I don't know if that it really mattered to anyone else, but it was, yeah, it was quite helpful for me to sort of enact that and try that out over Zoom. Whereas if I did something like that in the CCA and just stepped into the middle of room and just started doing my makeup—I just, I don't think I would have ever done that in the CCA. I think that just would have been too much or too frightening to do in a physical room. But who knows now afterward. (Argo, quoted in MacDonald et al., 2021)

Importantly, Argo notes that due to the homogenous layout of a Zoom screen, her contribution was only "one thing in many" of the boxes of performers on screen. In fact, she notes that while she felt the experience was "kind of political and quite powerful," she also positions this experience as a subjective one—one that was useful for her in a broader context to enact and try out in a musical setting, but not an action she undertook to enforce a political effect on the group. In fact, it was a creative interpretation of the theme of "colors".

Due to the richly populated visual layout of a Zoom screen, it is likely that the creative application of makeup was taken up and influenced some musicians' improvisatory responses, but it also could have been missed by others. It could have also been considered an "everyday" act that can be seen as a creative-adjacent contribution (e.g., where players often cook, speak with family, leave and enter a room, etc., which all contributes to the notion of the Theater of Home in the Zoomesphere). That is, contribution in the Zoom setting is intangibly performative; everyday tasks and the acts of living are both creative contributions but, at the same time, necessities. The blurring of boundaries, shaped by both the Zoom environment and the cultural practices developed by GIO through the use of the software, facilitates the merging of personal political acts into a powerful and exhilarating experience for the performer.

Simultaneously, these acts do not seem particularly out of place within the setting, highlighting the fluid and adaptable nature of the performance space. As Argo notes, she would most likely not have performed this action on the stage at the regular venue GIO uses (CCA). She expresses that taking such action in a physical space would be deemed "too much" or would evoke fear, reflecting the vulnerability associated with being a physical presence on a stage while engaging in a personal, visual, and vulnerable act. Additionally, the unconventional nature of using makeup as a performance in a traditional orchestral setting contributes to this hesitancy. In contrast, within the online realm of the Theater of Home, the dynamics of body politics carry less weight, allowing for a more liberated expression without the same physical-world constraints.

Moreover, it can be argued that the audio-visual nature of the digital improvisation setting provides an opportunity for individuals with previously marginalized visual qualities to assert their identities. The digital medium allows for a more inclusive platform where diverse visual expressions can be acknowledged and embraced—which at first seems strange. The enhancement of the visuals appears to be empowering those whose own visual identities are often the most misrepresented in canon. As previously discussed, this underscores the significance of extra-musical practices within the Theater of Home—specifically, the act of oversharing—as a means of empowering and celebrating forms of practice that have been historically marginalized. These practices overtly engage with aspects such as the body, visuality, and social positioning, reflecting the players' personal experiences of identity issues within a broader context. This context is shaped by the dual nature of making music while navigating the reality of creating music from a space that is minoritized. This once again emphasizes how the unique context of these online creative activities has beneficial effects related to participants' identity processes.

Education

Over the last 50 years, music education has experienced a progressive departure from the conventional classical music conservatory model, which followed a prescribed approach and a traditional notes-based understanding of virtuosity, as we have discussed in the previous chapter. Instead, there has been a transformation toward a more inclusive paradigm, encompassing a wide range of genres, including popular music, jazz, folk, and music from various cultures worldwide (MacDonald and Sarakallio, 2024; Odena, 2018; Sangiorgi, 2023).

There is now a broader acknowledgment of the importance of improvisation in musical education, reflecting a contemporary understanding of the evolving landscape of musical practices and technologies. The research presented here advocates for a more holistic approach to musical growth, recognizing the myriad ways—whether through digital platforms, machine-generated music, or artificial intelligence (AI)—that music, musicianship, and musical identities are expressed and integrated into our lives. This approach is in keeping with current developments seeking more participatory, inclusive, and innovative approaches to academic research (Tomas and Bidet, 2024). These approaches challenge conventional hegemonic power dynamics between researchers and participants and acknowledge the crucial contributions of research participants from planning through to the dissemination of research (MacGlone et al., 2023).

As explored in the preceding chapters, some of the emergent strategies within the GIO involved establishing virtual experimental and collaborative communities. For some of the players who also teach, aspects of the methodologies employed in GIO sessions came to be of use in the virtual classroom, particularly in university improvisation units, during the lockdown period of 2020–2021.

For example, Burke et al. (2021) observed that students, from an early age, are consistently immersed in interactive technologies such as phones, video games, computers, iPads, and more. Transitioning to online improvisation classes tapped the students' technical proficiency and their understanding of community dynamics through social media platforms—a culmination of a lifetime of exposure and immersion in interactive technologies. The incorporation of techniques such as digital backgrounds and the concept of the Theater of Home provided students with inspiration, new skills, and a heightened sense of community during a period marked by isolation.

> There was also an increased sense of a virtual collaborative bonding that was different from their normal approach to online communication through social media. In post-class discussions with staff, students spoke of a sense of progress, belief, satisfaction, and belonging and that ideas and opinions did not have the same bias and prejudice that can be present in jazz ensemble situations. (Burke et al., 2021, p. 10).

Feedback from the students included:

> I've developed more in this semester than at any other period of my life. It's definitely been a challenge adapting to this format, but it's forcing us to develop new skills as well as giving us the time to do a great deal of introspection.
>
> I've had some really awesome moments in my ensemble studies, being able to still interact with other students and teachers . . . it really felt like I was in the room with them. (Burke et al., 2021, p. 9).

Scottish musician, researcher, and pedagogue Una MacGlone (2023) conducted a study investigating the experiences of female students attending a university course and how the changed environment changed gendered dimensions that have had a history of being problematic due to hegemonic masculinity and male-dominated virtuosities (Reddan et al., 2022). MacGlone's work uncovered a range of strategies for adapting to online learning, while also exposing elements of the digital format which afforded benefits that were not possible in in-person sessions:

> If I had been doing this module in person, that is, a lot of other things that might be in my head about the way I'm sitting, or like what people judge, would people judge my posture? Like there were a lot of things like that that I mean. I feel like it takes up a lot of energy, but you don't realize it in your head and that's one of the big reasons that you're tired when you get home. So, and to add to that, I felt like breaks were different that I came back with a lot of energy. And that's because I was cool because I got to really switch off and like be cool and then come back. I feel like, if I had been outside I would have taken a break, but I would still be in a public space, sort of having to be public, yeah so um, for me personally, I think there are some things that I enjoyed about it being an online, Zoom class. (student quoted in MacGlone, 2023, n.p.)

Through this work, MacGlone investigated how digital work might contribute toward future face-to-face practices that capitalize on transdisciplinary practices and variation in "aesthetic material" which benefit students' experiences and has the potential to contribute toward positive shifts in expanding representation, instilling confidence, and responding to gender-diverse needs in improvised education. The current iteration of the course is led by author Sappho in collaboration with Henry McPherson. Although the course has returned to in-person sessions, both continue to lead classes focusing on telematic and audio-visual practices. These approaches have demonstrated their effectiveness in fostering improvisational skills among students with diverse abilities and creative backgrounds. This adaptation reflects a recognition of the ongoing relevance and utility of digital and collaborative practices in enhancing the learning experience for a diverse student body.

Implications

The GIO online sessions served as crucial experiences of social and artistic interaction and interventions for participants, especially when these interactions were notably limited. What has been discovered is that these artistic interventions, even when not explicitly framed within a clinical context, can yield positive effects. This observation underscores a robust connection between community-based art practices and more clinically oriented art practices, highlighting how artistic interventions hold agency for fostering positive change and facilitating discoveries. It emphasizes artistic engagement's broader impact and potential therapeutic value beyond explicitly clinical settings.

A significant implication also lies in the aesthetic domain, where completely novel creations emerged from the online context where no previous work of this nature had been generated. Navigating the recordings, both in terms of listening and watching, posed challenges in terms of how to engage with the overall aesthetic of what was produced. As a group of authors and participants in the sessions, we often spent time discussing the quality, context, and innovation of the outputs. This created issues around aesthetic judgments regarding quality due to the absence of a yardstick or framework by which to assess this type of artistic work. This situation highlights the ongoing subjective nature involved in assessing quality and creativity in artistic outputs more broadly. In an attempt to avoid what Maggie Nicols referred to as "aesthetic supremacy" during one of the online sessions during GIO's annual festival of improvisation in 2020 these types of critiques are important and impact the possible implications in musical aesthetic value, developed within creative cultures now evolving around these practices. The discourse on music aesthetics and critique extends to the education sector, where educators frequently face the task of assessing student work with reference to the quality of the output. One of the lessons learned could relate to the extent to which engagement in the artistic and collaborative processes is more important than the outputs, or certainly holds process-based criteria and output-based criteria in equilibrium (i.e., ability and expertise).

A key takeaway from our experiences emphasizes the significance of active participation in both the artistic and collaborative processes, potentially surpassing the importance attributed to the final outputs. This underscores the value of maintaining a balance between criteria that focus on the creative and collaborative journey itself and those that assess the ultimate results, considering factors such as individual ability and expertise. In essence, the lesson learned highlights that the depth of engagement in the creative and collaborative processes holds intrinsic value, advocating for a balanced approach that considers both the journey and the outcomes. Thus, creating the right social environment in which students can productively engage in artistic processes is an important way of helping students develop new ideas and creative breakthroughs in their practice. This resonates strongly with educational theory that emphasizes a more improvisatory or free-play approach to developing new skills and the effect of building a creative community of practice.

This observation also contributes to wider educational debates regarding how to teach skills that appear nebulous or non-specific, for example teaching a class focused on improvisation. In these contexts the classes may not be focused on developing a repertoire of specific skills, but rather on creating social contexts that facilitate learners to explore their own ideas and creativity in a supportive and encouraging environment. This context's specific skills may still emerge, but these skills will be contingent upon each student's unique requirements and experiences. The learning environments may also develop into what can be called a community of practice.

In the terms defined by Lave and Wenger (1991), a community of practice (CoP) is characterized as a collective of individuals sharing a common objective, aim, or focus in a specific domain. Members of this community come together to explicitly or implicitly work toward agreed-upon objectives within their shared area of interest. A key feature of the Zoom sessions undertaken by GIO is that the learning takes place through engagement within a facilitatory environment and not through the acquisition of new knowledge imparted by a powerful other. This is a cornerstone of communities of practice that is inclusive of sharing goals and similar practices while creating new knowledge to help facilitate musical interaction and group cohesion within the specific domain of professional practice (music). There is a move away from the development of facts and abstract ideas in more formal educational contexts toward more socially contextual and situated types of learning. Brown and Duguid (2002) underscore this point by emphasizing that conceptual online problem-solving leads to understanding and knowledge development through practical engagement. Gannon-Leary and Fontainha (2007) contribute to this discussion by addressing virtual educational online learning, suggesting that online CoPs are advantageous due to their reliance on collaborative learning. They argue that the knowledge generated through collaboration within CoPs surpasses the knowledge that individuals could acquire on their own (Johnson, 2001).

In this respect, the GIO sessions have many similarities to CoPs that have learned together informally throughout history. The term "community of practice" (CoP) was initially coined by cognitive anthropologists Jean Lave and Etienne Wenger (1991), who used it to describe learning models based on apprenticeships. The term highlights how a group of people support and transmit a body of knowledge in "living" form, by showing and doing with, by serving as exemplars for others. The GIO sessions also served as a CoP. Even without a formal apprenticeship system, GIO players began to mentor each other, modeling, scaffolding, validating, echoing, and sharing new techniques and skills that were learned by doing.

These developments carry both creative and psychological significance, as they open up possibilities for applying an improvisatory approach to education and healthcare objectives in the future. Future interventions could be designed to provide students with access to group music-making through online resources, as suggested by Lee and Quifan (2021). While the idea of online group music-making is not novel, the innovative aspect lies in adopting an improvisatory approach to the organization and delivery of these sessions. Moreover, online platforms could be used to deliver music therapy or community music with health and well-being objectives to groups of individuals dispersed nationally or even internationally, especially benefiting those facing challenges in organizing or affording transport or those who are home-bound (Quigley and MacDonald, 2024). These interventions would tap into a broadened perspective of aesthetic, creative, and technical aspects valued within music-making, specifically emphasizing new virtuosities and valuing the creative, interactive, and social engagement aspects of music.

In summary, this chapter has highlighted how the online sessions had beneficial implications for the identities of the participants. These identity developments were related to the collaborative creative activities and were clearly linked in positive ways to wider personal and social identities. The creative, social, and technological context of the work highlights the importance of personal agency, performativity, and empowerment within the creative processes. Of particular importance is the role of improvisation, which provides a process and context for participants to explore the development of agency, as part of a supportive social network, functioning as a CoP. These experiences clearly have positive benefits for the health and well-being of the participants, highlighting a wider relationship between general creative activities and explicitly clinically focused therapeutic practices. In addition to health-related developments, there are specific implications for formal educational contexts. For example, activities such as improvisation collaboration and process-based creative practices incorporating new technologies can be integrated into formal educational contexts. This is particularly important considering recent developments that seek to develop more inclusive, ecologically valid, post-colonial educational practices. In the following chapter, we discuss the implications of this work in terms of new approaches to improvisation activities.

9
New Insights into Understanding Improvisation

In this chapter, findings are drawn together from the analysis chapters to explore new understandings of improvisation through the experiences and discoveries of the participants performing in a virtual environment. In synthesizing the themes, we explore how collective music-making merges with the use of virtual backgrounds (photos/videos) and actual physical backgrounds/props to create a virtual habitat (either by digital techniques or by displaying objects/instruments/pets, costumes/bodily presentation, makeup, and apparel). We analyze these improvisational experiences and describe how they helped us to understand the genealogy of ideas and the influence of affordances inherent in the home environment which came to contribute to the improvisational process. Our analysis explores the rationale linked to the choices and decisions made and draws out implications for practice that extend beyond the confines of the virtual realm.

Post-Genre and Post-Disciplinary Implications

As discussed, one striking aspect of the sessions was that as the musicians adapted to the online environmental, technological, and cultural affordances, they began to experiment and perform in ways that were distinctly new. These novel approaches encompassed online practices that extended beyond their typical musical repertoire. Notably, participants were observed transcending, merging, and/or blurring conventional disciplinary boundaries. In this context, "transcending" refers to their exploration of new techniques and styles with their respective instruments and stylistic and technical repertoires, while "merging/blurring" denotes their increased involvement with film and photographic materials, leading to the creation of novel modes of communication (multimedia forms) and artistic expression. The shift to online collaboration redefined what qualified as "music" performance, significantly expanding its scope. This process also incorporated new elements as previously detailed, including domestic materials:

> What's been fascinating is finding objects, and finding things that I can use to create textures and stuff like that. Yes, you can play with the fabrics and stuff that's around. (Maggie Nicols)

Using new materials and blurring/merging disciplinary boundaries produced new freedoms for GIO members. It also began to deconstruct prescribed "correct" or "incorrect" modes of interaction, "musical" and otherwise. That deconstruction led to a post-disciplinary, post-genre mode of creativity that was, within GIO and beyond, genuinely unprecedented. The innovative nature of this work stems from a constellation of factors. While the integration of visual, theatrical, and musical elements within a composition is not novel, using these elements within an online environment where improvisation is the primary mode of expression is something new. Moreover, the unique pandemic context in which the musicians found themselves also helped to facilitate innovation and artistic interactions. In the next section, we discuss some of the implications of these innovative approaches. We employ case studies for this purpose.

A Bionic Patois

In Chapter 5, the notion of remixing to "build the world(s) we want to live in" (Russell, 2020, 133) was proposed. Here the notion of remixing in the literal sense (i.e., remixing elements of the recorded material to produce new work) was extended to include a metaphorical remixing; that is, remixing elements of players' identities as a result of participating in the online sessions, where the new artistic practices evolved from the unprecedented technological and social conditions of the time. Remixing therefore offered a way of tapping technological affordances collectively so as to re-create and explore questions around identity and culture. The methods employed in these experiments have been detailed in the preceding chapters. We have suggested that these methods played a significant role in shaping new opportunities for musical practice, technique, and virtuosity. In particular, we have described how using expanded tools for improvisation led to valuable visual and embodied experimentations. Moreover, we have described how experimentation with new digital tools became connected to the development of new music-making objects and innovative formats for presentation. This connection extends to the creation of spaces in which live performance can be combined and mutually interact, bridging the interplay between live performance, the physical realm, and the digital world. What transpired during these kinds of practices was a collective development of a new language—a mode of communication akin to what we outlined first in Chapter 2, through what Russell (2020) terms "a bionic patois" or a form of visual communication that is "suspended between on and offline. Eternally traversing this loop" (p. 45).

Consequently, this "patois" functioned as a transformative force. It challenged and disrupted established communicative categories, such as words and texts and routine musical practices. In doing so, it also redefined and reshaped the parameters of the space or place in which improvisation occurred. By disrupting this space, the patois questioned what counts and should count as given tenets of practice. In challenging the status quo, it prompted a critical reassessment of the foundational elements of understanding practice and, indeed, of the meanings of things more broadly.

We understand space as offering a habitat or place for action and experience. At the same time, we question the distinction between virtual and real spaces. Any space, whether online or in a physical location, is hybridized by imaginative engagement. That engagement projects meaning into spaces. Imaginative engagement furnishes spaces. It adds and modifies the meaning and potential affordances of what comes to count as the content of those spaces (DeNora, 2014). The new GIO improvisatory online space can, in this sense, be understood as a hybrid space: it offered a virtual/real habitat, an at-home space but also a welcoming into others' home spaces, and in ways that transformed each "home" and the experience of being at home. It became, in other words, a space in its own right, one in which creation and transformation into new entities became possible. That space afforded this kind of "becoming" because it blurred previous conventions, enabling both discovery and surprise. In this sense, what unfolded online exemplified a kind of "hoping for difference." In essence, it offered a means for imaginatively rethinking and, potentially, remaking meaningful worlds, understood as modes of relating, understanding, and existing in the world that is both within an online session and beyond, in terms of their "afterlife."

These practices accomplished much more than "music"; they were nothing less than performative practices of world-making (McPherson, 2023) that contribute to what comes to count as the shared meanings and assumptions and working procedures of social life and social perception/judgment. That process of world-making was in turn furthered by the collective myth-making (Sappho, 2022) that took place in GIO over time. We observed how the online experimentation developed new "skills" for practice but also facilitated a form of collective making of the ensemble's history. In this context, history is understood as a platform for the creation of new meaning (Lock, 2000; Onsman and Burke, 2018). Murray (2022) describes this process as "indices of style" that "enable ... the identification of the stylistic characteristics of the embodied music" (p. 3). Therefore, distinctive use of technology by players emerged that became recognizable to the group (as seen in Chapter 4), or moments/spaces are returned to in future improvisations (e.g., Maggie Nicols cooking in a number of different pieces). It offered a sense of continuity and shared history within the ensemble. In considering this collective shared memory as a narrative of self-generated mythology, we can also see how in any collective endeavor, and with any point of reference, there is always something up for "play." With GIO, there were events, objects, and acts that were malleable and that could be drawn across the digital and imagined space into shared history and understanding. We believe that the concept of boundary object (as discussed in Chapter 3) best captures what we mean by this phenomenon, emphasizing how what is initially drawn into the digital space as a mythic reality can find itself becoming, over time and through ritual en-actions, part of a shared, "real" reality. The role of boundary objects in facilitating improvisation and collaboration is crucial in this context.

It became clear that participants who consistently engaged in the Zoom sessions experienced changes in identity. These transformations of identity can be traced at both individual and collective levels, manifesting in small, sometimes microscopic ways, as well as in larger, more noticeable shifts that can be seen to be projected and publicized over time/space: the concept of the Theater of Home, the incorporation of new materials, the shift toward theatricality in "musical" performance, and the collective focus on materials and acts that afforded multiple meanings and yet seemed to carry stable, shared associations (the boundary objects). This facilitated the creation, at least in the online realm, of new—and highly visible and plausible—virtual/real worlds, myths, and shared realities. Moods could be lightened or intensified through the ways that materials—sometimes seemingly trivial ones, like a reference to "lemon cheesecake" or displaying a smiley face image on the top of a knitting needle—and those mood signifiers could be diffused across scenes and audio tracks as participants augmented them, adding, for example, a recipe for lemons (Chapter 6) to the topic of cheesecake, for example, or duplicating an image, such as a smiley face, from another screen. These acts simultaneously elaborated and validated new and initially tentative "furnishings" of the Zoomesphere, allowing new reality claims to be firmed up over time, during the duration of a session and from session to session. The impact extended beyond the confines of a session, influencing what occurred afterward or outside of it. For example, author DeNora experiences hearing the sound of water in her kitchen sink in new ways during a session, subsequently informing her approach to activities like dishwashing thereafter (Chapter 4).

Little by little, new worlds, associations, and affordances were discovered. As GIO piano player and general manager Gerry Rossi put it:

> So in a sense, it's a little utopia that we enter in from time to time... in a way that may sound a little bit corny. That's a world we want to live [in]. We don't want to spend 24 h a day making music on Zoom, but we want to be in a world that everybody has support for each other, everybody is equal, and they respect everybody for what they do. (Gerry Rossi)

These "little utopias" were as empowering as dreaming often is (DeNora, 2021). They scaffolded the increasingly politicized themes addressed in the sessions. The homeliness of the new virtuosity was, as we have described, also a resource for building community. The ways it supported, and indeed encouraged, over-sharing of the domestic and personal experience were also a resource for building confidence and for raising consciousness. From it, new identities emerged and were consolidated. Making new worlds involved and built upon appropriating new technologies for imagining altered realities. And in that imagining, new selves came into being. Thus, a bionic patois, an innovative mode of post-human communication, mediated by technology and consisting of linguistic, musical, and visual interactions, facilitated identity developments for the participants. Fundamental to this new communication and evolving identities was the social construction of shared realities (which then become collective histories) that helped sustain and enhance the group's work, well-being, and cohesion over the pandemic. We now move on to further explore these new realities in the next section

Politics and New Realities: A New Imagined Future?

> What I find most exciting is how it has transformed many of our performance practices. Performers are laughing in the face of mediation, consciously manipulating the digital self, blending live and prerecorded, and generating a regular space for temporary teleportation. (Argo, 2022, n.p.)

Reflecting on this shared world-making, we have come to see how the online experience provides a foundation for adjacent identity change. In GIO sessions, the boundaries between the real and imagined worlds often blur as players furnish the online world with what matters to them, in the moment, and around them in their domestic habitats and beyond. So, intertwined with technology's foregrounded presence in each session, it is possible to notice how participants are engaging in practices that assert needs, hopes, and glimmers of new possible worlds within which lie new possible identities, both personal and communal. These worlds are pressed into reality through players' acts of remixing materials, foregrounding and backgrounding things, introducing new elements, and combining the real (e.g., a chair in a room or a flute that is "really" being played) with the hyper-real (a video-background or a pretend flute or a video capture of another Zoom box where that "real" flute is really being played). Russell (2020) describes the significance of this process:

> The spirit of remixing is about finding ways to innovate with what's been given. Creating something new, from something that is already there. We are faced with the reality that we will never be given the keys to a utopia architectured by hegemony. Instead, we have been tasked with building the world or worlds we want to live in. (Russell, 2020, p. 99)

The remixing has been elucidated in previous chapters where, as we have described, it involves "stuff outside" sound. It encompasses the exploration by players or the group of various facets of what might be developed through the utilization of new tools contributing to the player's identity, as extensively discussed in Chapter 8. The point is that this exploration lies in the projection of imagined and aspirational modes of existence onto the display within the Zoomesphere, creating a manifestation of what might be. This display, in turn, serves as an exemplar, offering insights into the what and, to some extent, the how (methodologically) to effect change and to actualize what is initially performed as art. In this context, GIO's approach to art aligns, arguably, with the historical purpose of art—to find ways of framing and modeling realities. Through such framing and modeling, there is a reorientation of perception and imagination, aiming to integrate these frameworks and models into the "real" world. The anecdote of Picasso painting Gertrude Stein's portrait, with Stein exclaiming, "It does not look like me," and Picasso responding with the assertions that it will in time, underscores this transformative potential inherent in art.

Nonetheless, GIO advances this process further because of the integral role played by technology in its endeavors. What some might classify as "extra-musical" contributions—such as theatrical, visual, and Theater of Home practices—harmonize with the digital environment, augmenting participants' capabilities to depict mythic realities. In other words, the online, real-time format provided a new resource—one that was not possible within in-person contexts: precarity. Over time, the players began to learn a new form of virtuosity, one that merged precarity with extra-musical affordances such as domestic objects and video backdrops. This new virtuosity was particularly well-suited for asserting new identity claims, both individual and collective.

This new virtuosity has a lineage in the forms of social critique associated with earlier developments in the history of music improvisation. For example, the extra-musical toolkit (that is, the set of objects, frames, and practices drawn from outside music into the musical frame—using text in music, for example) has and continues to be used to assist in engaging with artist-led critique. That critique includes an analysis of both musical and social relations, along with an evaluation of prevailing musician values such as virtuosity, mastery, and aesthetics (Krekels, 2019; Reardon-Smith, 2020; Reardon-Smith et al., 2020). Additionally, it extends to a critique of relations in the broader world and the wider social context of works. Historically, this approach to critique can be found in the Feminist Improvising Group (FIG) and in Sun Ra's Arkestra. Both of these performing entities mobilized extra-musical practices in order to assert space for marginalized bodies and perspectives and for legitimate socio-creative identities. FIG aired the "hidden" by dressing in drag, personifying gender roles, and bringing the domestic to the stage. They storied their practice on living politics and tensions (Smith, 2001). Sun Ra intentionally expanded and mythologized the casting of self and community by developing the vision of a future utopian existence of traveling the "spaceways" from planet to planet (Lock, 2000). Sun Ra also proposed that alienation is a very pressing living experience and that therefore interstellar travel is the place to confront this (Szwed, 2020).

> I'm not real, I'm just like you. You don't exist in this society. If you did your people wouldn't be seeking equal rights. (Sun Ra in Coney, 1974, n.p.)

Indeed, these examples show how the GIO sessions evolved into a space of deep personal involvement with global issues, providing a platform to actively engage with politicization throughout this period. The ensemble proactively addressed critical themes; for example, the group explored elements of climate change and global impact in a work developed with Angela Hoyos Gomez for the annual World Listening Day with the World Listening Project[1] (see Figure 9.1; ▶ Film 9.1, June 22, 2021).

QR Code: Please follow this QR code to the ⓟ companion website to view additional content for Chapter 9. Alternatively, you can access the website using the link provided in the front matter.

The group also explored reflections on apocalypse and war as numerous contextual events influenced the thematic focus of the group (see Figure 9.2; ⓟ Film 9.2, September 28, 2021) and, on many occasions, the group embedded collective expressions of grief, mourning, and requiem into their practice. These poignant moments included expressions of sorrow for the immense losses during the pandemic (see Figure 9.3; ⓟ Film 9.3: June 13, 2020), a profound reaction to the murder of George Floyd (group responsive performance on June 2, 2020), and a solemn acknowledgment of the passing of a fellow player within the group (see Figure 9.4; ⓟ Film 9.4, January 19, 2021).

Returning to Russell's notion of bionic patois, it is at these intersections of enforced digital meetings amidst widespread global upheaval that the development of this techno-assisted social commentary and creative mediation was encouraged. In line with the existing link between social change/subversion/critique and the practices of free and improvised musics, the online sessions emerged as a platform for navigating and responding to pressing global issues, with new tools, from a new and more "unspecific" vantage point. GIO did not address politically charged themes from a shared experience or perspective but rather allowed each other to attend to a multitude of "pressing realities"

Figure 9.1. June 22, 2021, The Unquiet Earth by Angela Hoyos Gomez.

New Insights into Understanding Improvisation   163

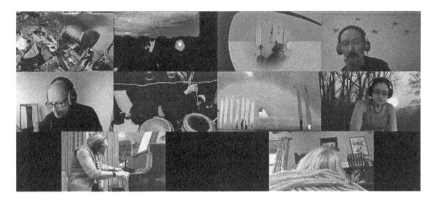

Figure 9.2. September 28, 2021, Apocalyptic Sunrise.

when they emerged within the group. Russell proposes that examples like this expose how our evolving digital languages are helping populate the "digital diaspora"—where bodies, groups, and movements "have no single destination but rather take on a distributed nature, fluidly occupying many beings, many places, all at once" (Russell, 2020, p. 2). For GIO, this facilitated not only identity developments but also significant engagements with global issues that all participants in the international community were experiencing in different ways. It nurtured a collective awareness and engagement with the world's challenges through a process that provides a space for the diversity of the group to drive the production of thematic and creative content. This engagement was further enhanced by the emergence of new virtuosities, developing

Figure 9.3. June 13, 2020, Requiem for the pandemic.

Figure 9.4. January 19, 2021, in memory of John Russell.

a deep connection with aspirational hopes for an imagined better future, as discussed in the next section.

From Activism to Change in Music and in Life

The excerpts from the interviews with GIO members presented throughout the book highlight the ways that GIO's newfound virtuosities also functioned as activist strategies, oriented to changing the scope of what—simultaneously—music and social formation could be and become. We have also observed how the online experience affected what happened after individual sessions and after the pandemic, particularly in live and hybrid performances. For example, during a hybrid performance at the Analix Forever gallery in Geneva (as discussed in Chapter 7, ⓑ Film 7.14), an online improvising group was integrated with the live performing band.

During GIOfest 2021, the concert premiered a collaborative composition titled *Foutraque*, created by the ensemble known as the Noisebringers (comprising author Sappho, Henry McPherson, Brice Catherin) and GIO member Rachel Joy Weiss, based in Miami. *Foutraque* offered a multidimensional, hybrid, transmedia experience, integrating augmented reality, an online and physical ensemble, and actants who facilitated the experience of these mixed realms for both a physical and digital audience. The piece employed a time-based score that encouraged members to self-select when to play based on sociopolitical prompts, resulting in a fluctuating density of performing players and unpredictable sonic and visual content. Within such a format, incorporating lived experiences into a critical analysis, *Foutraque* facilitated political critique illuminating through the detailed experience of individual lives. The inherent specificity, inclusive of its idiosyncrasy and personal features, adds nuance and granularity to otherwise more general issues of equity, justice, and challenge. By showcasing vulnerability, it amplifies the potential for empathy and understanding. Integrating lived experiences into critique, therefore, becomes a powerful tool for conveying political messages in a relatable and compelling manner, transcending traditional boundaries of political discourse. For example, Figure 9.5 (▶ Film 9.5) depicts the score and the corresponding moment in the live performance when the orchestra members were instructed to play "the last thing you play before you die"—but only if performers self-identified as being immigrants.

This format, itself a hybrid of the personal and the collectively produced, brings together elements of experimental music with agitprop theater, political manifesto, and a real-life rallying spirit. Certainly, its capacity to transcend conventional constraints, both in terms of verbal communication and musical genres, renders it a potentially powerful medium for protest music. By drawing from the lessons learned, this mode of expression replicates the complexities of lived experiences in ways that challenge genre constraints. Yet, because of the presence of mundane but profound, complex lived experience,

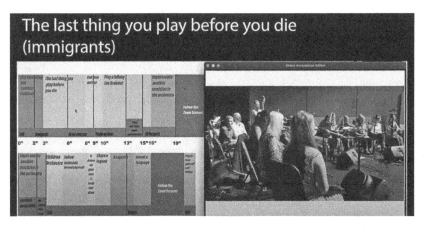

Figure 9.5. *Foutraque* at GIOfest 2021, with the Noisebringers and Rachel Weiss (score and live performance selection).

the format also supports a gentle kind of protest—one that shows rather than tells, orders, or proclaims, one that showcases issues and dramatizes them through the medium of platforming lived experience. This particular form of drama in turn renders protest more accessible and relatable, fostering a deeper connection with those involved and potentially increasing the impact of the political message.

As previously discussed, the development of a skill set that allowed the group to transition between online and offline work became an expression of agency for the group. It allowed the integration of online session practices into a wider transformative journey, fostering an examination of identities, creative processes, and (potentially) future trajectories. In essence, the sessions intertwined with the lives of the players. We presented examples of this integration through our own experiences, as documented in the auto-ethnographic commentaries in Chapter 4. But there were many more examples from the group, such as Faradina Afifi, for whom GIO led to: (a) an opportunity to work with Maggie Nicols, which she described as a dream collaboration; (b) meeting a new life-partner (Steve Beresford) in GIO that culminated in their marriage (they first "noticed" each other during the "glove"-themed improvisation described in Chapter 6); (c) establishing her own improvisation digital groups through which she (d) gained prominence in the UK improvising community and (e) founded *Noisy Women*, an improvisation group and multidisciplinary creative hub championing diversity and collective virtuosity.[2]

Transforming Materialities Through Collaborative Creativities

The preceding chapters and our interviews with the participants have illuminated various transformations occurring in the lives of individual members as a consequence of their engagement in the sessions. This transformative effect is evident in terms of both creative and broader psychological identities, as discussed in Chapter 8. Creatively, a significant transformation occurred with the use of "objects" (as opposed to sounds) as a foundation for collaboration, a point highlighted in the quote from Maggie Nicols early in the chapter. Meanwhile, psychologically, members described the mood-enhancing features of participation:

> Even if I wasn't sure if I was in the mood for it, I always kind of came away with a really positive energy from it as well. Well, I think a lot of people felt that. And so yeah,

> that was the main thing was just that feeling of being connected to other people when we were so disconnected.
>
> And so yeah, psychologically, it was. It was a benefit, I would say it was beneficial to my mental health during the lockdown, for sure. (Stuart Brown)
>
> GIO has been a very important part of nourishing me in a way that is, you know, lifting my spirits enough that I don't default to addiction. (Maggie Nicols)

These creative and psychological affordances of online and later hybrid working are mutually enhancing because, as previously discussed, the use of objects and, more broadly, personal experience as signified by objects enables the expression of politicized sentiments within improvisatory contexts. It also enables participants to "furnish" the improvisatory event with what could be termed "music-Plus," that is, with musical and creative acts that feature the materials of a life. For example, when Maggie Nicols speaks of the significance of "finding objects, finding things that I can use to create textures and stuff" they are also describing the way that the playful yet serious display of objects is "lifting" their spirit and keeping them aligned with habits and practices of well-being and health. The ability to integrate oneself more fully into the ongoing improvisation through the use of significant objects and personal experience is, in essence, a means of establishing a new forum for airing and sharing personal concerns and experiences. It is also a means for confirming and thus affirming the meaning and importance of the personal (objects, "stuff") in ways that, by bridging participants' domestic and wider worlds, also enhance the sense of well-being, lifting spirits and fostering a sense of ontological security. This sense, in turn, generates a foundation for empowerment within this setting, and as elucidated earlier, that empowerment extends beyond the improvisational setting, permeating other realms of life.

Analytically, this underscores one of the "mechanisms" or "active ingredients" responsible for the well-being effects that participants attributed to their GIO experiences. As discussed in Chapter 5, this concept of "making do" involved real-time ingenuity, a sense of being called upon to create something that would inspire or cheer other participants. This aspect became particularly evident in the "gallery view" display mode, where participants, spatially democratized in their own Zoom "box," contributed equally to the visual-sonic collective that defined the GIO habitat online for over 18 months.

Central to that habitat was its proximal materiality. Participants drew from readily available, "indigenous" materials, things that were literally "close to home," most typically things that lay at "arm's length." And over time, participants began to prepare the set of what would lie within reach for use in performance. These items included a variety of objects, such as photos, pots and kitchen utensils, favorite objects, artworks, quickly drawn cartoons, and messages on Post-its. This "close to home-ness" of materials imbued improvisations with an often homespun texture, a weave that was crafted from the personal fields of participants. And, if we agree that "the personal is political," then this proximal, praxial feature of GIO improvisations allowed for the new kind of virtuosic "over-sharing" that came to be a hallmark of GIO during lockdown and beyond. At times, as aforementioned in Chapter 6, those materials, which included masks and recipes for favorite lemon-based foods, became the integral threads of a tapestry woven around the theme of death and dying, exemplifying the phrase "when life gives you lemons."

Thus, the online format of GIO not only blended the "real" and the "virtual" in ways that subject both to deconstruction, but also facilitated for the fusion of the real and the virtual in ways that allowed the virtual to become a ground for the actual. For example, virtual flutes were able to interact by blending with real ones, or when sampled images of one person's screen in which domestic materials were featured were re-deployed on another person's screen as modified visual backdrops. In these ways, and in the fusing of what might (wrongly) be termed "fantasy" and "reality," GIO embodies the notion of "carrying" dreams, as described by DeNora, where dreams are brought into lived, actual experiences embodying realistic hope. The gallery view, in other words, became a way of showcasing everyday dreams, such as the dream of being together or reaching out to hug or touch—recalling the importance of hands close to the camera. These situations elevated mundane objects into works of art, illuminated by the camera lens, transcending their ordinary status. As such, this new virtuosity facilitated a participatory micro-aesthetic where everything had the potential to become art, momentarily, not just in principle but in reality. The latent, or potential artfulness, the beauty of things hitherto unsung in GIO improvisations—rubber gloves, a kitchen whisk, a cat or a dog, a leaf of kale—became manifest. Thus, the "local" became "global" as participants shared micro-features of their mundane existence from boxes that hailed from 20+ countries and 10 time zones. The aesthetic also offered a (democratic) WYSIWYG (what you see is what you get) principle, flattening hierarchies in the service of the Theater of Home and in the service of what participants came to speak of as a collective, online "Home."

In the context of this flattened aesthetic, the absence or potential absence of a backstage is notable. Information that is not typically shared finds expression, rendering the concept of "too much information" theoretically implausible (e.g., declarations like "I have not been kissed for six months"). Material ordinarily deemed unsuitable for inclusion in music improvisation is shared. Consequently, the inclusion of new materials becomes a deliberate, albeit occasionally unintended (e.g., when under the guise of humor), political act. This transcends the personal-political or the global-local dichotomy; it extends to procedural aspects, delineating how, within the realm of music, we establish paradigms for social behavior.

The technology and the way in which it was embraced afforded a radical political aesthetic. In the gallery view, where everyone sees everyone, boundaries are blurred between real and virtual, fantasy and reality, appropriate and inappropriate material, and avatars and real-world presences. These blurred boundaries enable a type of created results that lead to shared fantasies and co-created utopian dreams. During the challenges of lockdown, this new virtuosity, intertwined with a new communality, fostered hope. Through hope, a sense of well-being emerged. In this dreamscape, hope involves furnishing or fleshing out scenarios of what "might" happen and what can be built virtually and in reality, collaboratively.

Within the GIO online environment, seemingly trivial aspects, such as choices in attire, how players position themselves, and the objects individuals place in front of the camera, contribute to more enduring patterns. These patterns, as illustrated in the previous chapter, include experimenting with makeup, transitioning from instruments to light displays, and musically adapting their playing/use of instruments to "sound different." Moreover, participants showcased facets of themselves beyond their roles as musicians, assuming identities as cooks, gardeners, swimmers, walkers, cyclists, travelers, parents, and more. Collectively, these actions enable individuals and the collected gallery to present themselves in this new "theater" as different kinds of people and as a different kind of collective.

The materialities inherent in the Zoom session—household objects, clothes, instruments, furniture, and so on—underwent transformation through their deployment in a communal creative process. This transformation is facilitated by their close proximity to the creative activities enabled by the technology. Significantly, these creative activities would not have unfolded in the same manner if not for the social distancing regulations imposed by the pandemic. Therefore, we can assert that important materialities have been transformed through technology-mediated collaborative creativities

From Experiencing the Future and Adapting to the New

These social and artistic developments continued and evolved as the group moved back into the physical venue—the Centre for Contemporary Arts (CCA) in Glasgow—where GIO rehearses and performs in person. Notable changes in this transition back to in-person performances involve enfolding the outside environment into sessions, as discussed in Chapter 7. This includes how the members of GIO communicate, perceive, and integrate elements from their daily surroundings into the rehearsals. These carryovers help to consolidate identity stances that are taken from online learnings and into new arenas.

This chapter has synthesized a number of new insights into our understanding of improvisation through the analysis of the online sessions. We have emphasized how improvisation facilitated new types of post-genre and post-disciplinary artistic practices. The online sessions (Zoomesephere) have also facilitated the integration of local and domestic issues and contexts, encapsulated within the Theater of Home, into a global network of artists. The emergence of these new practices signifies the development of new virtuosities, not only acting as a foundation for artistic expression but also influencing broader life practices and sensibilities. It introduces what can be described as a new virtuosity of and in everyday life, highlighting the profound impact of improvisation on participants' daily experiences.

10
Beyond the Theater of Home

Toward Improvisational Hybridity

This chapter discusses the broader implications of our research and findings with a focus on how the possibilities explored through many hybrid environments came to be normalized in a post-pandemic global landscape. The discussion focuses on the insights gained from our work. It emphasizes the potential that online experiences offer for future creative practices. To that end, just as we began the book by sharing our initial experiences of being part of GIO during the pandemic, we close by sharing our experiences of what GIO over the past four years has meant to us and how it has had an impact on our daily lives and professional practice. Our individual reflections constitute one of the few occasions in this book where readers will be reading a paragraph—or for that matter, even a sentence—written entirely by one member of the authorial "quintet." Our final individual responses embody the twists and turns of a quintet of collaborative, creative, and occasionally over-sharing authors who embraced the notion and possibilities of "melding" together.

Duality of Identities—"I Zoom, Therefore We Are"

Undoubtedly, the prevalence of hybrid activity is increasingly evident in both the workplace and in personal contexts, with ongoing discussions exploring the opportunities and challenges associated with this trend. Consequently, identities associated with working environments will reflect virtual shifts that are inextricably linked to technology. As a result, negotiating the multiple concerns of in-person communication and virtual communication will remain a perennial topic for debate in the future. Ironically, our research suggests that performers working in isolation have, somewhat unexpectedly, created opportunities to discover innovative collaboration methods and to establish collective connections. Using technology to stay connected to wider communities has also precipitated new ways of viewing ourselves as individuals with both virtual and non-virtual identities coexisting at the

New Directions in Musical Collaborative Creativity. Raymond MacDonald, Tia DeNora, Maria Sappho, Robert Burke, and Ross Birrell, Oxford University Press. © Oxford University Press 2025. DOI: 10.1093/oso/9780197752838.003.0010

same time. Moreover, it has acted as a catalyst for reimagining communication in new and enhanced ways, extending beyond text to incorporate gesture and visual media. As depicted in this book, this transformative shift has reshaped the embodied nature of our communication. The convergence of virtual and non-virtual identities is palpable, manifesting both literally—through the simultaneous existence of a digital avatar and a physical person performing on Zoom—and metaphorically, as regular interactions reshape our self-perception. Conceptually, a new type of duality has emerged, virtual versus non-virtual, captured in the notion of "I Zoom, therefore we are." This encapsulates the essence of the communicative episodes outlined in this book. What is particularly intriguing is that this duality transcends simplistic binaries, that virtual and non-virtual identities can intertwine and blend, giving rise to new types of embodied communication. This novel type of creative collaboration also resonates with the concepts of distributed creativity discussed below.

Returning to Donna Haraway's provocation, "Why should our bodies end at the skin, or include at best other beings encapsulated by skin?" (Haraway, 1991, 178): our exploration of GIO and hybridity illuminates how technologies help us to reimagine how we communicate and connect, challenging traditional notions of physical, psychological, and technological boundaries and borders. Indeed, whatever we come to recognize as our body, our bodies are inevitably the outcome of our place in relation to materials, media, and technologies. We are, for example, weightless when in water or in outer space, less likely to perceive pain if engaged in something we value and find meaningful, beautiful, or interesting. Previously, the prevalence of more traditional forms of online real-time telecommunication was considered a "specialist" mode of communication, distinct from "normal" interaction. This perspective tended to overlook the fact that all communication is mediated by objects, technologies, and constructed environments. For example, we may speak in hushed voices when in a religious or sacred setting, shout to be heard across a crowded room, incorporate additional gestures in a noisy room, or employ props or imaginary props when recounting experiences (such as a symbolic phone, lifting a top hat, bows, etc.).

However, more recently, and as a response to the seismic changes in global communications precipitated by COVID-19 and the contexts of online communication platforms like Zoom, this dynamic has undergone a radical change. These platforms have acted as a catalyst, making visible the fluid and emergent nature of embodiment. For example, digital avatars merge with real-life bodies (as evidenced in many of our film examples), challenging the conventional notion that bodies are delimited by skin barriers. Instead, they can be understood to be extended entities that merge with avatars. This process of "merging" and emergent experiences fosters new identifications and new understandings of what it might be like to be another—another body, another kind of being. Just as our bodies have historically been extended or augmented by prosthetic technologies such as spectacles, artificial limbs, hearing aids, microscopes, and telescopes, we can now contemplate the notion of extended or augmented communities facilitated by prosthetic technologies. The process of "merging" and emergent experiences fostered by virtual technologies heightens and extends our sense of community. Additionally, the complexities of embodied communication, bodies, boundaries, and technologies not only challenge conventional concepts of communication and normal embodiment but also compel us to interrogate the evolving concept of what it means to be a human in the face of rapid technological progress.

Humanity is partially defined by the idea and practice of communication. A hybrid, virtual environment allows communication to evolve and widen in remit, to include embodied formats that do more than stand in for words; these formats enable communication to transcend words. In many ways, the same argument is often used for music, in that musical communication can often take place when verbal communication is not possible, and music can express ideas and feelings that words alone may struggle to articulate. The artistic collaborations we have discussed offer opportunities for emotional, conceptual, and community-based modalities of meaning; they allow matters that are part of our consciousness but which may be challenging to express explicitly to be shared and communicated with others—and with ourselves. In the following, we consider some examples of this evolving mode of communicative development.

The Growth of the Human Archive and Its Politics

A significant idea discussed throughout this book revolves around the adoption of the term "Theater of Home," which utilizes the fusion of private and everyday spaces as a starting point for creating a diverse and innovative performance stage. The genesis of this work began in intimate domestic spaces and gradually expanded to encompass more public spaces as the pandemic transitioned out of lockdown. Nevertheless, a pervasive theme of the works produced by GIO involved the development of blended realities, incorporating elements such as commutes, kitchens, holiday destinations, railway stations, airports, cafes, places of work, gardens, and more. Enabled by the Zoom medium, this new practice emerged and afforded players the ability to "over-share" and creatively utilize multifaceted portions of their life and identity in performance in ways that they had not aired previously. This capacity to amplify one's own lived experience has been seen to be both psychologically beneficial and personally valuable, providing a platform to articulate aspects that are often challenging to communicate in traditional physical world settings—in a sense, an amplified "selfie" in this new world!

Given that a major aspect of our research signifies a transformative shift toward inclusive and often more "intimate" global collaboration, it is important to consider the cultural and technological implications of how future advancements in technology further influence work in these domains. Digital events have undergone a clear revolution during the pandemic period, encompassing the use of software such as Zoom to host conferences, concerts, weddings, funerals, church services, and more. With the global acceptance of the concept of live-streamed events, advancements in technologies aimed at enhancing the experience of participating in these digital spaces are poised to gain significant traction. Significantly, the evolution of integrative technologies for wearable XR (extended reality) experiences is emerging, fueled by a renewed interest in these technologies during the pandemic which has already prompted digital initiatives for VR (virtual reality) artistic spaces, including VR artist residencies and gallery exhibitions. Closely following these developments are advancements in hardware, such as head-mounted-displays (HMDs) like the Apple Vision Pro, which are already entering the market, albeit at the high end of accessibility. Additionally, digital contact lenses are within reach of our technological capabilities (Lee and Quifan, 2021). When combined with the now commonplace live-streaming and mixed-reality spaces, a new narrative for the documentation and sharing of a plethora of human space appears poised to emerge. This suggests that, much like the adaptive and often unintended creative uses found for Zoom over the course of the pandemic, technology is emerging more and more as an intrinsic and influential agent in the development of new creative practices. Moreover, it serves as a marker for critical new sociopolitical conversations around our emergent techno-social worlds.

First, as XR devices become more affordable and accessible, they are likely to permeate the common world space on a large scale. In contrast to GIO's trajectory in developing the Zoomesphere, XR devices might initially be limited to home or work settings such as for conferencing/meetings or gaming. However, over time, they are expected to extend into the public sphere, influencing areas such as travel, shopping, and holidays. This development is noteworthy not only for the evident implications of an expanded integration of technology into social life but also because their increased presence in the broader public sphere will carry far-reaching consequences for the type of data that can be collected and documented about our human world.

Second, while not directly related to XR experiences, the emergence of automated vehicles serves as a relevant context to comprehend the implications of sophisticated new technologies entering public spaces. It is crucial to consider this aspect in order to understand the impact that technology is already having on our notions of privacy. At the time of writing, the California Commission has recently approved the operation of automated taxis in the San Francisco area (Bhuiyan, 2023). Activists opposed to the rise of automated vehicles highlight a core concern—these machines essentially function as giant 360 cameras, continuously driving around the city, documenting and storing all aspects of life in their surroundings (Roose and Newton, 2023). Companies operating these machines are already engaged in collaborative relationships with law enforcement and government officials, as the data collected from these vehicles hold significant benefits for crime prevention. Consequently, the resulting implications on personal privacy are pressing. In a future where automated vehicles become a commonplace technology, the value of our everyday public social actions undergoes a shift. It becomes highly lucrative for companies to own extensive amounts of human data. This example is significant because similar issues will inevitably be entwined with the development of wearable XR technologies, where users can integrate them into vast areas of their personal and public lives.

Third, a particularly promising domain where technology can make significant contributions is artificial intelligence (AI), which stands as one of the fastest-growing and controversial realms of technology-assisted art practices globally and merits some further discussion. AI, as a broad term, encompasses a diverse range of computer-based technologies that facilitate learning and decision-making in machines. AIs have the capacity to emulate specific types of decision-making skills found in the human mind, integrating problem-solving capabilities and automating tasks traditionally carried out by humans. With the abrupt rise of internet platform chat-based and multimodal AI machines, access to and experimentation with AI is now much more for specialists and non-specialists alike, prompting a major wave of arts-based AI practices now emerging. GIO, for example, has made several collaborative works with AI both during and post-pandemic in a series of hybrid improvisations and compositions. GIO continues to work in collaboration with the Swiss-developed "Chimère" AI,[1] made in partnership with the AiiA festival[2] and the Chimère Communities project—initiatives intent on questioning the significant access, marginalization, and dataset concerns of this new burgeoning field. One of the many worrying developments in this area is the growing alarm at the centrality of power—what companies control the markets and the tools, and the resulting continued and often noted warning that these groundbreaking new technologies are poised to further exacerbate global inequalities (Klien, 2023).

Moving beyond this project and contemplating a projected technological future, characterized by enmeshed techno-social worlds, raises questions about data collection, surveillance, and their impact on everyday human culture. The intention here is not to delve into the numerous geopolitical ramifications, which exceed the scope of this book, but rather to focus on the specific and related element of human cultural change that these machines will affect, with a particular focus on the role of art in responding to these shifts.

These numerous examples of the integration of how human cultural data are developed and employed in new technology prompt consideration of how we will adapt to a world with more opaque notions—of public and private space, of globality, human-machine relationships, and so on. Reflecting on the experiences of GIO offers valuable insights into how individuals may soon navigate decisions about what to reveal or conceal, which aspects of their identity to amplify, and ultimately, what versions of performance to experiment with as they integrate these technologies to meet personal needs and community goals. The examples from GIO are notably occurring within a closed and trusted community, contrasting with the overtly public nature of contemporary social media culture. However, GIO has nevertheless begun to navigate a changed world where the significance, meaning, and value of mundane and private actions undergo a re-evaluation; a sort of digital dada-ism, for example, might now be said to be emerging. In this future, where technology affords enhanced experiences in hybrid spaces, delving into realms of surveillance, or at the very least heightened documentation, we will enter a space where culturally we will face new questions about how these data should be used, stored, and monetized. These new sociocultural questions will undoubtedly be explored by artists as they hack and subvert these spaces, shaping and building alternative uses and responses to the rapidly shifting social contexts.

Global Connectedness

At the heart of the practices explored in this book are the narratives of intertwining social communities, global expansion, and generative new practices facilitated through the use of a range of new technologies. We have discussed how technology has impacted the generation and empowerment of digital identities. This exploration is underscored by such theories as techno-feminist and Harrawayan notions of the body in mix with technology, and the value of technology within these spaces to provide agency for novel globalized and marginalized perspectives. What we have discovered is, as in any other human time period, our "notions" of community are in flux and are prompting contemplation of how our cultures might leverage the new tools afforded to them, how these new mediums might affect our creative sectors, and what risks and benefits we might gain as a global society.

Theorists have continued to explore these issues, drawing inspiration from the works of Jacques Derrida, Félix Guattari, and Gilles Deleuze. These theorists advocate a more collaborative, less hierarchical, and less individualized approach to theory development, exemplified by rhizomatic theory, where ideas emerge, develop, and propagate via collective endeavors rather than solitary work (Ruud, 2022). Stacy Alaimo's concept of "Transcorporeality," built upon Haraway's work, highlights the ambiguous or even nonexistent boundaries between material bodies, technology, and theory (Alaimo, 2008). This perspective aligns with a meta-modern notion of identities that emphasizes oscillations, challenges conventional dualities and binaries, and opens up the possibilities of positioning post-human identities and transcorporeality as the very conditions of life (Kilicoglu and Kilicoglu, 2020; MacDonald, 2023). Like Haraway, Alaimo's concept of transcorporeality involves the blending of the human body with the external environment, as exemplified in our examples of individuals playing music on Zoom.

Transcorporeality emphasizes that our bodies are intertwined with nature and technology, so in the physical material world, our bodies are blended, mirroring the blended experiences of a Zoom call, as can be seen in many of the film examples in this book. Bodies blend into virtual backgrounds, hands playing instruments appear disembodied, and digital avatars merge with real people. Importantly, transcorporeality also highlights how this blurring of boundaries affects our sense of agency, creating numerous implications for our sense of agency. Thus, by harnessing this duality of expressive modality where in-person communication and virtual communication merge, new ideas can blossom and self-reliance in enhanced agency can be strengthened. At the same time, it can embolden the formation of community identities, as demonstrated in our interviews. This dynamic can be applied in formal and semi-formal contexts for educational, therapeutic, and social benefit, with music and the arts providing a unique context for these developments. In these contexts, the developments outlined in this book, driven by technological affordances, are clearly linked to global agendas where new technologies such as AI are facilitating a whole host of new artistic works, innovative collaborations, and are inviting us to reimagine what it means to be collectively artistic. These debates also precipitate more contentious debates regarding human agency, autonomy, control, and the extent to which AI might replace humans not only in artistic endeavors but also in the daily tasks of everyday life.

Accompanying these developments are discussions around the extent to which AIs can function independently of human involvement. These issues are not entirely new and relate to the nature of human consciousness. However, the rapid rise of AI and technologies such as Zoom has brought into stark relief the extent to which identity and consciousness may or may not be unique to our species. Panpsychism, the belief that all things, living and non-living, have a mind-like quality (Goff and Moran, 2021), articulates closely with these debates. Engaging in online collaborative creative activities, mediated by technology, facilitates an exploration of these issues. As we have shown, the processes and outputs of these activities involve rapidly evolving identities, as participants renegotiate the nature of their embodied communication, while at the same time establishing new social groups, utilizing new types of communication, and creating new artworks.

We propose that these new types of emergent communication represent new virtuosities. Moreover, we suggest that many of the new virtuosities exemplified in Chapter 7, the wider contributions for contemporary education, therapy, and community-building discussed in Chapter 8, and the implications for understanding creative practice and identity discussed in Chapter 9 will be central insights into ways socio-creative culture might be considered as the practices identified in GIO enter more elements of our lives. Given the speculation on the future technologies that are poised to advance these practices, it is worthwhile to consider some of the core cultural changes we see emerging in regard to the implications of GIO's experiences of building, sustaining, and ultimately normalizing this hybrid, "over-sharing," and globally connected techno-creative community.

What we posit is that the combined effect of the pandemic's unprecedented global social changes spurred a technological response to find new ways to keep people connected. Many of these approaches have become so ubiquitous that there is now a much broader investment in contributing to developing these tools, including the enhanced experiences possible with new kinds of technologies that contribute to a more digitally interconnected world (Koumaditis et al., 2021). For example, GIO has amassed over 500 hours of video-recorded weekly rehearsal sessions capturing not only artistic processes but also a rich tapestry of human experiences. GIO represents just one instance of a group leveraging the pandemic and technology in this manner. It is nearly inconceivable to quantify the countless hours of human activities documented since 2020. The archive of our human world has experienced an unprecedented expansion, not focused solely on carefully curated facets of life or a select group of "valued" individuals, but rather delving into the messy everyday realities of ordinary people engaged in extraordinary activities. This archive encapsulates improvisations in airports, celebrations of births, expressions of grief over deaths, casual conversations, parties, moments of joy and laughter, audio-visual records of human interactions, depictions of living spaces, expressions of fear, reflections and concerns over world events, and the evolution of communities, countries, and individual lives (Sappho, 2022). The divide between what constitutes performance and non-performance, private and public space, and what is suitable for recording has markedly shifted. Whether for better or worse, our daily actions, creative collaborations, and connections across vast distances have been meticulously documented and archived. This vast collection not only encompasses an array of unimaginable content for potential future exploration but also provides insight into how we have adapted to this new form of human documentation and the novel ways our communities navigate and normalize the expanded public-private space. The Theater of Home has become immense.

Nearly the Final Word

In the realm of experimental improvisation, the pursuit of generating new ideas collaboratively is the cornerstone that is embraced by improvisers who focus on innovation and are part of the "communal ownership" of the music (George Lewis in Onsman and Burke, 2018). This endeavor is intrinsic to our approach to crafting new creative projects and the shaping and evolution of artistic identity. By delving into uncharted territories of creativity, this book afforded us, the authors, the opportunity to make sense of further meanings of how experimentation informed creativity. This sense-making was achieved through the process of participating in the performance, learning, expressing, collaborating, and uncovering innovative approaches that influence the creative process in the journey of being an improviser and researcher in this field. What we have learned through this process is that the sociological, psychological, and practical constructs of this research have created the potential of participants to not only bolster a sense of agency and self-esteem in improvisation but also, more broadly, cultivate enhanced communication skills.

Those communicative and agentic developments have been central to the new identities linked to the overall well-being of participants and these, interwoven with constructs of learnings and experiences, constitute a new form of improvisational intelligence (Onsman and Burke, 2018), one that embraces an assemblage and actioning of both the tangible and intangible elements of this hybridity: the tangible encompassing the aforementioned technical elements, agency, and environment factors. In contrast, the intangible, involving the ineffable and ephemeral understanding of emotions such as trust, hope, and fear (Crawford, 2000), helped shape our identity as both individuals and as a collective (GIO) that foregrounded and backgrounded a shared passion, uniting us as kindred spirits in the pursuit of being creative beings. Finally, we argue that central to what constitutes new creativities—and the central thesis of this book—is the importance of the empowering agency of exploration and experimentation in improvisation. Through this, we assert that our discourse into an online and hybrid approach to improvisation has contributed to the notion of a new collaborative creativity. For each of us authors and artists, these new forms of creativity have resonated uniquely within our "quintet" and contribute individually to our creative journeys.

Final Words from the Authors

From Raymond: Remember Fun and Relational Quantum Mechanics

Stephen Nachmanovitch in *Free Play* (2024) emphasizes the importance of improvised play and fun in the development of social and artistic skills. As our sessions began in March 2020, I was struck by how much fun I was having. Indeed, at times we were conscious that in the midst of such global and local turmoil, we were having extremely enjoyable and rewarding and playful experiences. Looking back at recordings of those early sessions, which, at the time of writing, were nearly four years ago, I can appreciate how significant they were. Not least, because as well as creative breakthroughs emerging, new friendships were blossoming and old ones were flourishing. One important reason for these joyful advances was that we were all having fun! It was uplifting to see so many smiling faces on the recordings, and hear laughter, jokes, and camaraderie infuse the seriousness with which we engaged in our artistic work. However, I was also struck by the profound sadness and empathy that were also evident at times, particularly as we discussed world events and personal struggles. Sometimes the personal struggles were not explicitly mentioned but were evident in nonverbal communication. Reviewing the recorded material with the advantage of time, I can see how these highs and lows were profoundly important to us. They infused all the improvisations with an urgency, sometimes playful and fun filled, at other times mournful. However, the improvisations were performed with a seriousness that engendered an artistic and conceptual gravitas. This gravitas undoubtedly helped propel us into new uncharted areas.

Focusing on the specific socio-technological context of these new uncharted areas, we propose that improvisation offers a flexible, creative, spontaneous social process that can help people engaged in artistic endeavors use innovative technologies effectively. This engagement facilitates new creative insights, which can also have a positive impact on health and well-being. Moreover, engaging in this unique creative environment, the Zoomesphere, with technology at its heart, highlights the importance of embracing new approaches to musical engagement that move beyond what might be considered conventional craft-based conceptions of musicality. These new competencies, or new musical virtuosities, include a range of skills such as collaborating, listening, creative engagement, decision-making, and ethical interactions, emphasizing the broader relational aspects of music-making, some of which are unique to the process of musicking. These types of musical interactions, while unique, still influence, and are influenced by, everyday social interactions.

This link with everyday social interactions is crucial since it "normalizes" musical engagement and emphasizes our universal capacity for musicality. At the heart of these artistic, social, and psychological developments are musical identities that are evident in all the different types of musicking in which the participants engaged, as outlined in the preceding chapters. The nature of musical identities is fundamentally performative, evolving and influenced by specific situations and contexts (MacDonald and Saarikallio, 2022). The evidence gleaned from the interviews presented has demonstrated how these activities have had a positive impact on the musical identities of the participants. This contribution to the development of healthy musical identities has been suggested as a key goal for music education, facilitating lifelong engagement with music. Healthy musical identities are also linked to wider social and psychological developments that can develop with a fuller engagement with new musical virtuosities (MacDonald and Saarikallio, 2024). This work, in particular the collaborative nature of the working practices studied, also raises important issues of coauthorship and the importance of foregrounding aspects of co-creation and distributed creativity. The artistic processes and outputs of the sessions integrate diverse ideas from many individuals into specific outputs. This is an important aspect of the current work since it challenges individualistic notions of creativity, which view creativity as a singular process emanating from within any given individual. The reality of creativity is that it is socially constructed and distributed across many individuals and situations, as our work highlights.

From a personal perspective, one key aspect of this project was experiencing the nature of my embodied artistic communication change on a week-by-week basis. As I became more familiar with playing music on Zoom, I became fascinated by a new type of relationship between the visual and the musical. Seeing my saxophone and the other players on a computer monitor at the same time as playing completely changed my experience of improvisation. Since I heard my virtual colleagues through my small computer speakers, or occasionally through headphones, playing my saxophone as I had previously done was not appropriate in this context, and so I modified my playing to adapt to these new conditions. I found this process both liberating and exhilarating. I became interested in how my hands moved on the instrument and how small finger movements translated into sonic gestures and how those sonic gestures merged with the visual images on the computer screen. I also became interested in developing virtual backgrounds and blending them with sonic elements. Using virtual backgrounds to communicate with other musicians in different locations became another area for exploration. As the weeks progressed, I began experimenting by recording short films that could then be used during the session by integrating musical elements with the short films. It became possible to communicate with other musicians who were also experimenting visually and sonically with this new Zoom environment so that small subgroups would emerge within a larger improvisation. The Zoom context allowed these small groups to flourish while also contributing to the larger improvised structures being developed by the whole group.

While focusing on the personal, it would be remiss not to finish by emphasizing our collective experience. It was collectivity, community engagement, and a utopian (to quote Gerry Rossi from earlier in this book) sense of artistic togetherness that was one of the most important aspects of this project. On April 25, 2022, Alípio Carvalho Neto, one of the stalwarts of our sessions, arranged for a special online session. We performed *Bella Ciao*, a freedom song of resistance against fascism, as part of a solemn ceremony in the town of Rapolano Terme in Italy to mark the annual Italian "Day of Liberation" from Nazi fascism. This was a special performance; it emphasized the extent to which our online community had developed a sense of collectivity where we could perform as part of an important civic event as a band with an overarching identity that transcended the individual personalities of each member. This moment highlighted for me the extent to which the relational aspects of identities and the distributed nature of creative and collective endeavors were fundamental to our developing sense of the importance of the sessions.

Being engaged in a new activity, deeply personal, yet dependent upon the friendship, trust, and generosity of others, made me reflect on the importance of seeing my own personality, embodiment, and creative practice as merged and inextricably linked to others. We have discussed throughout the book how the understanding of participants' experiences takes place through a relational lens; that the experiences of the individuals foreground the importance of social contexts and networks of families and friends. The importance of understanding behavior by exploring relational features is not unique to social sciences. Carlo Rovelli, in his recent book *Helgoland*, proposes that in order to gain an understanding of the nature of tiny particles, such as electrons, we must understand their behavior in relation to other particles (Rovelli, 2022). When I first read these ideas, it made me immediately think of the online sessions, and how individuals' experiences of these sessions could only be understood by taking into account other people's experiences. Of course, psychology has offered multiple ways of viewing individuals as merged within a social context, whether that be from a social constructionist perspective (Potter and Wetherall, 1987) or a Jungian collective unconscious perspective (Stein, 1998) or many others. However, for me, participating in the online session gave new meaning and insight into the extent of our relational identities. Relational quantum mechanics emphasizes the fundamental importance of relations when trying to understand how the universe is constructed in much the same way that the online interactions gave me an even stronger appreciation of the relational aspects of personality and creative activities. Thus, not only are relational understandings fundamental to understanding collaborative creative practices, human behavior, and post-human psychology; an understanding of relational practices is core to understanding how the universe functions. Relating is at the heart of existence—from the smallest particles we know through to humans, pets, mushrooms, and post-human entities.

From Maria: Caring for a New Home

I am a baby of the nineties and therefore my entire life has felt like an entangled dance with the advance of (digital) technology in partnership with my cultural and contextual frames. As far back as I can remember, I have been building and caring for digital space and focusing on my hybrid presentation of self amidst others. When we were kids, we took care of NeoPets and learned a lot about caring for a digital being and operating as a digital human in a community space of peers. When we were pre-teens, we would secretly make Myspace accounts, learning to code—mine looked like a "pimp my ride" and played rap music—yet another example of my own path to coping with what digital version of myself, what elements of my culture, my interests, and my politics I wanted to foreground. Or when we had sleepover parties we would covertly explore Chat Roulette—a taboo and often risky space of the randomized video conference calls where you would be thrown into a conversation with anyone in the world—a now retro set of digital spaces that nevertheless were the locations of my first adventures in this very expanded internet age world.

Nevertheless, something seems to have taken place amidst this global pandemic and wider period of seemingly growing social unrest—the need and dangers of bionic adaptation seem hyper-present in new ways. Maybe the pandemic gave me new eyes to notice this shift, but the experiences of GIO helped me understand that the need to embed in learning to live and prosper in a techno-cultural world is, and has always been, the quiet drum, learning curve, and experimentation ground for the world I will continue to grow alongside.

This book has been about (in a broad sense) the role of new techno-social practices and their effect on challenging existing tensions, contributing toward dissolving disciplinary boundaries, questioning meritocracy, and further identifying hegemonic logics so that usable practices might be built and incorporated toward effective resistance and reform. But put in the subjective, the entangled techno-contextual development is more specifically a consequence influencing how we view our own reality and by proxy our creative influence on the world. And so in an attempt to summarize these thoughts, there are three major shifts (for me) that are products of this flourishing new creative practice, the writing of this book, and the solidifying of friendships and community over these past few tectonic years.

First, expanded realities are critical playgrounds, they are more obvious/accessible via a technology-enhanced practice—the x-reality or the *x-artist* offers alternatives for acting within a world. But these realities are not housed in the digital alone; once grasped, these new versions/possibilities for self and life might be drawn across to any other reality which we operate in, and this is powerful.

Second, as we free ourselves and wander in the expanded possibility of a reality, we are also confronted with a much more complex landscape brimming with new kinds of relationships. Surprisingly, living a life and building a community practice (a community resistance) online has brought me closer to physical bodies, soil, and alternate systems for sociality in fungal, plant, and human logics, too. We should continue to attend to this growing social virtuosity, which is as much a practice as it is a cultural power.

And finally, I keep returning to the notion of "care" as emblematic of this period, wrapped in the greater reality of a pandemic, made all the more palpable—through forced proximity with some, and isolation from others, through endless hours "stuck" in very real physical homes, to infinite possibilities of building new kinds of home-like spaces in hybrid and fantastical ways. I do believe that I have been part of a project which has built a home—a home that is in defiance of the master's tools, but also equipped with a table from which we might sit down and break bread with the major issues of our time, and which we are still developing a practice for taking care of as an amorphous bunch of roommates.

From Tia: A Force for Good

Writing this book about improvisation online, about GIO's discovery and elaboration of what we've called the Theater of Home, has been vitally important for me and for everything I have been doing since. To say that GIO has been a "force for good" in my life is an understatement. But it is also true that many of the research lessons I have learned in my various projects over the past four years have been traceable back to the ways they have interacted with what happened, and is still happening, in GIO and to the truly interdisciplinary character of our endeavor.

Before I was invited to join the then nascent GIO research project (and play as a "member of the band"—as Raymond once called me—a very proud moment), I had just begun work on the Care for Music project, in tandem with music therapists Gary Ansdell, Wolfgang Schmid, and Fraser Simpson. That work focused on how and under what circumstances people at or near the end of their lives might still "care for" music—how they engaged with, and actively made, music, and how they did this, as it were, in concert with others. We were exploring this theme in scenes of residential care—hospices and a "neurodisability care facility" (I prefer the term, a place where people are living, caring for, and being cared for). We were interested in the ways that caring for music might not only interact with but perhaps also help to structure the shape of care as demonstrated in more conventional ways. We were interested in how that musical care might affect things such as the quality of the relationship between care staff and residents. We were interested in, most broadly, what can happen when music happens, how and when music might (or might not!) support communicative action when other modalities were not readily to hand.

Then came the pandemic, and with it, lockdown. By December 2020, in Norway, Wolfgang was able to return to in-person music-making with hospice patients (Schmid 2020). Fraser was working online with the hospice choir and with individual service users. The choir recorded two beautiful songs, making them by asynchronous alignment of each voice to the next. But at the care facility where Gary was working, with people many of whom were not able on their own to use Zoom or to sing in a shared tempo or a shared pitch, what to do?

There was much discussion around "can this project be conducted remotely, online?" We quickly realized we had nothing to lose. We began to discover that not only Gary, but also the residents and the care staff, knew a thing or two about how to make it work, how to keep the music flowing, keep the social connection strong, virtually. . . .

Fast-forward to July 2020. Taking part in the World Congress of Music Therapy, a memorial session for Mercedes Pavlicevic, I attended the Congress's final online social gathering (it would have been a party-reception had the event been held in person). There were a few moments when no one remembered to mute. There were a couple of hundred of us. I remember thinking that the strange sounds emitted from my speakers were rather beautiful. And then Raymond wrote to ask if I would be interested in joining the team of GIO researchers.

This was a breakthrough moment, and a lot of the story of what it taught me has been recounted in the previous pages of this book. Those lessons had immediate, so-called "transferrable" effects on me—as a researcher, but also as a person, a person who likes to, and wants to, communicate.

There was an alchemy between what happened in GIO (both the sessions and the research project) and what was happening in Care for Music—and what I now see happening in a more recent project at Mountbatten Hospice, Isle of Wight (DeNora, 2023). The discovery of how, under some duress associated with the separation of people, it was still more than possible to connect and to connect through music (if not quite music as we knew it) was a watershed. New or renewed music and music-making/music-sharing practices, and the new technologies that afforded such practices, could draw otherwise separate people and groups of people back together again. It was incidental whether that separation was physical (due to the pandemic and lockdown), psycho-social-cognitive (due to some people's—the term used is—post-verbal situations), or the ultimate form of separation (due to some people being weeks or days away from dying, or some people actually dead while others remained bearing grief and engaging in remembrance). None of these divides was unbridgeable. In all cases, music could appear as a resource for that bridge-building. Music could be used to build the bridge which we could then traverse. But that traversal was very much dependent upon our willingness to adapt, to produce a new kind of adaptive music and thus a new kind of art, one that not only reassembled the way we think of music as a connector, but, indeed, the way we value music—what, in the end, we speak of as music's beauty and its truth.

From Ross: Toward an Ecology of Improvisation

As a temporal collectivity, an ensemble is not a closed totality but an open assemblage. An ensemble's constitution consists of porosity; it appears and disappears, mingles, intermingles, intra-mingles. An ensemble is not a solid entity or object, therefore, but a kind of fluid formation, ever-moving and ever-transforming. An ensemble is the intermingling and mixing of liquid identities. An ensemble improvisation in such a liquid state would be akin to a kind of musical cocktail party where there is no predefined recipe book for measuring and mixing the drinks. But when we shake up the mix, the consistency of the ensemble changes state, where it reveals that it was never really all liquid, acting more like a gas, becoming full of bubbles, a collision of effervescent forms, touching and displacing and destined to explode. This is the becoming-sound of an ensemble. Sound moves n-directionally, both mobilizing and becoming the atmosphere of the environment. In the sonic ecology of the ensemble, there is not both sound and surroundings. There is only the sound-contaminated and intermingled air that an ensemble breathes. In short, an ensemble is a contaminated assemblage. This is the porous *Umwelt* of ensemble improvisation.

Let us return to Uexküll's meadow for a moment. We have just considered GIO's online ensemble improvisations as a hybrid combination of sound and image, of physical and digital, of liquid and gaseous states which recombine to form what we earlier described as virtual foam. If you recall, according to Uexküll, the creaturely life of the meadow exists in an ensemble of isolated bubbles that interact in some way, as, to a greater or lesser extent, they exist in an interdependent, harmonious, and contrapuntal ecosystem, which Borgo likens to "a swarm of insects" or "insect music" (Borgo, 2006, pp. 3–4). To think of the ecosystem of the *Zumwelt* as swarm or meadow might help us visualize the online ensemble as an ecosystem in which there is performed a democratic distribution of bubble formations which find their own n-dimensionality in an improvisational virtual foam. However, such an image might not articulate or reflect sufficiently the hybrid status of the Zoom performances and recordings which together formed/foamed in the ecosystem of GIO's Theater of Home. The ecosystem which Zoom most resembles, therefore, is perhaps not the swarm or the meadow but an altogether more liminal and littoral zone—and one which is also an *interface effect*: the shoreline.

During successive lockdowns, GIO's global Zoom sessions became a kind of recurring island, a safe haven where improvising musicians and artists could visit or find themselves washed up on the welcoming shores; a free-form assemblage of musical flotsam and jetsam. (Is our cocktail party now a beach party?) More specifically, as an *Umwelt* (or *Zumwelt*), Zoom might be understood as an intertidal zone where the sea level rises and falls to reveal rockpools of emergent life. Virtual seafoam breeds in the liminal zones where the geologies of sound and image overlap, where liquid life meets the contingent formations of land. It is in the folds of this littoral and intertidal zone that we meet new hybrid formations. In terms of ecology, the life forms associated with the shoreline and the intertidal zone would include seaweeds, crustaceans, and invertebrates. However, in the early part of the twentieth century, the ecologist Frederick Keeble discovered a "worm-like" life form emergent in the intertidal zone. This hybrid life form, which existed between the states of plants and animals, Keeble called "plant-animals" (Keeble, 1910, p. v). Importantly for Keeble, the topography of the intertidal zone itself gave rise "not to a change of place, but to a change of state" (Keeble, 10, p. 58).[3] In terms of an ecology of improvisation as it manifests in an ensemble immersed in the technological affordances and digital contingencies of Zoom as an environment (and experiments with combinations of image and sound, physical and virtual tools and props), we might consider our post-human selves to be Haraway's cyborgs, as hybrid formations of the technological and the human. But maybe we are still altogether too fleshly, too full of liquid, gases, viruses, parasites, and symbionts. Perhaps we are only really beginning a new phase of post-human evolution, becoming a hybrid species more akin to intertidal plant-animals dwelling and dissolving amid the ebb and flow of shifting waters, feeding and picking among the swell of detritus—organic, plastic, metallic, digital—continually washed up along a fragile, fractal, and infinitely beautiful shoreline.

From Rob: Experimenting with Trust

Prior to the arrival of COVID-19, my improvisation practice and research included projects within my local community in Melbourne, Australia. Additionally, several times a year, I traveled overseas for recordings, performances at festivals and clubs, and presenting papers at conferences. These endeavors alternated between collaborating with familiar faces within my tribe and engaging with new collaborators. However, generally speaking, my collaborations were typically centered around colleagues based in Australia. As you are aware, Australia is geographically situated at a considerable distance from Europe, North America, and South America—with more proximity to Asia—so traveling overseas and being on a plane for 24 hours is a significant undertaking. With the arrival of COVID-19, the ubiquitous use of Zoom became the norm for virtually every aspect of communication. What came from this was an opportunity. Having previously collaborated on a recording (2022) and performances (2016 and 2019) with Raymond, I was afforded the opportunity and privilege of joining GIO online for weekly improvisation sessions. Following the first GIO performances, Raymond and I engaged in several brilliant discussions about this unfolding creative process, which led to an invitation to participate in a constellation of minds: a research group that Raymond was in the process of curating.

Up until this point, my research had been exploring the notion of improvisation through creativity and experimentation (Onsman and Burke, 2018) as an action theorist; investigations that focused on improvisation within the context of performance and artistic research (Burke and Onsman, 2017). However, through this online/hybrid experience, I was given the opportunity for my practice and research to embody a more global experience of improvisation. In essence, engaging in weekly improvisation sessions with a diverse array of amazing players from around the world has been profoundly inspiring for me. This experience has also granted me a newfound understanding of the meaning of improvisation, which holds a significant role in my ongoing narrative of discovery and experimentation.

From a research standpoint, I believe that this project has posited important new knowledge in music by first encapsulating and further developing the core elements of creativity: experimentation, novel ideation, incubation, and the cultivation of expertise (Wallas, 1926; Mumford & Gustafson, 1988; Sawyer and Henrickson, 2024). Second, the project embraces new, powerful ideas of creative, collaborative practices, not only involving the act of sharing our habitats but also forging new understandings of identities in improvisation. The collaborative nature of the project also extends to like-minded players engaged in analogous endeavors from diverse corners of the world—a laboratory of creating understandings of interaction and experimentation. And from these experiences, I know that the potentialities are boundless.

Finally, I loved the reaffirmation of the notion of social improvisation and engaging in both hybrid and online "busking" with my global friends.

However, the best thing for me in this project was working with such an exceptional team of creative thinkers, activists, and doers—remarkable individuals who brilliantly over-share. Working with such a collaborative team, I can think of no other words but friendship, care, and trust.

Technology, Improvisation, Collaborative Creativity, and the Mother of Invention

The email at the start of the Preface shows a modest invitation for GIO to gather online in an attempt to maintain social relations at what we now know was a precipitous and monumental point in global history. While that email gently steered us toward significant artistic and social developments that no one anticipated, we quickly realized that something special, which merited documenting, was in progress. In attempting to examine the process and outcomes of this artistic journey, we hope to have shed light on what it means to be musical and what it means to be creative, merging disciplines and artistic practices, while challenging conventional notions of artistic virtuosity. One of the defining aspects of creative work is improvisation, as it helps navigate complex technical, socio-artistic environments of the type described here. When domestic and work environments merge in creative and innovative ways, the Theater of Home, new artistic practices, and products can evolve. In this context, we have shown how technology can help ameliorate some of the effects of adversity and facilitate artistic developments that resonate beyond their immediate locality. This technological context, the Zoomesphere, articulates current global debates regarding the importance of technology within contemporary life and helps delineate the role that technology will play in mediating social relations in the future. Precisely how these technological advances will develop and how music, art, and other artistic practices will grow and further merge in a post-genre, post-discipline creative landscape is unknown; however, there is no doubt that technology-driven collaborative creativity will produce new practices and ideas that will help connect people psychologically, socially, and globally. While there is considerable debate regarding the role that technology will play in helping shape our lives in the future, we have shown how creative endeavors, when undertaken within a collective environment of trust, can help us understand how to communicate with each other and how to communicate with non-human entities.

How we communicate together, how we communicate with machines, and how we communicate with nature are the biggest challenges we face globally. Working collaboratively, in a technology-mediated creative environment, will not only produce innovative processes and products but also help us communicate more effectively among ourselves, with machines, and with nature. Necessity may be the mother of invention, but technology, improvisation, and collaborative creativity help the inventions to flourish in ways that can enhance our lives far into the future.

Notes

Chapter 1

1. https://www.youtube.com/watch?v=_LMq2Xr--18.
2. https://www.youtube.com/watch?v=Kny7lEPTb4E.

Chapter 2

1. https://careformusic.org/.
2. https://paulineoliveros.us/telematic-circle.html.
3. https://www.improvisersnetworks.online/telematic-improvisations.
4. http://www.avatarorchestra.org.
5. https://careformusic.org/2020/12/18/latency-whats-the-problem/.

Chapter 3

1. The Centre for Contemporary Arts (CCA) is one of Glasgow's arts hubs. They host a year-round program of exhibitions, events, films, music, literature, workshops, festivals, and performances. The CCA has also been GIO's primary rehearsal and meeting space since its inception; https://www.cca-glasgow.com/.
2. (Author Sappho) As the lockdown was announced, the university had sent a message out that we should gather everything that we would need for the foreseeable future. The common conception was "this will just be a few weeks, a month at most" and yet nevertheless my household (all featured in the first Zoom session, March 24) seized this opportunity to collect as many instruments from the university store as possible. For our household, "lockdown" meant nesting with music, and time to embed and practice. All in all we collected two lutes, multiple flutes (the piccolo in this film), synths and electronic instruments, a vibraphone, and a huge store of gear for recording. Some of these instruments we are each expert in, and others are entirely new to us; these were our safety objects for an expansive stretch of unknown time. And in hindsight it is clear that we were compelled to surround ourselves and fill our house with our comfort objects of "doing"—making and exploring sounds.

Chapter 4

1. https://johncage.org/pp/John-Cage-Work-Detail.cfm?work_ID=242.
2. https://www.youtube.com/watch?v=gXOIkT1-QWY .

Chapter 5

1. Although the prevailing tendency in academic studies is to describe online musical collaborations as Networked Music Performance (NMP) or Telematic Music Performance (TMP), in the context of GIO's Zoom improvisations we might advance the simple alternative of Internet Music Performance, which would carry the acronym "IMP," as this suggests both improvisation and the presence of the mischievous "imp" of improvisation.
2. Latency is "the delay between the moment a musician in one location makes a sound and the moment a second musician in a different location hears that sound" (Rofe and Reuben 2017, pp. 167–184).
3. https://www.falmouth.ac.uk/research/programmes/digital-creativity/online-orchestra (accessed July 4, 2023). This Online Orchestra project was also submitted as an Impact Case Study for UK REF 2021: https://results2021.ref.ac.uk/impact/3eb23c70-bbd3-4227-9cc4-6d88c8bf7bc9?page=1 (accessed July 4, 2023).
4. The conclusions of the Falmouth Online Orchestra are also drawn by Miriam Iorwerth and Don Knox from their study of NMP in communities in the Highlands and Islands of Scotland, published in 2019. "Meaningful musical relationships can be built and maintained using typical domestic equipment, and the network environment gives opportunities for musical creativity that would not be possible in a conventional rehearsal space" (Iorwerth and Knox, 2019, n.p.).
5. Becker writes: "A scientific work is, after all, inseparable from its social and historical context: the context is part of the intellectual and editorial fabric of the work itself." (Becker 1968, p. xv). Becker's vision of a unified science is closely related to the development of "contextual art" practice; see, for example, the Artists' Placement Group founded in 1965/1966 by John Latham and Barbara Steveni, whose guiding principle was "the context is half the work"—a form of artistic practice in which art is not autonomous or primarily an aesthetic endeavor but a social process and way of "being-in-the-world"; see also the writings of the Polish conceptual artist Jan Swidzinski (Swidzinski 1988).
6. See Hampton (2016) and Davide Sparti, "On the Edge: A Frame Analysis of Improvisation," both in Lewis and Piekut, eds. (2016); Peters (2009, p. 69); Luhmann (2000, p. 309); see also Rorty (1989).
7. Over two centuries earlier, Leibniz, in his essay "On Freedom," recognized the essential "contingency of things" (Leibniz, 1973, p. 107) In the current context, it is interesting to note Leibniz's distinction between necessary and contingent truths, whereby "the relation of contingent to necessary truths is somewhat like the relation of surd ratios (namely, the ratios of incommensurable numbers) to the expressible ratios of commensurable numbers" (Leibniz, 1973, p. 97). If improvisation in the Theatre of Home is the emancipation of contingency, and that contingency is akin to the numeral "surd" (or irrational number), then might not GIO's online ensemble improvisations signal a hybrid incarnation of the "theatre of the absurd"?
8. In this respect, it is interesting that Jakob von Uexküll's influential reading of the ecology of the environment (*Umwelt*) rests on the analogy with musical harmony and counterpoint (see Uexküll 2010).
9. In this context, Uexküll's reference to the buzzing insects of the meadow might remind one that Borgo (2006) likens ensemble improvisational music to "a swarm of insects" and

"insect music" (Borgo, 2006, pp. 3–4). And Bachelard quotes a poem by Rilke in which a house appears to become one with a "patch of meadow" (Bachelard 1969, p. 8).

10. For both Uexküll and Sloterdijk, in their various contrapuntal and co-fragile interactions, the ecological "bubble" remains an individual Leibnizian monad. However, we should recall that even the philosopher of the monad recognized "the mutual penetration and connexion of things" (Leibniz, 1973, p. 111).

11. In the context of art as the emancipation of contingencies, it is interesting to note Martha Buskirk's comments on the integral and performative role of photography in her study of the "contingent object" in contemporary art: "The more immediate, the more ephemeral, the more of-the-moment or of-the-place the work is, the more likely that it is known through images and accounts, the two sometimes working together, sometimes in isolation from one another" (Buskirk, 2003, p. 223).

12. "Enframing" as used here refers quite literally to the parameters or the screen as a visual interface, and therefore can only be interpreted as drawing in a limited capacity upon Heidegger's notion of *Gestell*. As Leighton Evans notes: "Enframing describes how humans come to relate to the world around them, or how they are orientated to the world around them" (Evans 2015, p. 53). The notion is employed as a register of GIO's playful experimentation with the screen-as-frame and not in the full Heideggerian sense of *Gestell* as a process whereby humans are "reduced to resources" and a "standing reserve" (see Evans, 2015, pp. 54–55).

13. Interestingly, Landow considers that "every hypertext reader-author is inevitably a *bricoleur*," as *bricolage* "provides a new kind of unity, one appropriate to hypertextuality" (Landow, 1997, p. 195).

14. On the importance of the image to theatre, Alan Read writes: "the essence of theatre is in its images.... The image is central to the act of theatre" (Read 1993, p. 63).

15. Winthrop-Young writes: "Webs versus bubbles, contact versus boundary, connection versus isolation, communication versus representation within— the tension between these poles will resonate throughout Uexküll and beyond." Geoffrey Winthrop-Young, "Afterword: Bubbles and Webs: A Backdoor Stroll Through the Readings of Uexküll" (Uexküll 2010, p. 214).

16. For more on the critical and aesthetic dimension of glitch, see Betancourt (2017). See also Russell (2020), where glitch is "celebrated as a vehicle of refusal, a strategy of nonperformance" and which proposes "glitch-becoming." For a discussion of the role of groove in jazz music, see Roholt (2014).

17. Individual audio stems from the GIO's Zoom sessions have also been remixed in the audio tracks for *Zumwelt* (2022), the "lead album" of TUSK Editions #6: https://tuskeditions.bandcamp.com/album/tusk-editions-6.

Chapter 7

1. https://youtu.be/_HO86JjtB2c.
2. http://www.akouphene.org/bricecatherin/GFsymphonieEN.php.

Chapter 8

1. https://youtu.be/2BfZCvhZK14?t=3424.

Chapter 9

1. https://www.worldlisteningproject.org/about-us/; https://youtu.be/n-hVaUbaLEs?t=23035.
2. https://www.noisywomenpresent.co.uk/.

Chapter 10

1. https://www.chimere.ai.
2. https://aiiafestival.org.
3. Like Uexküll's umwelt, Keeble describes this state change in terms of musical "tone" or "tonic effect" (Keeble, 1910, p. 58).

References

Acord, S. K. (2010). Beyond the Head: The Practical Work of Curating Contemporary Art. *Qualitative Sociology*, 33(4), 447–467.

Agamben, G. (2009). *What Is an Apparatus and Other Essays*. Trans. David Kishik and Stefan Pedatella. Stanford, CA: Stanford University Press.

Alaimo, S. (2008). Trans-Corporeal Feminisms and the Ethical Space of Nature. *Material Feminisms*, 25(2), 237–264.

Angelino, L. (2019). Motor Intentionality and the Intentionality of Improvisation: A Contribution to a Phenomenology of Musical Improvisation. *Continental Philosophy Review*, 2(November), 203–224. https://doi.org/10.1007/s11007-018-9452-x.

Ansdell, G., and DeNora, T. (2016). *Musical Pathways in Recovery: Community Music Therapy and Mental Wellbeing*. London: Routledge.

Argo, J. (2022). Telematic Music Making: Live Performance in the Time of COVID-19 with Jessica Argo | Audio Engineering Society. *Audio Engineering Society*, March 15, 2002. http://www.aes-uk.org/events/telematic-music-making-live-performance-in-the-time-of-covid-19-with-jessica-argo/?fbclid=IwAR3pxIf-tHwUEoFDXwRNkDLCSso5aI-x6CbVlUtAgWOA4VCsiHBTWoNiMVU.

Artaud, A. (1958). *The Theatre and Its Double*. Trans. Mary Caroline Richards. New York: Grove Press.

Bachelard, G. (1969). *The Poetics of Space*. Trans. Maria Jolas. Boston: Beacon Press.

Bailey, D. (1993). *Improvisation: Its Nature and Practice in Music*. Boston: Da Capo.

Baker, F. and T. Wigram (Eds.) (2005). Songwriting: Methods, Techniques and Clinical Applications for Music Therapy Clinicians, Educators and Students. London: Jessica Kingsley.

Barad, K. (2007). Meeting the Universe Halfway: Quantum Physics and the Entanglement of Matter and Meaning. Durham, NC: Duke University Press.

Barad, K. (2010). Re (Con)figuring the Ethico-Onto-Epistemological Question of Matter. *Interdisciplinarity: Methodological Approaches*, 7(1), 83.

Barad, K. (2007) Meeting the Universe Halfway: Quantum Physics and the Entanglement of Matter and Meaning. Durham, NC: Duke University Press.

Bate, J. (2000). *The Song of the Earth*. London: Picador.

Becker, E. (1968). *The Structure of Evil: An Essay on the Unification of the Science of Man*. New York, NY: The Free Press.

Bennett, D. (2008). Identity as a Catalyst for Success. In Michael Hannan (ed.), *Educating Musicians for a Lifetime of Learning: Proceedings of the 17th International Seminar of the Commission for the Education of the Professional Musician, International Society for Music Education*, 1–4. Spilamberto, Italy: International Society for Music Education.

Benson, B. E. (2003). *The Improvisation of Musical Dialogue: A Phenomenology of Music*. Cambridge: Cambridge University Press.

Berkowitz, A. L. (2010). *The Improvising Mind: Cognition and Creativity in the Musical Moment*. Oxford: Oxford University Press.

Berliner, P. (1984). *Thinking in Jazz: The Infinite Art of Improvisation*. Chicago Studies in Ethnomusicology CSE. Chicago: University of Chicago Press.

Berleant, A. (1992). *The Aesthetics of Environment*. Philadelphia: Temple University Press.

References

Bernstein, S. (1998). *Virtuosity of the Nineteenth Century: Performing Music and Language in Heine, Liszt, and Baudelaire.* Stanford, CA: Stanford University Press.

Betancourt, M. (2017). *Glitch Art in Theory and Practice: Critical Failures and Post-Digital Aesthetics.* London: Routledge.

Bhuiyan, J. (2023). San Francisco to Get Round-the-Clock Robo Taxis After Controversial Vote. *The Guardian, August 10, 2023.* https://www.theguardian.com/us-news/2023/aug/10/san-francisco-self-driving-car-autonomous-regulation-google-gm.

Biasutti, M., and Frezza, L. (2009). Dimensions of Music Improvisation. *Creativity Research Journal, 21*(2–3), 232–242.

Borgo, D. (2006). *Sync or Swarm: Musical Improvisation in a Complex Age.* New York: Continuum.

Bourdieu, P. (1977). *Outline of a Theory of Practice.* Cambridge: Cambridge University Press.

Bourriaud, N. (2002). *Postproduction: Culture as Screenplay: How Art Reprograms the World.* Trans. Jeanine Herman. New York: Lukas & Sternberg.

Brown, J. S., and Duguid, P. (2002). Local Knowledge: Innovation in the Networked Age. *Management Learning, 33*(4), 427–437.

Brümmer, L. (ed.) (2021). *The Hub: Pioneers of Network Music.* Heidelberg: Kehrer Verlag.

Burke, R., and Onsman, A. (2017). *Perspectives on Artistic Research in Music.* London: Lexington Press.

Burke, R. L. (2021). Analysis and Observations of Pre-Learnt and Idiosyncratic Elements in Improvisation. In Michael Kahr (ed.), *Artistic Research in Jazz: Positions, Theories, Methods,* 135–154. New York: Routledge.

Burke, R., Vincs, R., and Williamson, P. (2021). Teaching Undergraduate Jazz Ensembles Within Virtual Spaces. *Journal of Music, Health, and Wellbeing, 17*(65–72) https://www.musichealthandwellbeing.co.uk/musickingthroughcovid19

Burke, R. L., Sappho, M., Birrell, R., MacDonald, R., and DeNora, T. (2024). Opening up Openings: Zooming in on Improvisation in the Theater of Home. *Psychology of Music,* p.03057356241247528.

Burland, K. (2005). *Becoming a musician: a longitudinal study investigating the career transitions of undergraduate music students* [unpublished doctoral dissertation]. University of Sheffield.

Burnard, P. (2012). Rethinking "Musical Creativity" and the Notion of Multiple Creativities in Music. In Odena (ed.), *Musical Creativity: Insights from Music Education Research,* 5–27. London: Routledge.

Musical Creativity: Insights from Music Education Research, 5–27. London: Routledge.

Buskirk, M. (2003). *The Contingent Object of Contemporary Art.* Cambridge, MA: MIT Press.

Butler, J. (2004). *Undoing Gender.* London: Routledge.

Carôt, A., Renaud, A. B., and Rebelo, P. (2007). Networked music performance: state of the art. Paper presented at AES 30th International Conference, Saariselka, Finland.

Carvajal, M. A. (2020). Telehealth Music Therapy: Considerations and Changes During the COVID-19 Crisis. Unpublished doctoral dissertation, Florida State University.

Cavell, S. (1979). *The World Viewed: Reflections on the Ontology of Film.* Enlarged Edition. Cambridge, MA: Harvard University Press.

Coney, J. (1974). Space Is the Place [DVD, Plexifilm, 2003]. https://www.imdb.com/title/tt0072195/.

Coleman, B. (2011). *Hello Avatar: Rise of the Networked Generation.* Cambridge, MA: MIT Press.

Cook, N. (2001). *Analysing Musical Multimedia.* Oxford: Oxford University Press.

Cook, R. M., and Morton, B. (2008). *The Penguin Guide to Jazz Recordings,* 9th edition. London: Penguin.

Crawford, N. C. (2000). The Passion of World Politics: Propositions on Emotion and Emotional Relationships. *International Security, 24*(4), 116–156.

Cross, I. (2008). Musicality and the Human Capacity for Culture. *Musicae Scientiae, 12*(1 Suppl), 147–167.

Dant, T. (1999). *Material Culture in the Social World*. Buckingham, UK: McGraw-Hill Education.
Davidson, J. W. and MacArthur, S. (2021). Conceptions of musical ability and the expertise paradigm. In *Routledge International Handbook of Music Psychology in Education and the Community*, 153–168. Oxford, UK: Routledge.
Davis, T. (2019). Instrumental Intentionality: An Exploration of Mediated Intentionality in Musical Improvisation. *International Journal of Performance Arts and Digital Media*, 15(1), 70–83.
de Bruin, L. (2015). Theory and Practice in Idea Generation and Creativity in Jazz Improvisation. *Australian Journal of Music Education*, 2, 91–106. https://search.informit.org/doi/10.3316/informit.998936352073430.
de Bruin, L. R. (2018). Musical Play, Creativity and Metacognitive Processes in Developing Improvisational Expertise: Expert Improvising Voices. *International Journal of Play*, 7(3), 248–265.
DeLanda, M. (2016). *Assemblage Theory*. Edinburgh: Edinburgh University Press.
Deleuze, G. (1994). Difference and Repetition. Trans. Paul Patton. New York: Columbia University Press.
DeNora, T. (1992). Fast, Faster, Fastest: Comment on Chamblis' Mundanity of Excellence. *Sociological Theory*, 10(1), 99–102.
DeNora, T. (1995). *Beethoven and the Construction of Genius: Musical Politics in Vienna, 1792–1803*. Berkeley, Los Angeles, and London: University of California Press.
DeNora, T. (2000). *Music in Everyday Life*. Cambridge: University of Cambridge Press.
DeNora, T. (2013). *Music Asylums: Well-Being Through Music in Everyday Life*. Farnham, UK: Ashgate.
DeNora, T. (2014). *Making Sense of Reality: Culture and Perception in Everyday Life*. London: Sage.
DeNora, T. (2020). *Latency: What's the Problem? Care for Music*. Care for Music. https://careformusic.org/2020/12/18/latency-whats-the-problem/.
DeNora, T. (2021). *Hope: The Dream We Carry*. London: Palgrave Macmillan.
DeNora, T. (2023). Island Life and Death: studying cultural change around death, dying and bereavement. Project Website: https://islandlifeanddeath.org/
Deleuze, G. (1994). *Difference and Repetition*, Trans. Paul Patton. New York, NY: Columbia University Press.
Denzin, N. K., and Lincoln, Y. S. (2005). *The Sage Handbook of Qualitative Research,* 3rd edition. Thousand Oaks, CA: Sage.
Derrida, J. (1978). *Writing and Difference*, Trans. Alan Bass. Chicago, IL: University of Chicago Press.
Derrida, J. (1995). *Archive Fever: A Freudian Impression*. Trans. Eric Prenowitz. Chicago: University of Chicago Press.
Devenish, L., Hope, C., and McAuliffe, S. (2023). Contemporary Musical Virtuosities. In Louise Devenish and Cat Hope (eds.), Contemporary Musical Virtuosities, 1–13. London: Routledge.
Dewey, J. (1958). *Art as Experience*. New York: Capricorn Books.
Dewsbury, J. D. (2012). Affective Habit Ecologies: Material Dispositions and Immanent Inhabitations. *Performance Research*, 17(4), 74–82.
Devenish, L., Hope, C., and McAuliffe, S. (2023). Contemporary musical virtuosities. In Louise Devenish, Cat Hope (Eds.) *Contemporary Musical Virtuosities*, 1–13. London: Routledge.
Dezeuze, A. (2008). Assemblage, Bricolage, and the Practice of Everyday Life. *Art Journal*, 67(1), 31–37.
Duffin, R. W. (2008). *How Equal Temperament Ruined Harmony (and Why You Should Care)*. London: W. W. Norton.

References

Duman, D., Snape, N., Danso, A., Toiviainen, P., and Luck, G. (2023). Groove as a Multidimensional Participatory Experience. *Psychology of Music*, 52(1). https://doi.org/10.1177/03057356231165327.

Ericsson, K. A., and Harwell, K. W. (2019). Deliberate Practice and Proposed Limits on the Effects of Practice on the Acquisition of Expert Performance: Why the Original Definition Matters and Recommendations for Future Research. *Frontiers in Psychology*, 10, 2396. https://doi.org/10.3389/fpsyg.2019.02396.

Evans, L. (2015). *Locative Social Media: Place in the Digital Age*. Houndmills, UK: Palgrave.

Fisher, C. M., Demir-Caliskan, O., Hua, M. Y., and Cronin, M. A. (2021). Trying Not to Try: The Paradox of Intentionality in Jazz Improvisation and Its Implications for Organizational Scholarship. In R. Bednarek, M. P. Cunha, J. Schad, and W. Smith (eds.), *Interdisciplinary Dialogues on Organizational Paradox: Research in the Sociology of Organizations*, Vol. 73B, 125–139. Melbourne: Emerald.

Frank, C. (2021). Making with Agential Objects: An Autoethnographic Account of Fluidity in Artistic Practice. Unpublished doctoral thesis, University of Huddersfield.

Galenson, D. (2006). *Old Masters and Young Geniuses: The Two Life Cycles of Artistic Creativity*. Princeton, NJ: Princeton University Press.

Galenson, D. (2006). *Old Masters and Young Geniuses: The Two Life Cycles of Artistic Creativity*. New York: Princeton University Press.

Gannon-Leary, P., and Fontainha, E. (2007) Communities of Practice and Virtual Learning Communities: Benefits, Barriers and Success Factors. *Elearning Papers*, 5, 20–29.

Gay, P. (1981). *Voltaire's Candide: A Bilingual Edition by Voltaire*. Trans. and ed. Peter Gay, introduction by Peter Gay. New York: St. Martin's Press. https://www.oxfordreference.com/display/10.1093/acref/9780191843730.001.0001/q-oro-ed5-00011218.

Giddens, A. (1991). *Modernity and Self-Identity: Self and Society in the Late Modern Age*. Cambridge: Polity.

Gillies, S., and Sappho, M. (2021). Donohue+: Developing Performer-Specific Electronic Improvisatory Accompaniment for Instrumental Improvisation. *Organised Sound*, 26(1), 129–139. doi:10.1017/S1355771821000121.

Ginsborg, J. (2018). "The Brilliance of Perfection" or "Pointless Finish"? What Virtuosity Means to Musicians. *Musicae Scientiae*, 22(4), 454–473.

Goff, P., and Moran, A. (2021). Is Consciousness Everywhere? Essays on Panpsychism. *Journal of Consciousness Studies*, 28(9–10), 9–15.

Groce, N. E. (1988). *Everyone Here Spoke Sign Language: Hereditary Deafness on Martha's Vineyard*. Cambridge MA: Harvard University Press.

Guattari, F. (1995). *Chaosmosis: An Ethico-Aesthetic Paradigm*. Trans. Paul Baines and Julian Pefanis. Bloomington and Indianapolis: Indiana University Press.

Habermas, J. (1989). *The Structural Transformation of the Public Sphere: An Inquiry into a Category of Bourgeois Society*. Trans. Thomas Burger with the assistance of Frederick Lawrence. Cambridge: Polity Press.

Hallam, S. (2010). 21st century conceptions of musical ability. *Psychology of Music*, 38(3), 308–330.

Hallam, E., and Ingold, T. (eds.). (2007). *Creativity and Cultural Improvisation*. Oxford: Berg.

Hallam, S. (2010). 21st Century Conceptions of Musical Ability. Psychology of Music, 38(3), 308–330.

Hampton, T. (2016). Michel de Montaigne, or Philosophy as Improvisation. In G. Lewis and B. Piekut (eds.), *The Oxford Handbook of Critical Improvisation Studies*, Vol. 1, 227–238. Oxford: Oxford University Press.

Haraway, D. J. (1991). *Simians, Cyborgs, and Women: The Reinvention of Nature*. London: Free Association Books.

Haraway, D. J. (2016). *Staying with the Trouble: Making Kin in the Chthulucene.* Durham, NC: Duke University Press.
Haraway, D. J. (2003). *The Companion Species Manifesto: Dogs, People, and Significant Otherness.* Chicago: Prickly Paradigm Press.
Haraway, D. J. (2013). *Primate Visions: Gender, Race, and Nature in the World of Modern Science.* New York: Routledge.
Harrison, C., and Wood, P. (eds). (1992). *Art in Theory: 1900–1990: An Anthology of Changing Ideas.* Oxford: Blackwell.
Heidegger, M. (1962). *Being and Time.* Trans. John Macquarrie and Edward Robinson. Oxford: Blackwell.
Hennion, A. (1997). Baroque and Rock: Music, Mediators and Musical Taste. *Poetics, 24*(6), 415–435.
Hillis Miller, J. (1977). The Critic as Host. *Critical Inquiry, 3*(3, Spring), 439–447.
Holman Jones, S. (2016). Living Bodies of Thought: The "Critical" in Critical Autoethnography. *Qualitative Inquiry, 22*(4), 228–237.
Holman Jones, S. (2018). Creative Selves/Creative Cultures: Critical Autoethnography, Performance, and Pedagogy. In S. Holman Jones and M. Pruyn (eds.), *Creative Selves/Creative Cultures: Critical Autoethnography, Performance, and Pedagogy*, 3–20. New York: Springer International. https://doi.org/10.1007/978-3-319-47527-1_1.
Home, S. (ed). (1997). *Mind Invaders: A Reader in Psychic Warfare, Cultural Sabotage and Semiotic Terrorism.* London: Serpents Tail.
Huang, R. (2022). On Musical Labor, Talent and the "Deskilled" Artist in the Age of AI: AI Music Creativity. YouTube. https://www.youtube.com/watch?v=VvJkDUsPOJU.
Husserl, E. (1983). *Ideas Pertaining to a Pure Phenomenology and to a Phenomenological Philosophy, First Book, General Introduction to a Pure Phenomenology.* Trans. F. Kersten. The Hague: Martinus Nijhoff.
Ingold, T. (2010). Bringing Things to Life: Creative Entanglements in a World of Materials. *Working Paper #15, ESRC National Centre for Research Methods.* Manchester: University of Manchester.
Iorwerth, M., and Knox, D. (2019). Playing Together, Apart: Musicians' Experiences of Physical Separation in a Classical Recording Session. *Music Perception, 36*(3), 289–299. https://doi.org/10.1525/mp.2019.36.3.289.
Janicka, I. (2016). Are these Bubbles Anarchist? Peter Sloterdijk's Spherology and the Question of Anarchism. *Anarchist Studies, 24*(1), 62–84.
Johnson, C. M. (2001). A Survey of Current Research on Online Communities of Practice. *The Internet and Higher Education, 4*(1), 45–60.
Jordanous, A., and Keller, B. (2012). What Makes a Musical Improvisation Creative? *Journal of Interdisciplinary Music Studies, 6*(2), 151–175.
Kamoche, K., Cunha, M. P. E., and Cunha, J. V. D. (2003). Towards a Theory of Organizational Improvisation: Looking Beyond the Jazz Metaphor. *Journal of Management Studies, 40*(8), 2023–2051.
Kassabian, A. (2001). *Hearing Film: Tracking Identifications in Contemporary Film Music.* London: Routledge.
Keeble, F. (1910). *Plant-Animals: A Study in Symbiosis.* Cambridge: Cambridge University Press.
Kilicoglu, G., and Kilicoglu, D. (2020). The Birth of a New Paradigm: Rethinking Education and School Leadership with a Metamodern "Lens." *Studies in Philosophy and Education, 39*, 493–514. https://doi.org/10.1007/s11217-019-09690-z.
Kirshbaum, M. N., Carey, I., Purcell, B., and Nash, S. (2011). Talking about Dying and Death: A Focus Group Study to Explore a Local Community Perspective. *Nursing Reports, 1*(1), 8.

Klein, N. (2023). AI Machines Aren't "Hallucinating." But Their Makers Are. *The Guardian*, May 8, 2023. https://www.theguardian.com/commentisfree/2023/may/08/ai-machines-hallucinating-naomi-klein

Kotarba, J. A. (2023). *Music in the Course of Life*. London: Routledge.

Koumaditis, K., Mousas, C., and Chinello, F. (2021). XR in the Era of COVID-19. *Behaviour and Information Technology*, 40(12), 1234–1236. https://doi.org/10.1080/0144929X.2021.1988320.

Krauss, R. (1999). *"A Voyage on the North Sea": Art in the Age of the Post-Medium Condition*. London: Thames & Hudson.

Krekels, T. (2019). Loosening the Saxophone: Entanglements of Bodies in the Politics of Free Improvisation. Doctoral dissertation, University of Edinburgh.

Kroker, A. (2012). *Body Drift: Butler, Hayles, Haraway*. Minneapolis: University of Minnesota Press.

Landgraf, E. (2011). *Improvisation as Art: Conceptual Challenges, Historical Perspectives*. New Directions in German Studies, Vol. 1. London: Bloomsbury.

Landow, G. P. (1997). *Hypertext 2.0: The Convergence of Contemporary Critical Theory and Technology*. Baltimore, MD: Johns Hopkins University Press.

Latour, B. (1999). *Pandora's Hope: Essays on the Reality of Science Studies*. Cambridge, MA: Harvard University Press.

Lave, J., and Wenger, E. (1991). *Situated Learning: Legitimate Peripheral Participation*. Cambridge: Cambridge University Press. https://doi.org/10.1017/CBO9780511815355.

Lee, K. F., and Qiufan, C. (2021). *AI 2041: Ten Visions for Our Future*. London: Ebury.

Lefebvre, H. (2014). *Critique of Everyday Life: One-Volume Edition*. London: Verso.

Leibniz, G. W. (1973). *Philosophical Writings*. Trans. Mary Morris and G. H. R. Parkinson. London: J. M. Dent & Sons.

Lévi-Strauss, C. (1966). *The Savage Mind*. Chicago: University of Chicago Press.

Lewis, G., and Piekut, B. (eds.). (2016). *The Oxford Handbook of Critical Improvisation Studies*, Vol. 1. Oxford: Oxford University Press.

Lewis, G. E. (2000). Too Many Notes: Computers, Complexity and Culture in "Voyager." *Leonardo Music Journal*, 10, 33–39.

Lewis, G. (2017). "Let Your Secrets Sing Out": An Auto-ethnographic Analysis on How Music Can Afford Recovery from Child Abuse. *Voices: A World Forum for Music Therapy*, 17(2). https://doi.org/10.15845/voices.v17i2.85.

Lock, G. (2000). *Blutopia: Visions of the Future and Revisions of the Past in the Work of Sun Ra, Duke Ellington, and Anthony Braxton*. Durham, NC: Duke University Press.

Lorweth, M., and Knox, D. (2019). The Application of Networked Music Performance Technology to Access Ensemble Activity For Socially Isolated Musicians [conference paper]. Web Audio Conference 2019, Rondheim, Norway. https://www.ntnu.edu/documents/1282113268/1290797448/WAC2019-CameraReadySubmission-8.pdf/1bc3d35a-4edd-4ccf-d5b0-01cb7d33cc3e?t=1575329697561.

Lubet, A. (2018). Economies of Scales (and Chords): Disability Studies and Adaptive Music. In D. McDonald, and B. Hadley (eds.), *Routledge Handbook of Disability Arts, Culture, and Media Studies*, 250–263, London: Routledge.

Luhmann, N. (2000). *Art as a Social System*. Trans. Eva Knodt. Stanford, CA: Stanford University Press.

MacDonald, R. A. R (2019). *Exploring artistic, pedagogic, and therapeutic practices: Interdisciplinary knowledges for responsible research and innovation?* International workshop - Improvisation as a means to develop interdisciplinary knowledge. Bergen Norway 17–20 June 2019.

MacDonald, R. (2020). *This Is Not Improvised but That Is: Lockdown 2020*. Broadcast as part of Improvfest 2020, hosted by International Institute for Critical Studies in Improvisation, Guelph, Canada, August 7–8, 2020. https://www.youtube.com/watch?v=Kny7lEPTb4E.

MacDonald, R (2023) Music, Mess, Metamodernism, and Post-Qualitative Inquiry', in Margaret S. Barrett, and Graham F. Welch (eds), *The Oxford Handbook of Early Childhood Learning and Development in Music*, Oxford Handbooks (2023; online edn, Oxford Academic, 20 Nov. 2023), https://doi.org/10.1093/oxfordhb/9780190927523.013.50, accessed 19 Dec. 2023.

MacDonald, R. A. R. and Birrell, R. (2020) Flattening the curve: Glasgow Improvisers Orchestra's use of virtual improvising to maintain community during COVID-19 pandemic. *Critical Studies in Improvisation*, 14(2–3). https://www.criticalimprov.com/index.php/csieci/article/view/6384

MacDonald, R. A. R, Burke, R. L. De Nora, T, Sappho, M. and Birrell, R. (2021) Our Virtual Tribe: Sustaining and Enhancing Community via Online Music Improvisation *Frontiers in Psychology*. https://doi.org/10.3389/fpsyg.2020.623640.

MacDonald, R. and DeNora, T. (Forthcoming) Performing in *The Theatre of Home*: Autoethnographic perspectives on performer identities. *The Music Performer's Lived Experience*. Doğantan-Dack (Ed). London: Routledge.

MacDonald, R. A. R, Miell D., and Hargreaves, D. J. E. D. S. (2017). *The Handbook of Musical Identities*. Oxford: Oxford University Press.

MacDonald, R., and Saarikallio, S. (2022). Musical Identities in Action: Embodied, Situated, and Dynamic. *Musicae Scientiae*, 26(4), 729–745.

MacDonald, R., and Saarikallio, S. (2024). Healthy Musical Identities and New Virtuosities: A Humble Manifesto for Music Education Research. *Nordic Research in Music Education*, 5, 43–66. https://doi.org/10.23865/nrme.v5.5565.

MacDonald, R., and Wilson, G. (2014). Improvisation, Health and Welling: A Review. *Psychology of Well-Being*, 4(20). https://doi.org/10.1186/s13612-014-0020-9 http://www.psywb.com/content/4/1/20.

MacDonald, R. A. R., and Wilson, G. B. (2016). Billy Connolly, Daniel Barenboim, Willie Wonka, Jazz Bastards and the Universality of Improvisation. In G. Lewis and Ben Piekut (eds.), Oxford Handbook of Critical Improvisation Studies, 103–121. New York: Oxford University Press.

MacDonald, R. A. R., and Wilson, G. B. (2020). *The Art of Becoming: How Group Improvisation Works*. New York: Oxford University Press.

MacGlone, U. M. (2023) "Being Safe Means You Can Feel Uncomfortable": A Case Study of Female Students' Participation in a Higher Education, Online Improvisation Course. *Frontiers in Education* 8, 1068879. https://doi.org/10.3389/feduc.2023.1068879.

MacGlone, U. M. (2023). "Being Safe Means You Can Feel Uncomfortable": A Case Study of Female Students' Participation in a Higher Education, Online Improvisation Course. *Frontiers in Education*, 8, 1068879. https://doi.org/10.3389/feduc.2023.1068879.

MacGlone, U., Wilson, G. B, Vamvakaris, J., Brown, K., McEwan, M., and MacDonald R. A. R. (2023). Exploring Approaches to Community Music Delivery by Practitioners with and Without Additional Support Needs: A Qualitative Study. *International Journal of Community Music*, 15(3), 385–403.

Manovich, L. (2001). *The Language of the New Media*. Cambridge, MA: MIT Press.

Marx, K. (1975). *Early Writings*. Trans. Rodney Livingstone and Gregor Benton. Harmondsworth, UK: Penguin.

Mayall, J. (2021). Playing with Time to Escape Time: Mindful Online Slow Music Improvisation. *The Journal of Performance and Mindfulness*, 4(1). https://doi.org/10.5920/pam.966.

McFerran, K., Skinner, A., Hall, T., and Thompson, G. (2022). Structure, Agency and Community: Using Online Music Gatherings to Support Social Inclusion for People with

Disabilities in Australia During the COVID-19 Pandemic. *Nordic Journal of Music Therapy*, 31(3), 259–272.

McPherson, D. H. (2023). More than One Thing: A Practice-Led Investigation into Transdisciplinary Free Improvisation in Sound and Movement. Unpublished doctoral thesis. University of Huddersfield.

McPherson, G. E., Davidson, J. W., and Evans, P. (2006). Playing an Instrument In G. E. McPherson (ed.), *The Child As Musician: A Handbook of Musical Development*, 331–335. Oxford: Oxford University Press.

Messiaen, O. (2001 [1978]). *Lecture at Notre-Dame*. Trans. Timothy J. Tikker. Paris: Alphonse Leduc.

Miksza, P. (2007). Effective Practice: An Investigation of Observed Practice Behaviors, Self-Reported Practice Habits, and the Performance Achievement of High School Wind Players. *Journal of Research in Music Education*, 55(4), 359–375.

Mills, R. (2019). *Tele-Improvisation: Intercultural Interaction in the Online Global Music Jam Session*. New York: Springer.

Miyamato, Y., Nisbett, R. E., and Masuda, T. (2006). Culture and the Physical Environment: Holistic Versus Analytic Perceptual Affordances. *Psychological Science*, 17(2), 113–119.

Monson, I. (2000). Art Blakey's African Diaspora. In I. Monson (ed.), *The African Diaspora: A Musical Perspective*, 329–352. New York: Oxford University Press.

Mumford, M. D., and Gustafson, S. B., (1988). Creativity Syndrome: Integration, Application, and Iinnovation. *Psychological Bulletin*, 103(1), p.27.

Morris, L. B. (2017). *The Art of Conduction* New York: Karma.

Murray, J. (2020). Indices of Style in Free Jazz: Towards an Intersubjective Performance Framework. Doctoral dissertation, Monash University.

Mwamba, C., and Johansen, G. G. (2021). Everyone's Music? Explorations of the Democratic Ideal in Jazz and Improvised Music. *NMH-publikasjoner Utdanningsforskning i musikk – skriftserie fra CERM (Centre for Educational Research in Music*, 3(2). https://hdl.handle.net/11250/2826181.

Nachmanovitch, S. (2024). *Free Play*. Edinburgh: Cannongatge.

Nachmanovitch, S., and Krueger, A. (2022). "Comfortable with Being Uncomfortable" or "You, Me and the Latency . . .": A Conversation with Stephen Nachmanovitch. *Journal of Performance and Mindfulness*, 4(1).

Nicols, M. (2023). The Practice of Social Virtuosities. In Louise Devenish and Cat Hope (eds.), *Contemporary Musical Virtuosities*, 79–88. London: Routledge.

Nora, S., and Minc, A. (1980). *The Computerization of Society: A Report to the President of France*. Cambridge, MA: MIT Press.

O'Dea, J. (2000). *Virtue or Virtuosity?: Explorations in the Ethics of Musical Performance*. Westport, CT: Greenwood Press.

Odena, O. (2018). *Musical Creativity Revisited: Educational Foundations, Practices and Research*. London: Routledge.

Onsman, A., and Burke, R. (2018). *Experimentation in Improvised Jazz: Chasing Ideas*. New York: Routledge.

Orbell, S., and Verplanken, B. (2010). The Automatic Component of Habit in Health Behavior: Habit as Cue-Contingent Automaticity. *Health Psychology*, 29(4), 374–383. doi:10.1037/a0019596.

Pavlicevic, M., and G. Ansdell. (2004). *Community Music Therapy*. London: Jessica Kingsley.

Peters, G. (2009). *The Philosophy of Improvisation*. Chicago: University of Chicago Press.

Potter, J., and Wetherell, M. (1987). *Discourse and Social Psychology: Beyond Attitudes and Behaviour*. London: Sage.

References

Pressing, J. (1998). Psychological Constraints on Improvisational Expertise and Communication. In B. Nettl and M. Russell (eds.), *In the Course of Performance: Studies in the World of Musical Improvisation*, 47–67. Chicago: University of Chicago Press.

Prior, D., Biscoe, I., Rofe, M., and Reuben, F. (2017). Designing a System for Online Orchestra: Computer Hardware and Software. *Journal of Music, Technology & Education*, 10(2–3), 185–196.

Procter, S. (2011). Reparative Musicing: Thinking on the Usefulness of Social Capital Theory Within Music Therapy. *Nordic Journal of Music Therapy*, 20(3), 242–262.

Quigley, H., and MacDonald, R. (2024). A qualitative investigation of a virtual community music and music therapy intervention: A Scottish-American collaboration. *Musicae Scientiae*, 28(3), 573–590. https://doi.org/10.1177/10298649241227615.

Randles, C., and Burnard, P. (eds.). (2022). *The Routledge Companion to Creativities in Music Education*. New York: Taylor & Francis.

Ranmarine, T. K. (2009). Acoustemology, Indigeneity, and Joik in Valkeapää's Symphonic Activism: Views from Europe's Arctic Fringes for Environmental Ethnomusicology. *Ethnomusicology*, 53(2), 187–217.

Read, A. (1993). *Theatre and Everyday Life: An Ethics of Performance*. London: Routledge.

Reardon-Smith, H., Denson, L., and Tomlinson, V. (2020). Feministing Free Improvisation. *Tempo (United Kingdom)*, 74(292), 10–20. https://doi.org/10.1017/S004029821900113X.

Reason, M. (2023). Inclusive online community arts: COVID and beyond COVID. *Cultural Trends*, 32(1), 52–69.

Roholt, T. C. (2014). *Groove: A Phenomenology of Rhythmic Nuance*. London: Bloomsbury.

Rodgers, T. (2010). *Pink Noises: Women on Electronic Music and Sound*. Durham, NC: Duke University Press.

Rorty, R. (1989). *Contingency, irony, and solidarity*. Cambridge: Cambridge University Press.

Rofe, M. and Reuben, F. (2017). Telematic Performance and the Challenge of Latency. *Journal of Music, Technology and Education*, 10(2–3), 167–184.

Roholt, T. C. (2014). Groove: A Phenomenology of Rhythmic Nuance. London: Bloomsbury.

Rojas, P. (2015). To Become One with the Instrument: The Unfolding of a Musical Topography. Culture and Psychology, 21(2), 207–230.

Rolvsjord, R. (2010). Resource-oriented Music Therapy. Texas: Barcelona Publications.

Roose, K., and Newton, C. (2023). Don't Scrape Me, Bro, the Activists Sabotaging Self-Driving Cars and How Reddit Beat a Rebellion. *New York Times, November 8, 2023*. https://www.nytimes.com/2023/08/11/podcasts/dont-scrape-me-bro-the-activists-sabotaging-self-driving-cars-and-how-reddit-beat-a-rebellion.html.

Rottle, J., and Reardon-Smith, H. (2023). Companion Thinking in Improvised Musicking Practice. *Contemporary Music Review*, 42, 82–99. https://doi.org/10.1080/07494467.2023.2191070.

Rovelli, C. (2022). Helgoland: The Strange and Beautiful Story of Quantum Physics. London: Penguin.

Rowe, R. (1992). Machine Listening and Composing with Cypher. *Computer Music Journal*, 16(1), 43–63. https://doi.org/https://doi.org/10.2307/3680494.

Rowe, R. (1993). Chapter 5: Machine Listening. https://wp.nyu.edu/robert_rowe/text/interactive-music-systems-1993/chapter5/. (accessed July 14, 2023).

Russell, L. (2020). *Glitch Feminism: A Manifesto*. London and New York: Verso Books.

Ruud, E. (2022). *Toward a Sociology of Music Therapy: Musicking as a Cultural Immunogen*. New Braunfels, TX: Barcelona Press.

Sangiorgio, A. (ed.). (2023). *Creative Interactions: Creative Learning, Creative Teaching, and Teaching for Group Creativity in Music Education*. Munich: University of Music and Theatre Munich. Open Access ebook available at https://nbn-resolving.org/urn:nbn:de:bvb:m29-0000010661.

Sappho, M. (2020). Subverting by Not Subverting, Free Improvisation Dreams for Counter-Logic Activisms. *CeReNeM Journal, 7*. https://indd.adobe.com/embed/7bd9f6d8-ccdc-4c38-977a-6c81618f74e4?fbclid=IwAR2LdKnFTve_FhZBcZ68G0mQhSZybYc8TYEoUeV49yptGSKHp-BkaGEuQoM.

Sappho, M. (2022). The Improvisers Cookbook: Mythologising the Social in Experimental Improvisation. Thesis, University of Huddersfield.

Sappho, M. (2023). X-. *CeReNeM Journal, 8*. https://cerenempostgraduates.files.wordpress.com/2023/12/cerenemjournal-issue8.pdf.

Sawyer, R. K. (2006). Group Creativity: Musical Performance and Collaboration. *Psychology of Music, 34*(2), 148–165.

Sawyer, R. K. (2016 [1997]). *Pretend Play as Improvisation: Conversation in the Pre-School Classroom*. London: Routledge.

Sawyer, R. K., and Henriksen, D. (2024). *Explaining Creativity: The Science of Human Innovation*. Oxford: Oxford University Press.

Schafer, R. M. (1994). *The Soundscape: Our Sonic Environment and the Tuning of the World*. Rochester, VT: Destiny Books.

Scheer, J., and Groce, N. E. (1988). Impairment as a Human Constant: Cross-Cultural and Historical Perspectives on Variation. *Journal of Social Issues, 44*, 23-37.

Schegloff, E., and Sacks, H. (1973). Opening up Closings. *Semiotica, 8*(4), 289–387.

Schmid, W. (2017). Being Together—Exploring the Modulation of Affect in Improvisational Music Therapy with a Man in a Persistent Vegetative State: A Qualitative Single Case Study. *Health Psychology Report, 2*(5), 186–192. https://www.termedia.pl/Being-together-Exploring-the-modulation-of-affect-in-improvisational-music-therapy-with-a-man-in-a-persistent-vegetative-state-a-qualitative-single-case-study,74,28789,1,1.html (accessed July 10, 2020).

Schmid, W. (2020). I Take One of the Surgical Masks out of the Box That Is Placed on a Little Table in Front of Rebecca's Room.... *Care for Music Project Blog*, December 19, 2020. https://careformusic.org/2020/12/19/i-take-one-of-the-surgical-masks-out-of-the-box-that-is-placed-on-a-little-table-in-front-of-rebeccas-room/.

Schmid, W., and K. Fuchs. (2022). Stillwerden. *Musik Therapeutische, 43*(4), 392.

Schmid, W., F. Simpson, T. DeNora, and G. Ansdell. (2021). Music Therapy Research During a Pandemic: An Accidental Experiment in Caring for Music. *International Journal of Community Music, 14*(2–3), 311–330.

Shoemaker, B. (2023) *Music Farther Outside: Experimental Music During Brexit and the Pandemic*. Lanham, Maryland: Rowman & Littlefield Publishers.

Schroeder, F. (2013). Network[ed] Listening—Towards a De-centering of Beings. *Contemporary Music Review, 32*(2–3), 215. doi:10.1080/07494467.2013.775807.

Schumacher, C. (ed). (1989). *Artaud on Theatre*. London: Methuen.

Schumacher, C. (ed). (1989). Artaud on Theatre. London: Methuen.

Serres, M. (2008). *The Five Senses: A Philosophy of Mingled Bodies (I)*. Trans. Margaret Sankey and Peter Cowley. London: Continuum.

Siljamäki, E. (2022). Free Improvisation in Choral Settings: An Ecological Perspective. *Research Studies in Music Education, 44*(1), 234–256.

Sloterdijk, P. (2016). *Foams: Spheres*, Vol. III: *Plural Spherology*. Los Angeles: Semiotext.

Smith, H. and Dean, R. (1997). *Improvisation, Hypermedia and the Arts Since 1945*. London: Routledge.

Smith, J. D. (2001). Diva-Dogs: Sounding Women Improvising. Thesis, University of British Columbia.

Star, S. L., and Griesemer, J. R. (1989). Institutional Ecology, Translations and Boundary Objects: Amateurs and Professionals in Berkeley's Museum of Vertebrate Zoology, 1907–39. *Social Studies of Science, 19*(3), 387–420.

Stein, M. (1998). *Jung's Map of the Soul: An Introduction*. Chicago: Open Court.
Stern, D. (2004). *The Present Moment in Psychotherapy and Everyday Life*. New York: W. W. Norton.
Swidzinski, J. (1988). *Quotations on Contextual Art*. Eindhoven: Apollohuis.
Szwed, J. (2020). *Space Is the Place: The Lives and Times of Sun Ra*. Durham, NC: Duke University Press.
Tagg, P. (1979). *Kojak, 50 Seconds of Television Music: Towards the Analysis of Affect in Popular Music*. Goteborg: Musikvetenskapliga Institutionen.
Tamplin, J., F. A. Baker, R. A. R. MacDonald, C. Roddy, N. S. Rickard. (2016). A theoretical framework and therapeutic songwriting protocol to promote integration of self-concept in people with acquired neurological injuries. Nordic Journal of Music Therapy. 25, 2, pp. 111–33.
Tomas, L., and Bidet, O. (2024). Conducting Qualitative Interviews via VoIP Technologies: Reflections on Rapport, Technology, Digital Exclusion, and Ethics. *IJSRM*, 27(3), 275–287.
Tomas, L., and Bidet, O. (2024). Conducting qualitative interviews via VoIP technologies: reflections on rapport, technology, digital exclusion, and ethics. *IJSRM*, 27(3), 275–287.
Tonelli, C. J. (2015). Social Virtuosity and the Improvising Voice: Phil Minton and Maggie Nicols Interviewed by Chris Tonelli. *Critical Studies in Improvisation/Études critiques en improvisation*, 10(2). https://doi.org/10.21083/csieci.v10i2.3212.
Tsiris, G., Hockley, J. and Dives, T. (2022). Musical Care at the End of Life. In N. Spiro and K. R. M. Sanfilippo (eds.), *Collaborative Insights: Interdisciplinary Perspectives on Musical Care Throughout the Life Course*, 119–145. Oxford: Oxford University Press.
Uexküll, J. von. (2010). *A Foray into the Worlds of Animals and Humans, with a Theory of Meaning*, Trans. Joseph D. O'Neil. Minneapolis, MN: University of Minnesota Press.
Vellacott, C., and Ballantyne, J. (2022). An Exploration of the Practice Habits and Experiences of Professional Musicians. *Music Education Research*, 24(3), 312–326.
Wajcman, J. (2002). Addressing Technological Change: The Challenge to Social Theory. *Current Sociology*, 50(3), 347–363.
Wallas, G. (1926). *The Art of Thought*. New York: Harcourt, Brace, & World.
Walshe, J. (2009). *Grùpat*. Dublin: Pigeonhouse Books.
Waterman, E. (2014). Improvised Trust: Opening Statements. In *The Improvisation Studies Reader*, 59–62. London: Routledge.
Weiss, R., and MacDonald, R (2020). *Duet for Two People Who Have Never Met*. AudioVisual Composition broadcast, November 22, 2020, as part of The Huddersfield Contemporary Music Festival. https://hcmf.co.uk. https://www.ncbi.nlm.nih.gov/pmc/articles/PMC8778398/#B17-sensors-22-00514.
Wigram, T. (2017). *Improvisation: Methods and Techniques for Music Therapy Clinicians, Educators, and Students*. London: Jessica Kingsley.
Wildfeuer, J., Schnell, M. W., and Schulz, C. (2015). Talking about Dying and Death: On New Discursive Constructions of a Formerly Postulated Taboo. *Discourse & Society*, 26(3), 366–390.
Wootton, R. (1996). Telemedicine: A Cautious Welcome. *British Medical Journal*, 313(1). https://doi.org/10.1136/bmj.313.7096.1375.

Index

For the benefit of digital users, indexed terms that span two pages (e.g., 52-53) may, on occasion, appear on only one of those pages.

Figures are indicated by an italic *f* following the page number.

A-111, 87–89, 88*f*
adaptive creativity, 2–3, 5–6
Afifi, Faradina, 128–30, 131*f*, 166
AHRC. *See* Arts and Humanities Research Council
AI. *See* artificial intelligence
AJIRN. *See* Australasian Jazz and Improvisation Research Network
Alaimo, Stacy, 177
Ansdell, Gary, 28–30, 31, 185–86
Archive Fever, 89*f*, 89–90
Argo, Jessica, 45, 46, 125
    Cavanaugh and, 145–46
    in chat piece, 103, 104, 105, 107, 108, 109
    on color piece, 147–49
Artaud, Antonin, 71–72
artificial intelligence (AI), 175–76, 177–78
Arts and Humanities Research Council (AHRC), 72–73
assemblages, 70, 71, 76–77, 80, 81, 87–89
augmentation, 60–62, 68–69
Australasian Jazz and Improvisation Research Network (AJIRN), 124, 136*f*, 136
Avatar Orchestra Metaverse, 16–17

Bachelard, G., 194–95n.9
Bailey, Derek, 4–5
Bamford, Rick, 46
Becker, Ernest, 73, 194n.5
Beethoven, Ludwig van, 117
being-in-foam, 83, 92
being-in-the-world, 71, 92
Bella Ciao, 182–83
Beresford, Steve, 102, 166
Bergstorem-Nielsen, Carl, 44
bionic patois, 22, 156–59, 162–64
Birrell, Ross, 41, 44, 87–89, 88*f*, 187–88
Borgo, D., 50–51, 187–88, 194–95n.9

boundary objects, 38–39, 40, 51, 97–98, 144–45, 157–59
Bourdieu, Pierre, 56
Bourriaud, Nicolas, 76–77, 90–91
bricolage, 74–76, 87, 195n.13
Brown, J. S., 153
Brown, Stuart, 45, 66, 107, 108
bubbles, 76–78, 84, 187–88, 195n.10, 195n.15
Bulavina, Olenka, 128–30, 130*f*
Burke, Robert, 49, 50–51, 55–56, 67–68, 150
    in chat piece, 97–98, 102, 103, 104, 105, 107, 108, 109
    on experimenting with trust, 188–90
    MacDonald and, 14, 188–89
Buskirk, Martha, 195n.11
Butler, Judith, 70–71, 90–91

Cage, John, 57, 59
Care for Music, 16, 28–32, 185–87
Catherin, Brice, 127–28
Cavanaugh, Laura, 145–46
Centre for Contemporary Arts (CCA), 1–2, 45, 47, 48, 134*f*, 135, 170
"Cobra," 127–28
Coleman, Beth, 21–22
community of practice (CoP), 153–54
contamination, 37–38, 187
contingencies, 70–71, 72–74, 76–77, 79, 82, 188, 194n.7
conversations, 95–97, 109–12
CoP. *See* community of practice
Covid-19 pandemic, 1, 8, 122
    Care for Music and, 29–30, 31, 186
    GIO during, 1, 2–3, 6, 34, 48, 54, 69, 70, 71–72, 75–76, 113, 128–33, 140, 142, 143, 169, 171, 178–79
    global communications and, 172–73, 174, 188–89
    health and well-being during, 142

Covid-19 pandemic (*cont.*)
   human-machine creative cultures during, 16
   lockdown, 6, 9–10, 38–39, 48, 54, 78, 84, 113, 128–33, 186
   lockdown as creative constraint, 1, 2–3, 71–72
   Mopomoso TV monthly improvisation concerts during, 143–44
   networked music practices during, 17–18
   online communications during, 17
   online music therapy during, 26
creative constraint, 1, 2–3, 7, 32, 72–73
Cunningham, Suzi, 103
Cypher, 19

Davis, Tom, 65–66
DeLanda, Manuel, 71
Deleuze, Gilles, 71, 80–81, 92, 177
DelGiudice, Dylan, 48
DeNora, Tia, 28–29, 42, 56, 57–59, 61, 62*f*, 158–59, 168, 185–87
Denzin, N. K., 14
Derrida, Jacques, 76, 177
Dewey, John, 76–77
Dewsbury, J. D., 53–54
Dezeuze, Anna, 75
digital identities, 21–23
digital music cultures, music therapy and, 26–32
digital spaces, 23–26
   GIO and, 22–24, 25–26
   in telematic music, physical spaces and, 22–23, 23*f*, 24–25
disability studies, 35
Donohue+, 19
Dr. Mesmer's Private Army, 33
Duet for Two People Who Have Never Met, 9
Duguid, P., 153

ecologies of attunement, 78–80
ecology of improvisation, 187–88
emancipation of contingency, 73–74, 194n.7
embodied communication, 171–73, 178, 182
embodied expressions, 30–31, 64–65, 64*f*
embodied practices and habits, 53–55, 64–65, 66, 74
empowerment, 5, 37, 139–40, 141, 147–49
enfolding, 79, 80
enframing, 79, 80, 195n.12
entanglement, 80

Evans, Leighton, 195n.12
Evans, Sandy, 49, 107, 108
experimentation, 156–58
   habits and habitus of, 55–56
   improvisation and, 5–6, 53, 58, 68, 179
   with trust, 188–90
   in Zoomesphere, 141
expertise, habits and, 62–69
extended reality (XR), 174–75
extrinsic contingencies, 74, 76–77

Falmouth Online Orchestra, 72–73, 194n.4
Feld, Steven, 57
Feminist Improvising Group (FIG), 61, 161
Floyd, George, 162
Fontainha, E., 153
Foucault, Michel, 73–74
Foutraque, 164–65, 165*f*
free improvisation, 5, 19, 40, 75, 82, 143
Fuchs, Katharina, 99–100

Galloway, Alexander R., 73–74
Gannon-Leary, P., 153
gender, Butler on, 70–71, 90–91
Gestell, 195n.12
GIO. *See* Glasgow Improvisers Orchestra
GIOfest, 1–2, 48, 145, 164–66, 165*f*
Gladwell, Malcolm, 62–63
Glasgow Improvisers Orchestra (GIO)
   AI and, 175–76
   at CCA, 1–2, 45, 47, 48, 134*f*, 135, 170
   collective myth-making, 157–58
   during Covid-19 pandemic and lockdown, 1, 2–3, 6, 34, 48, 54, 69, 70, 71–72, 75–76, 113, 128–33, 140, 142, 143, 169, 171, 178–79
   digital spaces and, 22–24, 25–26
   expertise of players, 63, 65–66
   festivals of, 1–2, 25
   founding of, 1–2
   habits and expertise of, 62–69
   habits and habitus in experimentation, 58–59
   intentionality in improvisations, 64–65
   lay expertise and, 34
   lived experiences of players, 55
   music-learning approaches of players, 62–63
   online work ethos of, 46–48
Glasgow Improvisers Orchestra (GIO), on Zoom, 2–4, 18, 53–54, 70

Index

adjusting to setting, 40*f*
Apocalyptic Sunrise performance, 161, 163*f*
bionic patois and, 156–59
Birrell and, short film remixes by, 87–89, 88*f*
card piece, 128–30, 130*f*
chat piece, 98–109, 99*f*, 110–11, 125
cinematic, 40, 41–42
clap to open session, 40, 41–42, 41*f*, 44
color piece, 147–49
communicative practices, advancing, 144–46, 179–80
community opening, 48–50
conducting improvisations, 125–28, 126*f*, 127*f*
contingencies and, 73–74, 76–77
cooking piece, 124–25, 124*f*
as CoP, 153–54
digital hybrid performance, 135–36, 136*f*, 164
dualities of identities on, 171–73
ecologies of attunement in, 80
ecology of improvisation, 187–88
educational applications of strategies developed during, 150
emancipation of contingency and, 73–74
embodied expressions on, 64–65, 64*f*
empowerment through, 37, 139, 141, 147–49
endings, 93–96, 97–109, 110–12
expansion of spaces and development of new realms, 128–30, 129*f*, 130*f*, 131–36, 131*f*, 132*f*, 133*f*, 134*f*, 136*f*
first online improvisation, 39*f*
in gallery view, 81–83, 89–90
goodbye piece, 126–27, 128*f*
habits, habitat and, 64–65
health, identity and, 141–43
health and well-being and, 139–40, 141–44
Henderson improvising with light, 118–20, 119*f*
as hybrid space, 157
identity changes of participants, 158–59
implications of sessions, 151–54, 155–56
improvisatory agency, 140–41
instrument mirroring, 46–47, 47*f*
kaleidoscope effects on, 63, 64*f*
"lemons" session, 94, 97–98, 102–3, 110–11, 144–45
live graphic score, 126–27, 127*f*

Miniature on Infinity performance, 44*f*
in mise-en-scène of constraints, 71–73
music therapy and, 26
new modalities, toys and cooking as themes for, 120–25
new virtuosities and, 113–14, 115, 117–18, 120–22, 128–30, 137–38, 160–61, 164, 167–68, 169, 178
openings, 37–40, 41–42, 41*f*, 43–44, 45–52
over-sharing, 40, 48, 51–52, 123, 144–45, 149, 159, 167–68, 171, 173–74, 178, 189–90
performance in memory of Russell, J., 161, 164*f*
in pin view, 87–89
player country locations, 49*f*, 50*f*
politics, new realities and, 159–64, 162*f*, 163*f*, 164*f*
post-genre and post-disciplinary implications, 155–56
real and virtual fused in, 168–69
relationships with Zoom, 19–20
Requiem for the pandemic performance, 161, 163*f*
screen interface in, 79–80
short films, 87–89, 88*f*, 89*f*
sound and vision, integrating, 118–20
sound issues, 67
starting out, opening up, and boundary objects, 37–40
synchronous activity of, latency and, 6, 7, 8
Theater of Home and, 75–76, 117–18, 120, 122–23, 131–36, 132*f*, 133*f*, 134*f*, 136*f*, 158–59, 160–61, 168, 173–74, 185
"the end" sign, 46, 46*f*
toys piece, 120–24, 121*f*, 122*f*, 123*f*
transforming materialities through collaborative creativities, 166–69
The Unquiet Earth performance, 161, 162*f*
with virtual background, 46, 46*f*, 62*f*, 79, 92, 118, 119*f*, 122–23, 128–30, 129*f*, 130*f*, 136, 140–41
virtual foam and, 78, 92, 187–88
global connectedness, 176–79
Gomez, Angela Hoyos, 161, 162*f*
Gorman, Tony, 49
Guattari, Félix, 71, 79, 92, 177

Habermas, Jürgen, 71
habitats, 53–54, 64–65
habits, 55–59, 62–69

habituation, 53–55
habitus, 55–59
Hampton, Timothy, 73
Haraway, Donna, 60–61, 79, 172, 176–77, 188
health and well-being, 139–40, 141–44
Heidegger, Martin, 71, 92, 195n.12
Henderson, Robert, 108, 118–20, 119*f*
Huang, R., 116
Hub, The, 16–17
human-computer interface, 78
human-computer relationships, 18–20
human-machine creative cultures, 16
human-machine relationships, 17–18, 19–20, 176
Husserl, Edmund, 73

identity, 70–71, 139–40, 141–43, 158–59, 170, 171–73, 180
IMP. *See* Internet Music Performance
improvisation. *See also* Glasgow Improvisers Orchestra
　as art of becoming, 13
　audio-visual nature of digital, 149
　augmentation and, 60–62, 68
　Bailey on, 4–5
　as bricolage, 74–76, 87
　as collaboration, 42, 179, 189
　community, 48–49
　defining, 4–6
　ecology of, 187–88
　empowerment and, 5
　endings, 93, 94–95, 96, 99
　experimentation in, 5–6, 53, 58, 68, 179
　free, 5, 19, 40, 75, 82, 143
　fun in, 180–81
　gender as, Butler on, 70–71, 90–91
　habits and, 64–65, 67–68
　in health and well-being, 142
　human-computer relationship and, 18–20
　intentionality in, 64–66
　jazz, 65
　latency and, 6–8
　mirroring in, 46–47, 122
　within mise-en-scène of constraints, 70–74
　in music education, 149–50, 151
　Nicols on social virtuosity in, 115–16
　in online music therapy, 27
　online work ethos, 46–48
　openings in, 42–44, 50–51
　pre-composition *versus*, 10–13
　radical acceptance of contingency in, 73

　social, 43, 48, 51–52, 70, 115–16, 127–28, 189–90
　Zoom and, 4, 19–20, 34, 37, 40, 43–44, 64–65, 67, 70, 72–74, 76–77, 92
improvisatory agency, 140–41
Improvisers Network, The, 16–17
Ingold, Tim, 83–84
intentionality, in improvisation, 64–66
interface effect, 73–74, 76, 80–81, 83–84, 187–88
Internet Music Performance (IMP), 194n.1
intrinsic contingencies, 74–75, 76–77
Iorwerth, Miriam, 194n.4

Janicka, Iwona, 71, 75–76
Johansen, Guro Gravem, 147, 204
"Joy Against the Machine," 127–28

Kahlo, Frida, 61, 62*f*
Kaneko, Yasuko, 101, 108
Kazarian, Christine, 103, 104, 107
Keeble, Frederick, 188
Kerr, Fergus, 105, 106, 108, 120–21
Knight, Peter, 49
Knox, Don, 194n.4
Kokoro, 87–89, 88*f*
Krokek, Arthur, 61

LAA. *See* Latency Accepting Approach
Landgraf, Edgar, 70–71
Landow, G. P., 81, 195n.13
latency, 6–8, 33, 72–73, 194n.2
Latency Accepting Approach (LAA), 72–73
Latour, Bruno, 20
Lave, Jean, 153–54
Lee, K. F., 154
Lefebvre, Henri, 70, 85
Leibniz, G. W., 194n.7, 195n.10
Lévi-Strauss, Claude, 74–75
Lewis, George, 19, 48, 97–98, 99–100, 109
Lincoln, Y. S., 14

MacDonald, Raymond, 1–2
　on augmentation and improvisation, 68
　Burke and, 14, 188–89
　Duet for Two People Who Have Never Met by Weiss and, 9
　expansion of spaces by, 132*f*, 133–35, 133*f*
　on fun and relational quantum mechanics, 180–83
　in GIO, 42, 44, 46, 48, 97, 98, 99*f*, 100–1, 102, 103, 104, 105, 108, 109, 118, 119*f*, 125

hand conduction by, 125
Quigley and, 26–27
This is not improvised but that is by, 10–11
Weiss and, 9, 63
Wilson and, 13
MacGlone, Una, 66, 150–51
Manovich, L., 73–74, 78
McKenzie, Graham, 1–2
McPherson, Henry, 151
meadow, 78, 83–84, 187–88, 194–95n.9
merging, emergent experiences and, 172–73
meshwork, meadow and, 83–84
Messiaen, Olivier, 82
Miller, J. Hillis, 91–92
mirroring, 46–47, 47f, 122
mise-en-scène of constraints, 70–74, 78, 90–91
Monson, Ingrid, 65
Mopomoso TV, 143–44, 144f
Morris, Butch, 127–28
Mureddu, Libero, 127–28
Murray, J., 157–58
musicality, virtuosity and, 113–15, 117, 181–82
music education, 149–51
music therapy, 185–87
  conversation and, 109–10, 111–12
  digital music cultures and, 26–32
  mirroring in, 46–47, 122
  online platforms and, 154
  synchronizing in, 122
  virtuosity in, 114–15
Mwamba, Corey, 110–11

Nachmanovitch, Stephen, 180–81
Neto, Alípio Carvalho, 182–83
networked and telematic music, 16–18
Networked Music Performance (NMP), 72–73, 194n.1, 194n.4
Nicholson, Peter, 132f, 135
Nicols, Maggie, 41, 42, 61, 66–67
  on aesthetic supremacy, 152
  Afifi and, 166
  in chat piece, 100, 101, 102, 103–7, 108, 110–11, 144–45
  in cooking piece, 124–25
  expansion of spaces by, 128–30, 132f, 133–34
  on found objects, 157–58, 166, 167
  on social virtuosity, 115–16
  on toys piece, 122–24
NMP. *See* Networked Music Performance

Noisebringers, 164–65, 165f
Noisy Women, 166

Oliveros, Pauline, 16–17
OMax, 19
over-sharing, 40, 48, 51–52, 123, 144–45, 149, 159, 167–68, 171, 173–74, 178, 189–90

Pajunen, Anne, 48
panpsychism, 178
Parker, Evan, 1–2
Pavlicevic, Mercedes, 186
Peters, Gary, 73, 74, 86
Picasso, Pablo, 160
post-production, 90–91
precarity, 45, 160–61

Qiufan, C., 154
Quigley, H., 26–27

Ramnarine, Tina, 57
Rauschenberg, Robert, 81–82, 87
Read, Alan, 195n.14
Reardon-Smith, H., 37–38
relational art, 76–77, 90–91
remixing, 90–91, 156–57, 159–60
Rilke, Rainer Maria, 194–95n.9
Robertson, David, 134f, 135
rock 'n' roll music therapy, 26–28
Rofe, Michael, 72–73
Rohrer, Thomas, 103, 105, 109, 131f, 133–34
Rolvsjord, R., 109
Rossi, Gerry, 103, 106, 159
Rottle, J., 37–38
Rovelli, Carlo, 183
Russell, John, 97–98, 125
  in chat piece, 99–100, 101–2, 103, 104, 105, 106–7, 108, 110–11
  communicative practices and, 144–46
  on connection and belonging through GIO improvisation sessions, 141–42
  GIO performance in memory of, 161, 164f
  on Mopomoso TV, 143–44, 144f
Russell, Legacy, 22, 90–91, 156–57, 159–60, 162–64
Ruud, Even, 142, 177, 205

Sacks, Harvey, 95–96
Sappho, Maria, 19, 46, 48, 54–55, 60, 61, 62f, 100, 108, 128–30, 133f, 135, 151, 183–85
Schafer, R. Murray, 73–74

Schegloff, Emmanuel, 95–96
Schmid, Wolfgang, 99–100, 111, 185–86
Second Life, 16–17
Serres, Michel, 86, 92
Shirky, Clay, 21–22
Simpson, Fraser, 185–86
Skype, 29–30
Slaven, Ken, 46
Sloterdijk, Peter, 71, 75–76, 78, 81–82, 83, 84, 92, 195n.10
Snapcam, 63
social improvisation, 43, 48, 51–52, 70, 115–16, 127–28, 189–90
social isolation of lockdown, as creative constraint, 1, 2–3
social virtuosity, 115–16, 124, 184–85
Sonobus, 17–18
Sparti, Davide, 73
Spence, Alister, 49
Stein, Gertrude, 160
Steinberg, Leo, 81–82, 87
Sun Ra, 61, 161
"Symphonie pour une Femme Seule," 127–28
synchrony, latency as, 6–8

Telematic Circle, 16–17
Telematic Improvisation Resources, 16–17
telematic music, 16–18, 19–20, 22–23, 23*f*, 24–25, 35, 73
terminal exchanges, 95–97
Theater of Home, 26, 48, 54–55, 58, 173–74
　educational applications of, 150
　as emancipation of contingency, 194n.7
　empowerment in, 148–49
　expansion of, 131–36, 132*f*, 133*f*, 134*f*, 136*f*
　GIO on Zoom and, 75–76, 117–18, 120, 122–23, 131–36, 132*f*, 133*f*, 134*f*, 136*f*, 158–59, 160–61, 168, 173–74, 185
　mise-en-scène of constraints and, 78
　new virtuosities in, 117–18
　over-sharing in, 144–45, 149
　remixes and, 92
　Zoomesphere and, 8–10, 148, 170
Theater of Home Movies, 87–90
This is not improvised but that is, 10–11
Thomson, Walter, 127–28
transcorporeality, 177–78
Tremby, Marion, 128–30, 131*f*

Uexküll, Jakob von, 77–78, 83–84, 187–88, 194–95n.9, 195n.10

Umwelt, 76–78, 187
　Zumwelt, 77, 78–80, 91, 187–88
Usui, Yasuhiro, 59, 101, 102, 103, 105, 106, 107, 108, 109

virtual foam, 76, 78, 80, 92, 187–88
virtual reality (VR), 174
virtuosities, 113
　musicality and, 113–15, 117, 181–82
　new musical, 114–17
　new virtuosities through online music-making of GIO, 113–14, 115, 117–18, 120–22, 128–30, 137–38, 160–61, 164, 167–68, 169, 178
　social, 115–16, 124, 184–85
　technology and, 116–17
Voyager, 19
VR. *See* virtual reality

"Water Walk," 57, 59
Weiss, Rachel Joy, 9, 63, 105, 107, 109, 164–65, 165*f*
Wenger, Etienne, 153–54
Wigram, T., 122
Wilson, G. B., 13
Winthrop-Young, Geoffrey, 84, 195n.15
World Congress of Music Therapy, 186
World Listening Day, 161
Wylie, Allan, 48, 101, 103, 104, 105, 106, 107

XR. *See* extended reality
X reality, 21–22, 184

Zoom, 14, 17–18, 27. *See also* Glasgow Improvisers Orchestra, on Zoom
　active view, 80–81
　apparatus of, 73–74, 79, 80, 84–86
　audio recording settings, 83
　augmentation and, 60
　Care for Music and, 30–31, 186
　embodied expressions on, 30–31, 64–65, 64*f*
　gallery view, 80–83, 84–86, 87–90, 167
　host and parasite, 91
　improvisation and, 4, 19–20, 34, 37, 40, 43–44, 64–65, 67, 70, 72–74, 76–77, 92
　interface effect on, 187–88
　pin view, 80–81, 86–90
　Snapcam and, 63
　speaker view, 80–81, 84–86, 87–90
　technology in creative practices and, 174

transcorporeality and, 177–78
virtual backgrounds, 46, 46*f*, 62*f*, 79–80, 92, 118, 119*f*, 122–23, 128–30, 129*f*, 130*f*, 136, 140–41, 177–78, 182
as *Zumwelt*, 77, 78–80, 91, 187–88
Zoomesphere, 158–59, 181, 190

aspirational modes of existence in, 160
experimentation in, 141
new communicative practices in, 146
Theater of Home and, 8–10, 148, 170
Zorn, John, 127–28
Zumwelt, 77, 78–80, 91, 187–88